BUILT BY COLE CONSTRUCTION

CLASSIC HOUSES OF SEATTLE

CLASSIC HOUSES
OF SEATTLE

High Style to Vernacular
1870–1950

CAROLINE T. SWOPE

TIMBER PRESS

Frontispiece: A Victorian house with Queen Anne design elements in the
Capitol Hill neighborhood, East Pine and 11th Streets, Seattle, 1909.
James P. Lee. University of Washington Libraries, Special Collections, Lee 177.

Published in 2005 by

Timber Press, Inc.
The Haseltine Building
133 S.W. Second Avenue, Suite 450
Portland, Oregon 97204-3527, U.S.A.
www.timberpress.com

Reprinted 2006

Printed through Colorcraft Ltd., Hong Kong

Library of Congress Cataloging-in-Publication Data

Swope, Caroline T.
  Classic houses of Seattle : high style to vernacular, 1870-1950 /
Caroline T. Swope.
      p. cm.
  Includes bibliographical references and index.
  ISBN-13: 978-0-88192-717-7
  ISBN-10: 0-88192-717-1
  1. Architecture, Domestic—Washington (State)—Seattle. 2. Seattle
(Wash.)—Buildings, structures, etc. I. Title.
  NA7238.S4S94 2005
  728'.37'09797772—dc22
                                                    2005001448

A catalog record for this book is also available from the British Library.

TO DAVID

Non Semper sub Umbra

CONTENTS

PREFACE

MY INTRODUCTION to historic architecture came at an early age. My paternal grandfather lived in an old brick farmhouse just down the road from us in southwestern Virginia. Built in the Civil War era, it was a simple structure, with a dirt cellar and a large barn in the backyard. My maternal grandmother lived hundreds of miles away, in a "newer" house, built around 1890. Both of these homes had undergone major remodelings over the years, with layer after layer of paint and wallpaper applied, porches removed, bathrooms added. Doors never shut properly, windows rarely opened, and the floors creaked. I *loved* both of those houses: they were puzzles, waiting to be solved. What had the front porch originally looked like? Why did the kitchen have such a strange floor plan? What about that odd room off to the side—what possible purpose could it have had?

These houses were so different from the one I lived in, a 1970s split level with an avocado green kitchen. Yes, our house functioned better with an efficient kitchen and more convenient bathroom placement, but where was the mystery, the fun? I loved the older houses both for what they were and for what they had the potential to be. I could see under the peeled wallpaper, and imagine the original hallway. My high school classmates selected colleges based on closeness to home, or potential majors. I chose one with the oldest buildings possible—I fell in love with the dormitory built in the 1780s. How could one not be entranced by old handmade bricks, with multicolored swirls?

My interest in historic buildings eventually led to graduate work in historic preservation in the Midwest and doctoral studies in architectural history across the country in Seattle. The Pacific Northwest was filled with a fresh array of historic buildings and styles. Craftsman houses, a style I was relatively unfamiliar with, were everywhere. So were Seattle variations of the Four-Square style house. In the late 1990s, the Ballard Historical Society, a northwest Seattle neighborhood group interested in promoting local history, started a lecture series on older homes, and asked me to

speak on historic architectural styles. I set off to survey the neighborhood in preparation for my talk. First, I studied the classic regional styles, such as Craftsman. Next, I studied hybrids—Victorian mixed with Colonial Revival, and Colonial Revival mixed with Craftsman—buildings that did not fit neatly into the categories I had learned. I also examined numerous vernacular homes, ones with minimal stylistic details. Folk housing of this type, while quite common, is sometimes less clearly identified stylistically than the grand, heavily ornamented residences. As I talked with property owners after the lectures, many invited me to visit their homes, or their neighbor who found something odd while remodeling. Their houses were rarely the architect-designed residences that were prominently depicted in period magazines. They were middle-class homes riddled with various changes made over time: funny closets added, original siding covered, porches replaced. The questions homeowners constantly asked were, "What style is my house? How do I bring back some of the old charm?" Many of them were familiar with the grand architectural examples of a style, and did not recognize smaller, vernacular versions.

This book, in part, came out of the lecture series, and is designed to help Seattle homeowners to identify the style of their house and to recognize the prominent features of that style. This guide can be used to understand the history of your home, as well as to plan future improvements. I have selected a dozen or so houses for the most prevalent domestic architectural styles in Seattle and devoted a chapter to each, explaining origins, exterior variations, and interiors. Whenever possible, I have included floor plans to help the reader understand how interior space functioned. I used two criteria to select the houses featured in this volume. The first was historical significance. I selected numerous houses from the local and state register that are either superb examples of an architectural style or had well-documented owner histories. The second factor was the availability of images. To adequately convey the features of each style, quality images of the exterior (and the interior, when available) of the house were needed for the book. Historic photographs were given priority, and numerous hours were spent digging through archives in search of period photographs. Those photographs are augmented by my own photographs, taken on many a long afternoon driving up and down the side streets of Seattle.

When possible, houses featured in each chapter are identified by original owner's name, address, and construction date, and architect or builder when known. Many of these have two-part name designations, for example, the Raymond-Ogden residence. The first name is generally the historic owner of the house, while the second often denotes the homeowner at the time of landmark designation. Occasionally, I've used period photographs to illustrate style, even if additional information is unknown. The text is concluded with a detailed discussion of how to go about tracing the history of your own house or one that interests you.

There are two house locators in the back of the book, each designed to help readers locate homes. The first is organized by style, in the order featured houses are discussed in text. The second lists featured houses by neighborhood and is accompanied by a Seattle neighborhood map. A glossary explains unfamiliar architectural terminology. A bibliography lists sources consulted in my research, and an index completes the book.

Because this book is designed to address predominantly single-family residences, commercial architecture is not included. This volume showcases the most common styles seen in Seattle, the hybridized styles that were the result of period transitions, and the broader social trends that shaped all of these houses. While basic stylistic trends are the main focus, the book does introduce the reader to some of Seattle's best period architects, including Bebb & Mendel, a firm that specialized in historical revival styles, and Jud Yoho of the Seattle Bungalow Company. Period floor plans for different styles are illustrated with diagrams from Victor W. Voorhees's *West Home Builder* (circa 1910 edition). Voorhees, partner in the Ballard firm of Fisher & Voorhees, worked in a number of eclectic architectural styles.

By the early twentieth century, Seattle had an amazing collection of high-style (elaborate, highly detailed interpretations of style) and vernacular (simple, folk) residences. Booster publications indicate that the city took great pride in its houses. But unfortunately, time has not always been kind to historic structures. Some of the buildings illustrated in this book are no longer standing, some have been changed beyond stylistic recognizability, and a few are in poor condition. I debated the merits of including photos of now-demolished structures, particularly if there were existing versions of the style, such as Queen Anne. I decided to include some houses that no longer ornament Seattle's cityscape, because an important part of understanding current history is an awareness of the past

In the race to regrade, build roads, and expand business districts, Seattle has lost countless historic structures. Historic architecture, commercial and residential, is the soul of a city. Can you imagine Boston without its Beacon Hill residences, or San Francisco without her painted Victorians? Can you envision Seattle without her Craftsman houses? Our built environment is one of the most important legacies we possess. The past should not be confined to a museum; it needs to be evident in our neighborhoods and homes. Understanding the history of Seattle's residences will help ensure their preservation for future generations.

ACKNOWLEDGMENTS

ANY PUBLICATION OF THIS NATURE owes substantial thanks to those who helped behind the scenes, and this book is no exception. The board and membership of the Ballard Historical Society has encouraged my research for many years now. Mary Fortino, Martha Obenauer, Jenny Joyce, and John O'Hare deserve special mention, as do all the homeowners who graciously allowed me access to their property over the years. Myke Woodwell lent me historic images of the Belltown Craftsman Bungalows. Carol Rosen Neiman spent an afternoon sharing family photographs of the Rosen residence, and made arrangements for photo reproduction. Andrea Mercado of the West Seattle Historical Society spent hours helping me access their historic photograph collection, even when it meant meeting late at night to accommodate both our hectic schedules. Larry Kreisman at Historic Seattle provided me with contact information and additional resources.

Some of the information for this book came from student research. In the spring of 2001, I taught a Washington State architecture class at the University of Washington. Angela Berry, Julia DiMartino, Allison Dunn, Jennifer Griffith, Barbara Manning, Anna Schafer, and Alex Wilson completed historic structure reports for the class, some of which provided information for this book.

Most of the historic images in the book came from museum archives. Nicolette Bromberg, curator of photographs and graphics at the University of Washington, and her assistant, Lauren Manes, spent untold hours locating historic photographs and arranging for reproduction. Carolyn Marr, librarian at the Museum of History and Industry, suggested sources on houseboats and located dozens of historic images. Elaine Miller, Washington State Historical Society, Tacoma, helped me sift through hundreds of Asahel Curtis photographic negatives. Rayette Wilder, Northwest Museum of Arts and Culture, Spokane, located images of Kirtland Cutter's Stimson-Green mansion. Jodee Fenton, of the Seattle Public Library, arranged for photo reproduction from *Bungalow Magazine*. Photographic reproduction was made possible with a grant from the Margaret Ann Klein Foundation.

City and state offices helped me locate historical research documents on landmark-designated buildings. Beth Chave at Seattle's Department of Neighborhoods provided access to landmark files, and put me in touch with some of the property owners. The staff at Puget Sound Regional Archives in Bellevue pulled dozens of property tax cards for me to examine, and Greg Lange provided a critical eye by reviewing part of the manuscript. A special thanks to architectural historian Michael Houser, at the Washington State Office of Archeology and Historic Preservation, who suggested sources on contemporary residential architecture, read many manuscript drafts and was a great sparring partner for hashing out the problematic issue of "style."

Friends and family also provided necessary support. Amy Fink endured countless hours of car and walking tours, trying to help me locate historic structures. No small feat considering how many houses we viewed. She also patiently listened to my rampages over ineptly remodeled houses and neglected landmark buildings. Allan Fink, aka "computer god," removed the pesky wording from the historic tax assessor's photos; the difference between before and after images is truly amazing—now we can actually see the buildings! Friends Jo Heiman, Isaac and Kristen Miyakawa, and my father, Fred C. Swope, came to my rescue on countless occasions and watched my dog Henry, so I could spend full research days at the archives.

My husband, David Waring, deserves special thanks. He volunteered to act as chauffeur on his days off, driving me from one historic house to the next, and provided unending support, never saying a word as our house turned into a repository for historic images, film, and manuscript drafts.

IN MEMORIAM

In memory of Seattle's fantastic vintage buildings that have fallen victim to fire, inept remodels, or development.

The demolition of the Stacy mansion after a fire, in 1960. *Museum of History and Industry, Seattle, 7169*

The Martin van Buren Stacy residence (1885), originally located at 308 Marion Street. Modern addition by Paul Thiry in the 1930s. *Museum of History and Industry, Seattle, 4134*

INTRODUCTION

A Brief History of Seattle's Residential Architecture

The first house in Seattle (built circa 1851, torn down in 1891). *Seattle Public Library, 20779*

IN NOVEMBER 1851, two dozen settlers, led by David Thomas Denny, established a small settlement on Puget Sound in the area that is now West Seattle. They took shelter in a log cabin constructed during an earlier reconnaissance mission. The party was cold and wet, and while the structure was certainly welcome, it did not offer the comforts of their Midwestern homes. This structure represented Seattle's early residential architecture. The site lacked suitable farming land and deepwater anchorage, so within a year many of the settlers moved across Elliott Bay, naming their new settlement Seattle, after a Coast Salish tribal leader. In 1853 Henry Yesler built the first steam mill on Puget Sound, and Seattle's hills were eventually stripped of their huge trees. Wood waste and later regrade sluicing helped fill in the mud flats near Pioneer Square.

The new community was small and grew more slowly than its leaders had hoped. In 1862, a decade after the Denny party had landed, Seattle's population was a meager 182. Growth was stalled by the Civil War, and major transportation routes were waterways that did not provide easy access to the area. The completion of the transcontinental railroad in 1869 allowed faster settlement of the West Coast. The Northern Pacific Railroad selected Tacoma, some thirty miles south, as the terminus of its first line to the Puget Sound region in 1873, dismaying Seattle boosters.

View from Seattle's Elliott Bay, 1878. *Seattle Public Library, 5064*

View from Broadway and James Street, 1889. *Seattle Public Library, 5111*

Throughout this early period in Seattle's history, most buildings were made from wood. Historic photographs show rows of neatly constructed gabled, framed buildings. Most were one and a half stories. These dwellings were simple, easy to construct, and followed basic vernacular, or folk, housing traditions. As Seattle's commercial center slowly grew, these structures were replaced by businesses, and new residences were built on the community's edges. By 1880, Seattle's population had climbed to more than 3500. The city continued to grow, in part spurred by a transcontinental rail connection, which had finally reached Seattle in 1883.

The Seattle Public Library, the former Henry Yesler mansion, circa 1899.

Anders B. Wilse. Museum of History and Industry, Seattle, 88.33.1

The remains of the Henry Yesler mansion after the fire of January 1, 1901.

Museum of History and Industry, Seattle, SHS165

Tragedy struck when Seattle's original commercial district was engulfed by fire in 1889. Seattle was subsequently rebuilt, with bigger, fire-resistant structures. Brick became the preferred building material for commercial structures, while residential buildings were still constructed primarily from wood. This left the residential structures vulnerable to fire, and the Henry Yesler mansion, built by Yesler, the founder of Seattle's first timber mill, ultimately fell victim to this fate. The mansion was a grandiose structure that showcased the ornate possibilities of wood. Henry and Sarah Yesler's home, built on the present site of the King County Courthouse, was rented by Seattle's public library in 1899. Although the home survived Seattle's Great Fire of 1889, it burned to the ground in 1901.

Early residences that survived the perils of fire had to find ways of adapting to encroaching commercial districts. In many cases, they were overrun by the commercial districts, and fell into disrepair and eventual ruin. Attorney James McNaught's mansion was typical of the elaborate dwellings that were once home to the city's elite. The building, constructed in 1883, was inhabited by McNaught for a short period of time. It then became home of the Rainier Club, and by 1893 it was used as a boarding house. The mansion was moved to make room for the Carnegie-funded Seattle Public Library building of 1906. Even commercial buildings faced uncertainty, and the Carnegie-funded Seattle Public Library was demolished in 1956.

In 1893, a national economic depression brought a quick end to the booming growth of the 1800s. Building in the region slowed considerably until the discovery of gold in

James McNaught mansion (1883), circa 1891.

Museum of History and Industry, Seattle, SHS260

Alaska. The Klondike Gold Rush, which started in 1897, helped Seattle's economy greatly. The topography of the city, however, was not conducive to urban expansion. To the west lay water, to the north were Denny and Queen Anne Hills, to the northeast lay Lake Washington, with Capitol and First Hills to the east. In today's automotive age such natural features would hardly impact development, but in the age of horse-drawn transportation, the hills were formidable.

City engineer Reginald H. Thomson, a firm believer that the city should expand north, knew that hydraulic mining techniques could level Seattle's hills. Thomson set his sights on Denny Hill, which rose north of Pine Street, and started regrad-

Denny Hill regrade, circa 1910. *Asahel Curtis. University of Washington Libraries, Special Collections, UW4812*

ing the area between 2nd and 5th Avenues. The regrades continued in fits and starts until 1930, when the final stage was complete. Many residences that had once occupied the hill were destroyed, including one of the old Denny houses. The Denny residence typifies a style known as an "I-House," a building type common in their native Midwest, defined by its two-story rectangular massing, side-facing gables, centered front door, and symmetrical windows. This example has Victorian detailing on the front porch.

Seattle's population grew rapidly in the early 1900s, and by 1910 the city had more than a quarter of a million residents. Seattle's population growth came at a time when home ownership was a national preoccupation. Prior to World War I, the real estate community promoted individual residences, encouraging people to leave the crowded, apartment-filled city in search of suburban homes. Residential construction peaked, and a slew of architects and design professionals were ready to help home owners move out of cramped cabins and into platted residential neighborhoods. While most homeowners lived modestly, a number of large residences were built on Queen Anne and Capitol Hills.

Middle-class residents lived in builders' houses, in any one of the prevailing styles: Craftsman, Tudor Revival, or Colonial Revival. A 1910 booster publication for West Seattle showcased Victorian, Dutch Colonial, Tudor, Craftsman, and Four-Square homes, boasting of their fine housing stock. (The Four-Square house has four rooms, one in each corner, and a pyramidal or hipped roof.) Seattleites outfitted their homes with the latest in modern labor-saving technology. An annual report from the Seattle Light Department showed the dining room and kitchen of a contemporary home filled with electric lighting, a toaster, coffee pot, range, hot water heater, and even a vacuum cleaner.

The trend of individual home ownership gained renewed impetus after the war. An annual "Better Homes Week" was declared by the Better Homes in America movement. President Harding visited the Washington, DC, model home, and later, President Hoover helped reorganize the movement as a national education corporation. Seattle was one of thousands of cities across the country that participated. Special exhibits, model homes, and newspaper articles besieged Seattleites, who were told that "The

Denny Hill regrade, 1911. The house on the bank is one of the old Denny homes.

Museum of History and Industry, Seattle, Pemco Webster and Stevens Collection, 83.10.6981

Houses showcased in the 1910 edition of *Beautiful West Seattle*. Many are still standing. *Southwest Seattle Historical Society, P286*

A "modern" dining room, complete with the newest in electrical technology, circa 1915. *Museum of History and Industry, Seattle SHS8921*

A "modern" kitchen, with the newest appliances, circa 1915. *Museum of History and Industry, Seattle, 8896*

A Seattle family in front of their cabin, circa 1910. *Museum of History and Industry, Seattle, Moen Collection, 1980.6880.926*

strength and future of America will depend in large measure upon the quality of the American home. Every community which realizes its need for citizens of physical and moral sturdiness will applaud the Better Homes in America movement." Photos of recently completed Tudor and Colonial Revival houses were shown in the Seattle *Daily Times*. In support of the movement, *House and Garden* sent a touring show of four model homes around the county in 1925, stopping in Seattle. These two-foot model homes showcased the Georgian, Tudor Revival, and Spanish and French Revival styles, and were on display for the general public. Although many Seattleites lived in houses that were similar to those in other parts of the country, there were variations. The Ramsing house, built in 1908, is an example. The entire structure was covered with fancy sawn shingles, even under the eaves.

One of Seattle's most distinctive vernacular forms is the houseboat. While many contemporary houseboats are luxurious dwellings, their origins were much simpler. Some of the earliest floating houses were constructed in the 1880s by mill workers on the West Coast, but by the early 1900s many families saw the "temporary" dwellings as delightful cottages, well suited for weekend nature retreats. In 1905 there were more than thirty houseboats on Lake Washington, north of Madison Park. Some were described in the Seattle *Post-Intelligencer* as a single-room, floating cottage, while others were two stories, with "every convenience of a city home." It was estimated that the number at this location would more than double in the coming year by families who wanted to spend their summers relaxing on the lake. By the 1920s there were an estimated 2500 floating houses in Seattle. By the 1950s their number had declined, in part because of new ordinances addressing sewage, zoning, and taxes. The largest houseboat community in Seattle is currently located on the eastern shore of Lake Union.

Capitol Hill residences, circa 1906. *University of Washington Libraries, Special Collections, UW9375*

Capitol Hill residences, circa 1913. The Parker-Ferson residence is on the left. *Museum of History and Industry, Seattle, Pemco Webster and Stevens Collection, 83.10.8771.1*

Builders' houses on North 76th Street, photographed in the 1950s.
Museum of History and Industry, Seattle, 4259

The shingle-covered Ramsing residence, photographed in the 1950s.
Seattle Public Library, 22453

PHOTO BY NOWELL & ROGNON.

House-Boats on Lake Washington, near Madison Park, Seattle.

Houseboats on Lake Washington near Madison Park, 1915. *University of Washington Libraries, Special Collections, UW23432*

FOR SALE

Houseboat "IDAWIS" on Lake Washington. Furnished Complete, Five Rooms
Call North 664, or East 84

Seattle houseboat for sale, 1911.

University of Washington Libraries, Special Collections, UW4701

A casually furnished houseboat interior, early twentieth century.

Museum of History and Industry, Seattle, Pemco Webster and Stevens Collection, 83.10.7356.1

A large, well-maintained houseboat, early twentieth century. The porch supports have Victorian scrollwork. Location undocumented.

Museum of History and Industry, Seattle, Pemco Webster and Stevens Collection, 83.10.7356.3

Late nineteenth-century Victorian house, torn down circa 1940, 12th Avenue and Yesler Way. *Museum of History and Industry, Seattle, 86.5.11865.1*

Family in a crowded apartment, circa 1940. *Museum of History and Industry, Seattle, Seattle* Post-Intelligencer *Collection, PI23744*

With the advent of World War II, days of carefree living in Seattle quickly came to an end. War industries impacted population shifts, and Seattle's population grew from approximately 370,000 in 1940 to 482,000 in 1944. Between 1940 and 1942, the number of employees in Seattle's manufacturing industry doubled. The Great Depression had decreased the number of new housing starts, and wartime building material shortages also impacted the market. In the summer of 1941 housing vacancy rates dropped to almost 1 percent, and rents skyrocketed. Inflation in Seattle climbed 74 percent from 1939 until 1947. As a result, new homes were smaller, and more minimal in their design details. The city had already started to address crowded and substandard residential quarters with public housing. In 1937 the city received funding from the Federal Housing Authority to construct a low-income housing project. The site selected for redevelopment was on the south end of First Hill, an area originally developed by some of Seattle's wealthy citizens. The Victorian houses had already been subdivided to provide cramped quarters

for local workers. The site was cleared in the early 1940s, and a group including architects John T. Jacobsen, J. Lister Holmes, and Victor Steinbrueck designed more than 850 housing units, modeled after Swedish worker housing. The resulting complex, called Yesler Terrace, is now partially changed by demolition and remodeling from the construction of Interstate 5. The project showed sensitivity to human scale that was uncommon in public housing at the time.

These historical events have all had a major impact on the current landscape of Seattle's historic residential architecture. The Great Fire of 1889, coupled with the urban expansion highlighted by the massive Denny Hill regrade, resulted in the loss of many historic residences from the late 1800s. The tremendous population growth of the Seattle area during the early 1900s resulted in the construction of thousands of Craftsman, Tudor Revival, Colonial Revival, and Four-Square homes, many of which remain, defining the historic landscape of Seattle today. By understanding and celebrating the heritage of these dwellings, we can ensure that history does not repeat itself, and that these structures will continue to stand as testament to the quality craftsmanship of past. Even today, many of these historic structures are at risk, through continued efforts of urban expansion or massive home remodels.

Yesler Terrace, period photograph. John T. Jacobsen, J. Lister Holmes, and Victor Steinbrueck, architects.
University of Washington Libraries, Special Collections, DM01978

Houses in West Seattle, circa 1960. *Southwest Seattle Historical Society, 1992.002.0069*

1

VICTORIAN

Italianate, Queen Anne, and Folk Victorian

The Arthur Armstrong Denny residence (1865), southeast corner of 1st Avenue and Union Street (demolished 1900), period photo. *Museum of History and Industry, Seattle, SHS269*

Houses at 319 and 325 8th Avenue North, in 1911. The house at 319 is a small Folk Victorian, minimally articulated; 325 is a larger Queen Anne house, with Classical decoration. *James P. Lee. University of Washington Libraries, Special Collections, Lee 595*

VICTORIAN ARCHITECTURE is one of the more easily identified styles. While most people recognize the towers, ornate woodwork, and multicolored stained glass, many are unaware that "Victorian" is not a single architectural style, but a conglomeration of styles ranging from Gothic Revival to Queen Anne and Eastlake. Most of these styles share irregular massing, ornate exterior decorations, and a number of different design influences, including English, French, Italian, and Swiss. Plain elevations are uncommon, since large-scale Seattle mill operations supplied inexpensive, mass-produced molding, ornate doors, windows, and decorative details, providing designers a plethora of choices. The Victorian styles began in England under the reign of Queen Victoria (1837–1901) and arrived in the United States through the influence of such architects as Andrew Jackson Downing and Richard Norman Shaw. Seattleites enjoyed building in these elaborate styles. A particularly interesting Seattle house was the Arthur Armstrong Denny residence, a rare example of a Carpenter Gothic Victorian, built in 1865. Carpenter Gothic houses had steeply pitched, cross-gabled roofs decorated with ornate vergeboards.

Preceding pages: (far left) James Nugent residence (1892), in 1898, at the corner of Cherry and 12th Streets. *Anders B. Wilse collection. Museum of History and Industry, Seattle, 88.33.431*; (chapter title page, upper left and below) Victorians in Ballard; (upper right) Italianate residence at 716 Nob Hill, in 1957. *Werner Lenggenhager. Seattle Public Library, 22461*

Ornate Victorian row houses (1890), corner of Boren Avenue and Yesler Way, in 1909. Towle and Wilcox, architects. *Museum of History and Industry, Seattle, 8837*

The flexible combination of floor plans, building materials, and ornamentation associated with the Victorian styles made them attractive to many different social and economic groups. As a result one can find Victorian commercial buildings, apartments, single-family houses, and large mansions throughout the city, many dating from the late nineteenth century. While one can still find an occasional Italianate house, the most common Victorian substyles in Seattle are Queen Anne and Folk Victorian.

ITALIANATE (1850–1885)

Italianate houses are often two-story, rectangular structures, with a low-pitched, hipped or pyramidal roof. Roof eaves have wide overhangs with decorative brackets beneath. Windows are tall and narrow, and frequently have elaborate window crowns. Window sashes usually have only one or two lights, and are double hung. Square towers are common and porches, while generally present, are only single story and somewhat restrained in decoration when compared to other design elements on the house. As with the following Queen Anne style, this style originated in England and was popularized through the pattern books of

Budlong residence on North 34th Street, period photo.
Seattle Public Library, 14270

American designer Andrew Jackson Downing. This style was common nationally from 1850 to 1885, but there are only a few surviving examples in Seattle. In part this is because Seattle's population grew rather slowly until the 1880s, and by then the Italianate style was outmoded.

An elaborate Queen Anne style house, the George Bowman residence (1890s, demolished), period drawing. Willis A. Ritchie, architect. *University of Washington Libraries, Special Collections, UW4749*

Urban regrading projects, growing business districts, and economic pressures have also contributed to the small number of surviving Italianate structures.

QUEEN ANNE AND FOLK VICTORIAN
(1880–1910)

Queen Anne houses typify what most people visualize when they hear the term "Victorian." Most Queen Anne houses have two full stories, although large three-story mansions and smaller one-and-a-half-story or one-story Folk Victorian versions occur as well. The massing is irregular, and a dominant street-facing gable is usually present on an asymmetrical façade. Towers are commonly found on the main elevation in the larger, more elaborate manifestations. Roof forms are normally hipped or cross gabled. Windows are often one over one (a single pane for the top and bottom halves), and double hung. Stained glass or leaded glass appears in even some of the simplest examples. A particular design feature of this style is the Queen Anne window, which is double hung with a single light (pane of glass) on the lower portion while the upper portion has a single large pane surrounded by smaller square panes, usually made from colored glass. Large one-story porches are ubiquitous, accenting the irregular plan of the façade, while recessed porches and balconies appear on upper floors. Queen Anne houses are easily recognized by an abundance of decorative wooden gingerbreading (sometimes called spindlework), used to detail porches and accent doorways, gables, and bay windows, and by heavily textured wall surfaces that use an abundance of patterned shingles. While wooden examples are most common, brick versions occasionally appeared, achieving the ornate layering of texture through different brick patterns, colors, or even half-timbered elements.

The term "Queen Anne" is a misnomer, since this style has little in common with the formal Italian Renaissance Revival architecture that was popular during Queen Anne's reign in England from 1702 to 1714. Instead, Queen Anne designers borrowed architectural forms from the preceding Elizabethan and Jacobean periods. English architect Richard Norman Shaw (1831–1912) borrowed design elements from half-timbered medieval architecture. Several sketches of his work were published during the 1870s in the journal *Building News*. Shaw was one of the most popular designers of late Victorian houses, and developed early Arts and Crafts designs, popularized by William Morris, in addition to the Queen Anne style. Smaller, vernacular versions of the Queen Anne style are sometimes referred to as Folk Victorian. These structures also have spindlework, front porches, and a dominant front gable, but are usually only one or one and a half stories with considerably less ornamentation than their larger cousins.

Americans who were unable to travel abroad would have seen examples of the nascent Queen Anne style at the 1876 Philadelphia Centennial International Exposition with buildings designed for the British commissioner and delegates. These irregularly massed buildings with half timbering, extended bays, steep roof lines, and multilighted windows were illustrated in *American Building Magazine* and *Building News*. The first American example of this style is the Watts-Sherman House (1874) at Newport, Rhode Island, designed by Henry Hobson Richardson. Architects and designers could peruse Queen Anne design elements in illustrated style books of the period, including E. C. Gardner's *Illustrated Homes* (1875) and Bicknell and Comstock's *Specimen Book of One-Hundred Architectural Designs* (1880).

The development of the Queen Anne and the Folk Victorian styles was, in part, made possible by a fundamental change in construction technology—the balloon frame. This streamlined construction technique was first used in Chicago and became the major building method. It is still the most common method of frame construction in the United States. The new lightweight framing technique replaced the heavier braced-frame construction. Braced-frame construction required heavy corner posts and hewn joints. In contrast, the balloon frame has corner posts built from several two-by-fours and uses only nails to join framing members. This newer structural system allowed

Two late Victorian houses, 36th Avenue North, period photo. Bebb & Mendel, architects. *University of Washington Libraries, Special Collections, UW23563*

both cheaper and more rapid construction than hewn joints and also allowed greater freedom in creating the irregular floor plans common in these styles.

Victorians loved color, texture and pattern, but it is often difficult to tell how paint was used on their homes. Period photographs help in establishing structural design, but the black-and-white medium offers little information regarding original color schemes. Scraping the paint back to its original layer is not always reliable, since pigments can change color over time, and distinguishing primers and undercoats from finish coats can be difficult. Exterior color choices were considerably more limited than the thousands of shades available to contemporary homeowners. Gray, various shades of green, and brown were frequently used. Blues, yellows, purples and bright reds were not often used since these colors were seldom colorfast. Smaller houses often used two similar colors, one for the main body of the house, the other for trim—window frames, cornices, brackets, and porch railings and supports. Sometimes an additional color was used for window sashes. More elaborate houses might have six or more paint colors. Late Victorian buildings often used softer paint colors, particularly if they had Colonial Revival or Neoclassical design elements. Pastel yellows and blue-grays were common, and trim might be white, instead of the darker colors preferred in earlier decades.

Two residences at 12th Avenue between Cherry Street and Spring Street, in 1909. *James P. Lee. University of Washington Libraries, Special Collections, Lee 115*

INTERIORS

Both large and small Victorian residences usually had a front entry hall. If there was a second floor, the main staircase was immediately accessible from the front hall, and could be quite articulated, with decorative spindles, a massive newel post, and occasionally a paneled sidewall. A

Victorian living room, Anson S. Burwell residence, with elaborately patterned wallpaper, period photograph.
Museum of History and Industry, Seattle, 18784

secondary staircase for servant use was occasionally located in the back of the house. An important piece of furniture from this time period, the hall stand, would have been displayed in the front hallway. Hall stands provided convenient pegs for gentleman guests to leave their hats, a mirror where one could quickly check appearance, a place for the newly popular umbrella to rest, and an area for both ladies and gentlemen to leave calling cards.

A parlor for receiving guests was frequently located off the front hallway. This room usually had a fireplace and was the most likely location for a bay window. Elaborate Victorian houses would also have a library or sitting room off of the parlor, where the family would spend their private time. Frequently the parlor was connected to the hallway by a set of large pocket doors, which had the advantage of disappearing into the interior walls when not in use rather than taking up wall space. A formal dining room was also located on the main floor and was often separated from the parlor by a set of pocket doors as well. If a house were large enough to warrant a pantry, it would lie between the dining room and the kitchen, providing storage for china, silverware, and glassware, in addition to providing a buffer between the

smelly, noisy kitchen and the family's dining space.

Victorian kitchens were spacious, but poorly laid out for modern conveniences, with tables providing much of the workspace, and a relatively small amount of cabinet space. The pantry provided the main storage area for the dining and cooking areas of the house. Victorian kitchens, with one door leading to the pantry and usually another to the outside or a back hallway, not to mention numerous windows providing ventilation and light, frequently lacked expanses of unbroken wall space. Kitchen countertops were usually wood, and cabinet doors were designed to set flush within their frame. Linoleum was popular for kitchens, baths, and even some hallways.

Bathrooms were usually tiled, with small hexagonal tiles covering the floor, and larger, rectangular tiles on wall surfaces. Tubs were freestanding, and few would have had shower fixtures. Most homeowners simply used water pitchers to pour water over their heads while sitting in the bathtub. White was the color of choice for bathrooms, because of its connotations with hygienic conditions. Console sinks with their exposed plumbing were popular until the late 1900s when pedestal sinks became common.

Living rooms and bedrooms were ornate by contemporary standards. Wood floors, either oak or fir, were accented with Oriental rugs. Sanitary concerns discouraged wall-to-wall carpeting, which was difficult to clean. Large machine-made Brussels (looped pile) and Wilton (cut pile) carpets were common, and could be taken outside and beaten. Wealthier home owners favored carpets manufactured by Axminster, which imitated some of the complex patterns found in hand-knotted Oriental rugs and provided a wider range of colors than either Brussels or Wilton carpets. Designers in the late Victorian era (1870–1910) called for less cluttered rooms, more subdued wall colors, and simpler window treatments than earlier styles. "Simpler" is a relative term with window treatments, which still had two or three different types of fabrics, albeit fewer swags and trims than earlier styles. A number of British designers were important in developing late Victorian interiors, including William Morris, Stephen Crane, and Charles Eastlake (author of *Hints on Household Taste*, 1872). While the brackets, grooves, spindles, and inlays common in Victorian furniture styles may look overly fussy to modern eyes, they are in many cases far more restrained than the preceding Renaissance Revival and Rococo Revival styles from the 1850s. Favored interior paint selections included rich burgundies, deep golds, peacock blue, and plum. Wallpaper was extremely popular during this period and multiple patterns in one room were not uncommon, with rooms having several horizontal layers of pattern. If a homeowner's resources allowed, ceilings were even papered or stenciled with decorative patterns.

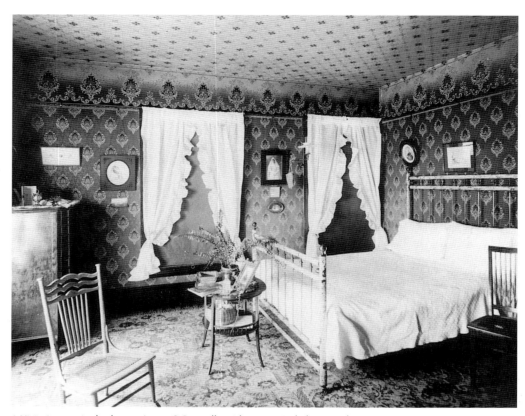

A Victorian master bedroom, Anson S. Burwell residence, period photograph.
Museum of History and Industry, Seattle, 18785

A little girl's bedroom with typical Victorian furnishings, Anson S. Burwell residence, period photograph. *Museum of History and Industry, Seattle, 18786*

V. W. VOORHEES, ARCHITECT, SEATTLE, WASH.

DESIGN NO. 38 B.

Width of this seven-room house is 26 feet; length 40 feet; height of first story 9 feet; height of second story in the lowest place 7 feet; height of second story 8½ feet.

Exterior finished with siding and shingles.

Approximate cost of construction, $1,500.00.

Cost of one set of plans, specifications and details, $13.00.

Cost of two sets of plans, specifications and details, $15.00.

(Any plan can be reversed to suit location.)

A Victorian house featured in Seattle architect V. W. Voorhees's pattern book, *Western Home Builder*, circa 1910.

University of Washington Libraries, Special Collections, UW23600

VICTORIAN HOUSES

Italianate (1850–1885)

circa 1870–1880	Corliss P. Stone Residence
circa 1873	Dexter Horton Residence
1882	George W. Ward Residence
1890	James Bard Metcalf Residence
circa 1890	Mills Residence
1901	Italianate Victorian

Queen Anne and Folk Victorian (1880–1910)

1883	Turner-Koepf Residence
1885	George C. Kinnear Residence
1888	David T. Denny Residence
circa 1890	D. Thomas Denny Jr. Residence
circa 1890	Charles H. Lilly Residence
1890	Henry Van Asselt Residence
1890	Victorian Builders' Row Houses
1890–1909	14th Avenue Housing Group: Gilman and Torbatica Residences

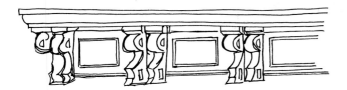

Italianate cornice treatment, with paired brackets.

Victorian shingled gable, with canted corners.

Hooded Italianate window.

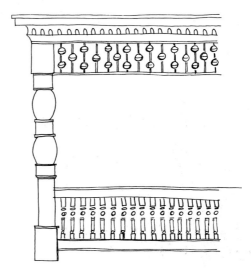

Victorian spindlework, with a turned porch post.

1891	Victor Steinbrueck Residence
1892	List-Bussell Residence
circa 1892	Fisher-Howell Residence
1894	William H. Thompson Residence
1892–1893	23rd Avenue Houses Group, 800 Block
1899–1902	Yesler Residences
circa 1890	Various Victorian Residences
circa 1900	Capt. M. T. Powers Residence

ITALIANATE (1850–1885)

Corliss P. Stone residence, period photograph. *University of Washington Libraries, Special Collections, UW23564*

Corliss P. Stone Residence (circa 1870–1880)

Corliss P. Stone was associated with the Seattle Timber Preserving Company of Ballard and served as partners with Lewis Rowe in a carriage business. His house typifies a simply ornamented Italianate dwelling. Predominantly rectangular in plan, the structure has a hipped roof with decorative brackets under the roof eaves. Although the second-story windows do not have elaborate crowns, the first-floor windows and doors have stronger articulation. While the front windows appear to be two over two, double hung, the side windows appear to be a mix of four over four and one over one. Typical of the Italianate style, the front porch is relatively simple with a minimal porch railing.

Dexter Horton residence (demolished), corner of 3rd Avenue and Seneca Street, period photograph. *University of Washington Libraries, Special Collections, UV/13782*

Dexter Horton Residence (circa 1873)

The Dexter Horton residence was a typical example of the Italianate style, with massive eave brackets and narrow articulated windows. The ornate balustrade along the top of the dual-pitched roof, decorative wall treatments above the windows, and the elaborate front door were design features that added a strong visual presence to the structure, and made it considerably more imposing than the Corliss P. Stone house. The implied importance of the homeowner was unmistakable.

The man with resources to build such an ornate structure was Dexter Horton, a major business leader in Seattle's early development. Horton, originally from New York, moved as a child with his family to Illinois. He married at age nineteen and traveled with his wife, Rebecca, by wagon train to the Pacific Northwest. He arrived in the Puget Sound area in 1853, via Salem, Oregon. One of his first jobs was sawing shingles for Yesler's Mill. An early business venture was starting the first private bank in Washington Territory. In later years he sold the bank and spent his time developing real estate. He was active in the religious life of his community, and served as Sunday school superintendent for the Methodist church.

George W. Ward residence (1882), in 2004.

George W. Ward Residence (1882)

The George W. Ward residence is thought to be Seattle's oldest extant house, and is typical of towered Italianate buildings. The two-story structure has irregular massing, with a three-story tower marking the front entrance. Roof pitches are low, in keeping with the style, and are accented with nonstructural brackets. Windows are one over one, double hung, and are articulated with moderately ornate caps. The main entry is shielded by a small L-shaped porch, which is ornamented with delicate spindlework. The front door surround is moderately ornate as well, echoing the window caps.

One of the last surviving Italianate buildings in Seattle, the house was built by George W. Ward in 1882. Born in New York, Ward moved to Seattle in 1874 with his wife, Louise, and two children. He became a contractor and builder, eventually heading the Llewellyn and Ward Company, which specialized in real estate, insurance, and loans. He served as president of the Washington State Mutual Accident Association, and was a justice of the peace. In his private life he served as a deacon in the Baptist church. Although this house was built during a prosperous period for the family, they sold it a decade later, after the 1893 economic crash. In 1905 the property became a hotel and housed boarders during the 1909 Alaska-Yukon-Pacific Exposition. The structure was originally located at 1025 Pike Street. It was slated for demolition in the 1980s until Historic Seattle, a preservation advocacy group, helped relocate the structure and convert it into office space.

James Bard Metcalfe residence, period photograph. *Museum of History and Industry, Seattle, 1231*

James Bard Metcalfe Residence (1890)

The James Bard Metcalfe residence is an example of an asymmetrical Italianate house. The two-story structure had both front and side porches that were capped with a low wooden balustrade. An ornamental iron balustrade and small decorative brackets accented the shallow hipped roof. Spaces between the brackets were further articulated by raised rectangular molding. The main floor of the house had an extended bay to the left, followed by a recessed double bay section. Windows, while paired on the projecting bay, were singly placed on the rest of the main façade. The house had a mixture of window types. While all appear to have been double hung, some were two over two and the narrower examples were one over one. This house was an imposing, stately residence, befitting the social status of its owner, James Bard Metcalfe, and his wife Louise Boarman Metcalfe.

Metcalfe was a native of Mississippi, and served the Confederacy during the Civil War. He studied law after the war, then decided to move west for greater career advancement, settling in San Francisco. He visited Seattle in 1883 and decided to stay, opening a law office the following year. A few years later he entered into partnership with Junius Rochister, forming the firm of Metcalfe and Rochister. Metcalfe had several different legal partnerships over his professional career, with the last being Metcalfe and Jury. One of his sons, James Vernon, was also a lawyer, and graduated from the University of Washington in 1909.

Mills residence, photograph date unknown. *Ballard Historical Society, Seattle, 002/19932840002*

Mills Residence (circa 1890)

Some houses do not fit neatly into one particular style. This example might very well be a transition between the Italianate Victorian and the later Queen Anne style, or an Italianate remodeled at a later date. The major footprint of the building is square, which was common for Italianate structures. The small brackets under the eaves are also typical of the Italianate, not the Queen Anne style. The front porch treatment, with turned porch supports and delicate gingerbreading, is more indicative of a Queen Anne structure. The smaller second-floor portion of the bay window is unusual.

Italianate Victorian house originally located at 208 13th Avenue South, in 2004.

Italianate Victorian porch detail, 208 13th Avenue South.

Italianate Victorian Residence (1901)

This two-story building was one of a pair that were almost identical, both having hipped roofs, and similar floor plans and window articulation. The main distinguishing feature was the porch treatment. The house at 208 13th Avenue South has two porches, one on each floor. The main-level porch has gingerbreading, while the second-floor porch has columns and arch decorations. The house at 210 13th Avenue South (destroyed by fire) had a covered entry porch with an ornate column. These buildings were originally single-family houses, but were subdivided into apartments. The residence at 208 13th Avenue South was later moved to 1414 South Washington Street for the construction of the Bailey Gatzert Elementary School.

Italianate Victorian house located at 210 13th Avenue South, in 1937.
Puget Sound Regional Archives

QUEEN ANNE AND FOLK VICTORIAN (1880–1910)

Turner-Koepf residence, in 1937.
*Washington State Archives,
Puget Sound Regional Branch*

Turner-Koepf Residence (1883)

This two-story house, thought to be the first house erected on Beacon Hill's summit, was built by Edward A. Turner in the Italianate style. The massing of the original house was rectangular in plan, with a pyramidal roof, quite common for Italianate homes at that time. The main façade originally had a two-story bay window and small, ornamented porches on both the front and the side. A subsequent owner, Frederick Koepf, remodeled the structure around 1907. During the remodeling process the double stacked bays were extended, causing them to look more like a tower than bay windows. The Italianate brackets were removed, rafter tails exposed, and a large wraparound porch was added with Tuscan columns and a pediment marking the front entry. The end result resembles a Queen Anne "Free Classic" subtype, which is identified by Classical ornamentation applied to Victorian massing.

Turner, a Maine native, arrived in Seattle by 1875. He began working for the *Daily Tribune*, which was acquired by the *Daily Intelligencer* by 1879. After several years in the newspaper business, Turner ventured into real estate and was a principal in Turner, Engle, and Lewis Real Estate,

Loans, and Insurance Company. When the house was built in the early 1880s, it was several miles south of the city. In fact, it was so far removed from named streets that its address in city directories was "ridge 1 ¾ miles south of post office." By 1896 electric streetcars connected this area to the downtown. Turner and his wife appear to have lived in the house only a few years. Frederick Koepf, who purchased the house in 1898, was chief draftsman for the city's engineer's office.

The house was moved when 15th Avenue South was graded. The property was purchased by the Jefferson Park Ladies Improvement Club in 1916, shortly after Mrs. Koepf's death. The club, founded in 1912, had a civic interest in improving education and living conditions, and in contributing to community enrichment projects. The ladies had planned to enlarge the home by adding a hall, complete with stage, to seat 600. Although the side porch was enclosed and the living room enlarged (by removing most of an interior wall), the plan never materialized. The property now serves as headquarters for the Washington State Garden Club.

Drawing of original Edward A. Turner residence based on a historic photograph in the building's state historical register file.

Tower detail, Turner-Koepf residence, in 2004.

Interior detail, Turner-Koepf residence, in 2004.

George C. Kinnear residence, front view, period photograph. *Museum of History and Industry, Seattle, 4288*

George C. Kinnear Residence (1885)

The George C. Kinnear residence, designed by the Syracuse, New York, architectural firm of Kirby & Randall, was one of many stunning Queen Anne houses that gave the Queen Anne neighborhood its distinctive architectural character. The house, built in 1885, was an excellent example of late Victorian architecture. While exterior wall treatments were relatively sparse and lacked the usual array of applied gingerbreading, the house was rich with multiple projecting gables, a large tower, porches, and balconies. Queen Anne–style windows are evident in the structure's second floor and in the decorative multilighted windows that graced the turret.

Kinnear was born in Ohio, moving to Indiana and then Illinois as a child. He came to the Northwest in 1874 and returned with his family in 1878. He quickly became involved with real estate, promoting road construction through Snoqualmie Pass and organizing an immigration board for the city. He was also treasurer of a local power company and a railroad. In 1887 he gave fourteen acres of land, located on the west side of Queen Anne Hill, to the city of Seattle for a park. He bequeathed his house to his church for use as a retirement home. While the house no longer stands (destroyed in 1958), the retirement and assisted-living home, Bayview Manor, still occupies the original site.

George C. Kinnear residence, side view, period photograph. *Museum of History and Industry, Seattle, 6530*

David Thomas Denny residence, circa 1900. *University of Washington, Special Collections, UW13792*

David Thomas Denny Residence (1888)

The David Thomas Denny residence was a particularly elaborate example of Queen Anne architecture, with octagonal and round turrets, complex rooflines, and a substantial wraparound front porch. The articulated chimneys and porch gingerbreading were accented by multiple colors of paint. While windows on the upper stories have multiple lights and even a horseshoe arch-shaped window, the majority of the windows are rather simple one over ones, perhaps selected to frame territorial views. Seattleites were aware of architectural trends back East through architectural journals. This residence is almost identical to one illustrated in the *Scientific American Architects and Builders Edition* of 1888. The house was later moved and converted into apartments before being demolished in 1938.

The David Thomas Denny residence, nicknamed "Decatur Terrace" after a fort that served as their protection during the Seattle Indian conflict of 1855–1856, was a lavishly decorated mansion that symbolized the success and wealth of Seattle's founders. Denny had left the Midwest for the Pacific Coast, arriving in Oregon to work in the lumber camps. He was one of the first settlers to arrive in Seattle, and he became involved in almost every aspect of the new city's life. He eventually platted seven additions for the growing city. His interest in electric transportation led to his involvement in electric and cable streetcars. He helped build and equip an electric road to Ravenna Park. His business involvements also included presidency of the city's water company, and serving as chief executive for several

SUPPLEMENT TO THE SCIENTIFIC AMERICAN-ARCHITECTS AND BUILDERS EDITION-MARCH 1888.

A suburban residence, 1888, illustrated in *Scientific American Architects and Builders Edition*, similar to the David Thomas Denny residence.
Scientific American Architects and Builders Edition, *March 1888*

large mining companies. He was a member of the city council and was involved in education as well, serving for twelve years as the school director of Seattle's school district 1 and as a regent for the Territorial University. Other civic involvements included his charter membership in the Knights Templar fraternal organization, work with the Prohibition party, and a pro-woman's suffrage stance. In his leisure time he enjoyed hunting and is rumored to have killed the last elk in the Seattle area.

D. Thomas Denny residence, period photograph. *University of Washington, Special Collections, UW23566*

D. Thomas Denny Jr. Residence (circa 1890)

David Thomas Denny Jr., known as D. Thomas Denny, inhabited a large Queen Anne house as well. While the house was ornate, it was considerably less decorated than his father's, with only a single tower and a smaller porch. The chimney stacks and the main porch were also less ornamented. The house had an irregular roof massing, with an octagonal tower on the front corner, and cross gables on both the front and the side. The front cross gable added emphasis to the main entry, while the side cross gable had canted corners. Dentil work formed a delicate stringcourse dividing the second floor from the attic space. Windows were primarily one over one, double hung. A period interior photo of the main stairwell shows a grand front hall with a staircase, and a wood paneled hallway. The ornate newel post, complete with electric light fixture, was common in larger homes.

Interior, main stairwell of the D. Thomas Denny residence, period photograph. *University of Washington, Special Collections, UW23565*

Charles H. Lilly residence, 1913. *University of Washington, Special Collections, UW3494*

Charles H. Lilly Residence (circa 1890)

The Charles H. Lilly residence shows typical Queen Anne massing, with its bell tower, cross gables, and large wraparound front porch. The Palladian window in the upper gable (a tall arched window flanked by two smaller rectangular windows) and the paired Tuscan columns on the front porch are illustrative of a Queen Anne subtype sometimes referred to as "Free Classic." While many people do not think of Classical columns and Palladian windows as particularly Victorian in style, perhaps one third of Queen Anne homes had such details. This stylistic variation became increasingly common after 1893, due in part to Classical design influences from the World's Columbian Exposition in Chicago that year.

Charles H. Lilly arrived in Seattle from Illinois in 1889 and worked as a street contractor hauling building mate-

rial. He soon formed a business partnership with E. F. Bogardus, which led to the establishment of Lilly, Bogardus, and Company, the largest hay and grain business in the Northwest. By 1904 Lilly took sole control of the company and added seed stock to his sales line. Many of the seeds were grown in La Conner, Washington, and were sold in Hawaii, Alaska, Asia, and Europe. His company also owned the New North Coast Flouring Mills. In addition to his many business ventures and his active involvement with the local chamber of commerce, Lilly was involved in community life through the Presbyterian Church, and the fraternal orders of the Knights Templar and the Shriners.

Henry Van Asselt Residence (1890)

Henry Van Asselt residence, period photograph. *Museum of History and Industry, Seattle, SHS1106*

Henry Van Asselt residence, in 1955. *Museum of History and Industry, Seattle, 5503*

The Henry Van Asselt residence typifies the Queen Anne architectural style in some of the movement's most characteristic details: irregular massing, a steeply pitched cross-gabled roof, first-floor canted corners with end brackets, an ornately decorated front porch (including a horseshoe arch), and Queen Anne windows. Images of this house suggest how houses can change over time. The photograph taken in 1955 shows a monochromatic paint job, an added second-floor window, perhaps for a bathroom (far right), and the removal of the gingerbreading (including the ornate horseshoe arch) from the front porch. It is likely that the porch gingerbreading was removed because of rot in the original decorative elements. The second floor window addition is trimmed with molding representative of the Craftsman design movement, and was perhaps undertaken during the 1910s–1920s.

Van Asselt was among the first settlers to arrive in the Seattle area. A native of Holland, he moved to New York in 1877 and then traveled westward to Iowa and then Oregon. By 1850 he lived in Oregon City, and is rumored to have lost his home during an Indian conflict of the 1850s. He made several trips to the Puget Sound region, settling there in 1889. Van Asselt was a jack of all trades, and worked as a farmer, shingle maker, carpenter, and cabinetmaker at various times in his life. He was also an expert marksman, a valued skill during the settlement era.

Victorian builders' row houses, period photograph. *University of Washington Library, Special Collections, UW13787*

Victorian Builders' Row Houses (1890)

Row houses were a common urban housing type during the late nineteenth century. They provided individual family homes, but their smaller floor plan, shared wall construction, and small yards made them more affordable than large, free-standing houses. This particularly fine example epitomized the style, with irregular massing, a steeply pitched roof, and a decorative ridge crest with finials. The walls were articulated through a variety of materials, including shingles, vertical siding, and horizontal siding. Windows were predominantly one over one, double hung.

Canted corner windows on the second floor were accented with ornate scrollwork. Stained glass windows in the center section were on a half level, most likely indicating a staircase. The front entries were lavishly decorated with a wide variety of turned wooden ornamentation, even a small sunburst located in the crest of the porch gable. While black-and-white images are not helpful in ascertaining original paint colors, the tonal contrasts clearly show the use of at least five different hues.

14th Avenue housing group, in 2004.

14th Avenue Housing Group (1890–1909): Gilman and Torbactia Residences

These houses were built on lower Queen Anne Hill in an area once known as Smith's Cove. At this time, Puget Sound's tide extended along 15th Avenue West, and these homes were only one block from the waterfront. The Gilman house, located at 2016 14th Avenue West, was constructed in 1891. The two-story structure has a gabled roof, an angled bay window on the main floor, and a rectangular tower. Historic photographs of the buildings show milled brackets and posts, now missing, although the main gable still has remnants of elaborate Victorian scrollwork. The Torbactia house, at 2014 14th Avenue West, was constructed a decade later in 1901. Similar in plan to the Gilman house, it lacks the rectangular tower. Angled bays are on both the first and second floors. Sections of the original bracketing are intact. Other houses in the neighborhood are Victorian as well, including those at 2000 and 2006 14th Avenue West and at 1311 West Newton.

At the time of construction these houses were located in a Finnish fishing community, which encompassed several blocks. By 1915 increased Slavic emigration to Seattle changed the area's ethnic character; the Slavs also had a maritime heritage. By 1916 Herman Hentschke purchased the house at 2010 14th Avenue West, and the Slavic names of Zorovich, Brusich, and Damoulow can be found as owners of nearby residences.

Gilman residence (1891), 2016 14th Avenue West, in 2004.

Torbactia residence (1901), 2014 14th Avenue West, in 2004.

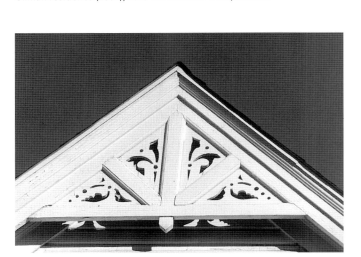

Gable detail on the Gilman residence.

Detail of canted corner on the Torbactia residence.

Victor Steinbrueck residence, in 2004.

Victor Steinbrueck Residence (1891)

This two-story wood-clad house has cross gables, a tower on the left front, and a wraparound porch on the main façade. Victorian details include turned balusters and gingerbreading. Side windows have canted corners and decorative brackets. Fish-scale shingles adorn all the gables while the front cross gable has spindlework that is repeated on the wraparound front porch.

Victor Steinbrueck, a Seattle architect, lived in this house and was instrumental in getting it listed as a landmark example of a middle-class Victorian residence. Steinbrueck, one of Seattle's most eloquent preservation champions, was an important figure in the city's urban planning and public policy development. Deeply concerned with the relationship between people and their cultural and built environments, he was a major advocate for preserving Seattle's Pike Place Market in the 1960s.

List-Bussell residence, period photograph. *Courtesy of Darren Pritt*

List-Bussell Residence (1892)

The List-Bussell residence, a remodeled Queen Anne, was covered with stucco in the late 1920s. The structure retained its roof massing, canted corners, turret, decorative glass, and interior woodwork. The house is large, fifteen rooms, and was sited to take full advantage of Lake Washington and mountain views. As a result, the front of the house faces away from the street. The original siding was horizontal wood with half-timbered detailing, decorative shingles, and ornate millwork. In 1928 new owners hired contractor W. H. Dye to conduct an extensive exterior remodel. Dye recounted that the new owners were influenced by Hollywood films showing Spanish and Italian architecture, with smooth stucco exteriors. Thus, Dye removed all decorative trim, wire meshed the exterior, and stuccoed the entire structure. The stucco has been removed in recent years. The interior of the house has a large entry foyer, with an oak staircase. The newel post is edged with carved oak leaves. Oak was also used for flooring, wainscoting, and window trim on the main levels.

The original owners of the building were George S. and Julia Gooch List. List was a real estate investor, and was partners with James Upper. Their firm helped develop the city's Lakeside and Rosedale Additions. List was also a general agent for the Great Northern Railroad and Wells Fargo Express. In 1900 the house was sold to Charles and Nina Bussell. Bussell was a businessman who invested in real estate, mining, lumber, shipping, and canneries. In 1889 he began to purchase tidewater land and became one of the largest holders of tidal land in Seattle. While many considered his tidal investments unwise, he was able to sell most of this land to the railroads in 1906, for the considerable sum of $1.5 million. The profits made from this

List-Bussell residence, in 2004.

List-Bussell residence, in 1937. *Puget Sound Regional Archives*

venture allowed him to further expand the Bussell Land Company and the Weber–Bussell Canning Company. The house was designed by the architectural firm of Flynn and Rockmark.

Fisher-Howell residence, in 1937.
Puget Sound Regional Archives

Fisher-Howell Residence (circa 1892)

While difficult to see through the dense plantings in front, this landmark house showcases a variety of Queen Anne detailing. Elaborate gingerbreading, cut vergeboards, and decorative shingles accent the cross-gabled roofline. A large front porch supported by turned pillars covers most of the front and side elevations.

Bidmead and Annie Wright purchased this lot in 1891 with hopes to build a mansion that would rival the Dennys' in both scale and decoration. However, they fell on hard times, and Charles E. Owings acquired the property in 1898. Owings finished the house over a number of years, but appears to have not had the funds to sufficiently maintain the property. In 1900 he is listed in the Polk Seattle city directory as renting beds in the house. He sold the property a few years later and the house was eventually purchased by a Mr. Saylor in 1906. Saylor's two daughters began a candy company in the house, the Canterbury Candy Makers. The company's first factory was located on Boylston Avenue East, just one block away from the home.

Gable detail of the Fisher-Howell residence.

William H. Thompson residence, period photograph. *Washington State Historical Society, Tacoma, 1967.45.2.1*

William H. Thompson Residence (1894)

This large Queen Anne structure was designed as a single-family home, although it was used as a boarding house and then as a sanatorium for a number of years. It has a high, hipped roof with dormers on both front and sides, and a three-story tower. A large wraparound porch extends along the front and east side of the building. Paneling and decorative shingles ornament gable ends. Most of the windows are single paned and double hung, although the front door has a transom and sidelights with a diamond-paned window pattern. The interior of the building was subdivided and modified for its use as a sanatorium, although the original oak staircase remains.

The builder of the house was Ernest A. MacKay, who applied for a permit to construct the dwelling in April 1894.

Estimated construction cost was $4,500. MacKay, who built the house for himself, appears to have been a prosperous citizen of Seattle at that time. The Polk Seattle city directory lists him as secretary-treasurer of the Puget Sound Glass Company in 1897, the year that the house was sold to William H. Thompson, who lived in the residence from 1897 to 1917. Thompson, a Georgia native, had moved west at the end of the Civil War. Originally trained in civil engineering, he began a law career in Indiana and moved to Seattle in 1889, eventually establishing his own firm, Thompson, Edsen and Humphries. Well known for his oratory skills, he served on the Democrats' State Central Committee, which debated Washington Territory's admission as a state. Thompson was also known for his literary writings, including the poem, "The High Tide at Gettysburg," which was published in several languages.

23rd Avenue Houses Group, in the 1960s. *Werner Lenggenhager. Seattle Public Library, 22444*

23rd Avenue Housing Group, 800 Block (1892–1893)

The Victorian houses on the 800 block of 23rd Avenue are considered the finest extant grouping of Folk Victorian architecture in Seattle. Constructed in 1892–1893, the buildings have nearly identical plans and elevations. All of the houses are one and a half story, with steep gabled roofs, and machine-milled wooden gingerbreading, gable ornaments, and turned posts. These small houses were designed to include a parlor, dining room, and kitchen on the main floor, and bedrooms on the second level. Bathrooms appear to have been located outside the buildings originally, which was not uncommon for this time period. Historic Seattle played a major role in preserving the current structures and restored four of the buildings in the late 1970s before selling them with protective covenants.

These row houses are located in Seattle's Central district, an area that underwent tremendous real estate development during the late 1880s when a cable car line connected it to Lake Washington. The houses occupy part of a twenty-two block subdivision, commonly called the Walla Walla Addition, platted by H. H. Hungate, Charles A. Hungate, and James F. Cropp. The developers of the addition were eastern Washington investors. Dr. James F.

23rd Avenue Houses Group, detail of gable end, in 2004.

Cropp was a physician in Walla Walla and Charles Hungate was a partner in a Seattle real estate investment firm. There were six Folk Victorian houses built on this block originally. The builders remain unknown. Residents of these homes were middle class, including Lucilla Kinsman, a grocery store clerk, and James McCarthy, a blacksmith.

Yesler residences, in 2004.

Yesler residence, gable detail, in 2004.

Restored Yesler residence on the left, next to one of the residences that has lost its architectural detailing through siding, in 2004.

Yesler Residences (1899–1902)

The Yesler residences, built in a middle-class neighborhood, served as rentals for years before they were abandoned. During the 1980s a failed renovation gutted the structures, leaving them vacant for years. In 1996 Historic Seattle purchased the houses and has facilitated their preservation. The buildings were originally constructed as rentals for Dr. Alexander L. Prevost of the Copland Medical Institute. Prevost, born in Canada, moved to the United States with his parents in 1853, becoming a naturalized citizen in 1870. He is thought to have had some medical training in New York and arrived in Seattle between 1893 and 1896. The residences cost $2000 each when built by

contractor Emil Kriegel, a German citizen who emigrated to the United States in 1882 and resided in Seattle by 1890. A carpenter, he most likely found Seattle a lucrative place to engage in business after the Great Fire.

The home at 103 23rd Avenue was rented by James and Isabel Wallace, who moved in with their two children shortly after the building's construction in 1899. Wallace originally worked for the Seattle Harness Company but started his own hauling service, Lloyd Transfer Company, in 1901. Construction of 109 23rd Avenue was in 1902, also by Emil Kriegel. By the 1920s this building housed a bakery run by the Lippman brothers (Otto, Harry, and Frank).

An ornate Queen Anne residence (circa 1890), in 1909. *James P. Lee. University of Washington Libraries, Special Collections, Lee 154*

Various Victorian Residences (circa 1890)

These three houses illustrate the range of smaller Victorian residences that were once prevalent in Seattle. The most ornate of the three was probably the most typically urban in style. While small in size, all had the elaborate Queen Anne details found in much larger examples, including multiple surface treatments, clipped corners, and gingerbreading. The first example, 1009 East Madison, was the most ornate, and had irregular massing and a prominent front gable. Shingles and wood siding cover the structure. A Queen Anne door, without colored glass, is similar in form to a Queen Anne window. The front façade had canted corners with decorative scrollwork. Patterned shingles and an ornamented vergeboard decorated the upper half of the structure.

The house on 62nd Street is the largest example but the simplest in its ornamentation. The lot it sits on is large, suggesting a suburban setting. It shares massing similarities with late nineteenth-century farmhouses found in the region. It may very well have been part of a larger landtract, eventually subdivided as urban areas encroached. The simple, almost austere building form was accented with ornate gable scrollwork and turned porch posts.

The one-story Victorian probably had the smallest square footage of the three examples. Some might describe it as a "Victorian Bungalow" because of its small size or a "Folk Victorian" due to its simple ornamentation. Representative of small vernacular housing stock, ornamented to fit contemporary trends, the simple pyramidal roof of the building was masked by the gabled bay extension, a gabled dormer, and a small front porch. As a result, massing became one of the structure's major design elements. Victorian trim was minimal, and is evident only in the slender window surrounds, shingled front gable, and Tuscan porch columns.

A cross-gabled, two-story Victorian (circa 1890–1900), in the early twentieth century. *Ballard Historical Society, 001/19931340001*

A small pyramidal-roofed
Victorian (circa 1900), in 1921.
Ballard Historical Society, 001/19880370001

Capt. M. T. Powers
residence, period photograph.
*University of Washington, Special
Collections, UW3583*

Capt. M. T. Powers Residence (circa 1900)

This residence, although imposing in structure, was sparsely decorated, appropriate perhaps for Seattle police officer Capt. M. T. Powers, who lived here. In fact, the only thing that truly indicates its Victorian style is the irregular massing created by the double-story bay, and the shingle-accented cross gable. This house is an excellent example of what is now called a Free Classic Victorian, a house style that is often simpler in plan, with restrained ornamentation that echoes the Classical style. Although the exact construction date for this residence is undetermined, it was likely built around 1900. During this time Classically inspired details were popularized by the 1893 World's Columbian Exposition held in Chicago. By 1900 the Colonial Revival and Neoclassical Revival styles had begun to surpass the Victorian styles in popularity.

2 CLASSICAL REVIVALS

Colonial Revival and Neoclassical Revival

nial and early Federal styles were loosely based on Greco-Roman design sources in an attempt to associate the greatness of past civilizations with our nascent democracy. The revivalist styles continued in their popularity, particularly at the end of the nineteenth century. The 1913 Seattle publication, *Homes and Gardens of the Pacific Coast*, noted the public acceptance of the style, and commented that, "There is no type of architecture which the American People more admire and none that is more appropriate for them to use than the 'colonial.' " In Seattle, European-born architects Bebb and Mendel were often retained by clients interested in Classical Revival designs.

COLONIAL REVIVAL (1880–1955)

While people from many countries lived in colonial America, the term "Colonial Revival" in architecture generally refers to houses based on early English and Dutch designs. The symmetrical Georgian and Federal style buildings had a number of architectural features that found favor, including extensive paneling of entryways and primary living spaces, center hallways, four-square plans, Palladian windows, Classical columns, and shuttered multilighted windows. Secondary influences came from Dutch Colonial examples, which sport a gambrel roof, sometimes described as a "barn" roof. While the dominant architectural style at the time of the Philadelphia exhibition was Victorian, it did not take long for designers to add Palladian windows and Classical columns to rambling irregularly massed Victorian structures, which are often identified as Queen Anne Free Classics. Colonial Revival styles gained further publicity when the well-known architecture firm of McKim, Mead, and White designed a Colonial Revival house in 1882 for H. A. C. Taylor of Newport, Rhode Island, a summer playground for America's elite.

A variety of design details used in English Colonial revival homes include the following: they generally have regular massing, with hipped or side-facing gables. Windows are evenly spaced, with the front door frequently holding the center position. A columned porch or small portico marks the primary entrance, and the paneled door is surrounded by sidelights and occasionally a Federal style fanlight above. Windows are double hung, with both sections displaying multiple lights. During the Colonial

Georgian plantation of Westover, Virginia (circa 1750), in 1993.

Dutch Colonial house in Colonial Williamsburg, Virginia (late 1700s, reconstruction), in 1993.

I N THE UNITED STATES, the Colonial Revival and Neoclassical Revival styles share some Classical design features. The Colonial Revival style, where architectural massing and details are copied from period Colonial examples, originated with the Philadelphia Centennial International Exposition of 1876. A growing wave of historical patriotism found visual form through historic interiors as well, designed to show how our founding fathers lived during the late 1700s and early 1800s. In turn, many Colo-

Preceding pages: (far left) Edwin G. Ames Colonial Revival residence, 808 36th Avenue North. *University of Washington Libraries, Special Collections, UW2462*; (chapter title page, upper left) Colonial Revival house, Mount Baker neighborhood; (upper right) Neoclassical Revival residence, 310 19th Avenue East, in 1951. *Werner Lenggenhager. Seattle Public Library, 22417*; (below) Colonial Revival house in Ballard.

period, large windows required the joining of multiple small panes of glass, since window glass was imported from Europe and large sheets were expensive and prone to breakage on the long sea crossing. Thus, for these revival styles, "old fashioned" multilighted windows were often specified. Palladian windows were popular: a tripartite design with either a larger central arched window or a regular window topped with an arch flanked by smaller double-hung windows.

Shutters reappear in Colonial Revival styles as well. Solid and louvered shutters were operable during the Colonial period, and could be used to block light or protect windows. Shutter catches—small pieces of metal hardware—held the shutters open against the side of the house, and could be turned to release the shutters for closing. While shutter catches were used in many early Colonial Revival homes, later examples often omit the catches. Some Colonial Revival houses may lack shutters entirely, since they were no longer functional by the late 1800s and were

purely decorative. (Most Victorian, Craftsman, and Tudor Revival styles lacked shutters, due to their obsolescence and because the combination of two or three windows together would not allow functional shutters.) Roof eaves are articulated with multiple layers of molding. Dentil work, a series of small square blocks, is one of the more typical examples. Some houses sport quoins, masonry details on the corners of buildings, distinguished from the primary masonry by size, texture, and/or color. Occasionally even wood clad houses have quoins. Quoins accented a building's corners, making them appear large and structurally sound. Other design details might include a balustraded roof, or widow's walk, and pediments over doors or windows.

Early examples of Colonial Revival were rarely historically accurate copies. Instead they were rather loose interpretations of the style. Colonial Revival homes were built from the late 1800s, and while their popularity has fluxuated, they remain popular to this day, particularly on the East Coast where the style originated. In 1898 *The American*

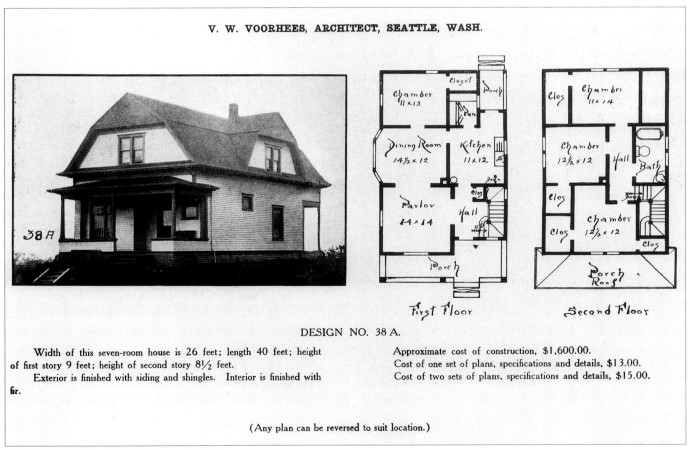

V. W. VOORHEES, ARCHITECT, SEATTLE, WASH.

DESIGN NO. 38 A.

Width of this seven-room house is 26 feet; length 40 feet; height of first story 9 feet; height of second story 8½ feet.
Exterior is finished with siding and shingles. Interior is finished with fir.

Approximate cost of construction, $1,600.00.
Cost of one set of plans, specifications and details, $13.00.
Cost of two sets of plans, specifications and details, $15.00.

(Any plan can be reversed to suit location.)

Dutch Colonial house featured in the V. W. Voorhees pattern book, *Western Home Builder*, circa 1910 *University of Washington, Special Collections, UW23599*

Parson Capon House, 1683, Topsfield, Massachusetts, in 2003.

Architect and Building News published a series of photographs and measured drawings of Colonial architecture. (They were republished in 1923.) Other publications, including Boston architect Joseph Chandler's *Colonial Architecture of Maryland, Pennsylvania, and Virginia* (1892), and Fiske Kimball's *Domestic Architecture of the American Colonies and of the Early Republic* (1922) also enhanced interest in the style, as did the much publicized documentation and restoration of Colonial Williamsburg during the 1930s. Williamsburg had been the capital of Virginia during the eighteenth century, and the multimillion dollar restoration and reconstruction of the town by John D. Rockefeller Jr. attracted national attention. One result of this intense documentation is that Colonial Revival houses constructed between 1910 and 1935 were more likely to duplicate the original prototypes. The style continued to be popular after World War II, but designs were usually simplified for economic reasons.

Dutch Colonial Revival houses achieved popularity somewhat later, around 1900. The Dutch Colonial, with the second story placed up under the roof, was a favorite of house plan books, and appeared frequently in the Standard Homes Company (Washington, DC) plan books from the 1920s. Most people were probably unaware of the style's Dutch origins, since the plans were given English names like "Oxford," "Washington," and "Jefferson." A jettied Colonial variation is more common post World War II, which has a second floor slightly overhanging the first, based on examples like the Parson Capon House of Topsfield, Massachusetts (1683). Smaller one-story or one-and-a-half-story Colonial Revivals appear in the twentieth century

as well. These examples frequently retain the multilighted windows, shutters, and occasional front portal pediment, but remove many of the more complex (and expensive) design details. The 1976 U.S. bicentennial celebration kept Colonial Revival forms in design periodicals during the late twentieth century.

NEOCLASSICAL REVIVAL (1895–1950)

Another architectural style that utilizes some of the same design elements as the Colonial Revival style, although frequently in different proportions, is the Neoclassical Revival, sometimes referred to as Beaux Arts. The Neoclassical Revival style was popular from about 1895 to 1950. As with its Colonial Revival cousin, façades are generally symmetrical, and roof types are commonly side gabled or hipped. The style was also popular during two main periods, the first from 1900 to 1920 and the second from the 1920s until the 1950s. The first version of the style utilized hipped roofs and elaborate Ionic or Corinthian columns. The later version has more examples of side-gabled roofs, and columns typically are simpler. Unlike the Colonial Revival style, Neoclassical Revival houses are generally grand, and smaller vernacular examples are almost unknown.

Neoclassical Revival houses generally have porches that are monumental in scale, reaching the full double-story height of the building. As a result the columns are large, usually referred to as "colossal." Porticos, instead of full façade porches, are common, further emphasizing the height of the columns. Windows and doors are placed symmetrically, and the multiple lights that were common with Colonial Revival are less frequent, with sometimes only the top portion of the window having multiple panes. Clustering multiple windows is more likely in this design than in the Colonial Revival style. Other features are side wings, roofline and porch-level balustrades, exaggerated broken pediments, and paneled front doors.

Neoclassical Revival architecture developed in part from the public's earlier interest in Colonial Georgian and Federal forms. But other styles blended into the mix, including civic architecture from Greece and Rome, and Neoclassical forms from the Italian Renaissance (which were loosely based on Greco-Italian forms). Designers blended architectural details from these periods. The World's Columbian Exposition of 1893 in Chicago displayed many Neoclassical buildings to the American public. The fair, a celebration of America's discovery by Columbus in 1492, was monumental. The event's planners

V. W. VOORHEES, ARCHITECT, SEATTLE, WASH.

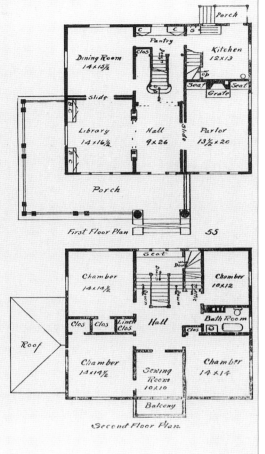

DESIGN NO. 55.

This beautiful Colonial residence combines an artistic and attractive exterior with a well arranged, convenient and harmonious interior.

All the living rooms open into the main hall. The chambers are large and there is ample closet space on the second floor. This residence will cost approximately $5,500.

Cost of one set of plans, specifications and details, $40.00.
Cost of two sets of plans, specifications and details, $45.00.

(Any plan can be reversed to suit location.)

A Neoclassical Revival house featured in the V. W. Voorhees pattern book, *Western Home Builder*, circa 1910.
University of Washington Libraries, Special Collections, UW23596

selected a classical theme, to the dismay of some architects (including Chicago's Louis Sullivan) who wanted to showcase a more modern or "American" style. Some of the best-known architects of the time designed monumental colonnaded buildings, all arranged around a central fountain court. The buildings were temporary, and most were constructed of white plaster, earning the exposition the nickname "the White City."

The huge, gleaming buildings, lit up at night and filled with fountains, flowers, and statuary, were unified through design and arranged around public spaces. An interest developed in recreating this type of urban environment. Consequently numerous cities across the country developed Beaux Arts plans for their downtowns. (Seattle, too, was not immune from this trend. The ambitious Bogue Plan [1911] drawn up to unify the commercial district failed to receive adequate support.) The exposition was widely publicized and heavily visited, with more than 27 million visitors during the year. While the main exhibition halls were large and weren't easily modified prototypes for residences, their grandeur could easily be adapted to the large mansions of Newport, Rhode Island and other wealthy enclaves. Individual states had smaller pavilions at the fair which were more domestic in scale. Virginia, Connecticut, Kentucky, Ohio, Utah, Nebraska, and South Dakota all had buildings with columned entry porches. Massachusetts, New York, and West Virginia's buildings had Colonial or Neoclassical detailing.

Library, Frederick K. Struve residence, period photograph. Furnishings for this "gentleman's" room are darker than those of the "ladies' " drawing room in the home. *University of Washington Libraries, Special Collections, UW13839*

INTERIORS

The interiors of Colonial Revival and Neoclassical Revival houses vary almost as much as their exteriors. Foyers with grand staircases are usually visible in the larger homes. Staircase railings and newelposts are often simpler in form than their Victorian counterparts. The section of the banister that meets the newelpost sometimes spirals back, mimicking curved bottom stairs. Wood paneling is common in the main rooms, sometimes Georgian and geometric in pattern, other times more fanciful, carved with swags and other Neoclassical ornamentation. Woodwork is either darkly stained or painted white. Fireplaces often have marble surrounds with Classical pilasters and sometimes overmantel paneling. Plasterwork can be elaborate in larger houses, particularly on ceilings where it would accent chandeliers. Stained glass sometimes appears over particularly

lavish central staircases. Smaller working-class houses might have little if any interior details to suggest the period—perhaps a simple paneled fireplace, or a deeper plaster or wood ceiling molding. Some original Colonial buildings had vibrant paint colors. The dining room at Mount Vernon, for example, was originally painted a vivid blue-green. But historical revivalists were unaware of the original colors and revival style dwellings were more likely to be painted in subdued shades of mustard yellow, dusty blue, rose, and soft greens. White was also popular.

Colonial Revival furniture was easily acquired, since a great number of furniture manufacturers reproduced the style. Even Gustav Stickley, a proponent of the Craftsman movement, admired Colonial architecture and furniture. His earliest experimentation in furniture was a chair

Drawing room, Frederick K. Struve residence, period photograph. The delicate wall paneling is more Louis XV than American in its style. The Struve residence, at 1221 Minor Avenue, was destroyed in 1958. *Museum of History and Industry, Seattle, 12294*

inspired by a simple, "old Colonial Windsor" example, which was different from mass-produced, intricately carved Victorian pieces. While most of his work remained Craftsman in style, his company also made traditional style Colonial Revival pieces, including Windsor and Jacobean pieces. Sears and Roebuck sold inexpensive examples of the style, while wealthier patrons could acquire original antiques or a number of finely crafted period reproduction pieces. Mahogany, cherry, and maple were common furniture woods; most decorative lock plates and handles were brass.

Colonial furniture came in a variety of styles. The Queen Anne period (1730–1760) was known for curved cabriole legs, pediments, and crests. Tables, chairs, combination desk and bookcases, high chest of drawers, and four-poster beds were the most common pieces of furniture from this period. Chippendale furniture (1755–1790), with its graceful lines and ornate decorations, was popular as well, and was ornamented with occasional Chinese details, Gothic arches, floral elements, and ornate carvings. Occasionally these were combined with details from the Queen Anne period. Claw-and-ball feet were frequent in later examples. Some homeowners decorated with Folk German or Pennsylvania Dutch style furniture which featured painted flora and fauna, hearts, or stars.

V. W. VOORHEES, ARCHITECT, SEATTLE, WASH.

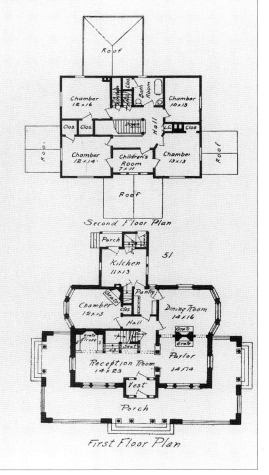

DESIGN NO. 51.

The first story of this modern Colonial residence is built of red pressed brick. The porches and terrace are also of brick. The second story is of frame construction. There is ample space for three servants' rooms on the third floor. The chamber on the first floor may be used for a library. This house to be heated with a hot water system. The approximate cost of this house is $10,000.

Cost of one set of plans, specifications and details, $90.00.
Cost of two sets of plans, specifications and details, $100.00.

(Any plan can be reversed to suit location.)

A Colonial Revival house featured in the V. W. Voorhees pattern book, *Western Home Builder*, circa 1910.
University of Washington Libraries, Special Collections, UW23594

CLASSICAL REVIVAL HOUSES

Colonial Revival (1880–1955)

1909	William C. Phillips Residence
1902	William Bell Phillips Residence
1903	Caroline Kline Galland Residence
1905	Reginald H. Parsons Residence
1905	David E. Skinner Residence
1906	Edwin G. Ames Residence
1908	Edgar H. Bucklin Residence
1912	Dr. Waldo Richardson Residence
1912–1913	Raymond-Ogden Residence

1915	Nathan Eckstein Residence
1917	Dr. Albert S. Kerry Residence
1913	Lloyd Tindall Residence
1915	A. Morris Atwood Residence

Neoclassical Revival (1895–1950)

1900–1901	Ballard-Howe Residence
1902	Dr. Adolph O. Loe Residence
1903–1909	Harvard Residence
1903	John C. McMillan Residence

A Colonial style balustrade.

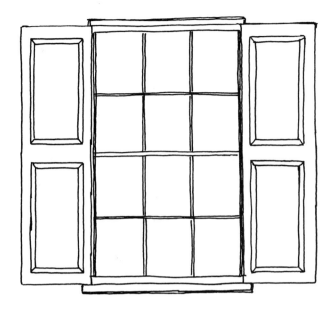

A Colonial Revival window with multiple lights and full, fitting shutters.

Colonial Revival doorway with a broken pediment, slender Tuscan columns, fanlight, and sidelights flanking the center paneled door.

A Palladian window decorated with Ionic columns.

1907–1908	Arthur E. Lyon Residence
1908	Henry Owen Shuey Residence
1909	Parker-Ferson Residence
1909–1910	Richard Dwight Merrill Residence
1909–1910	Samuel Hyde Residence
1901	Horace Adelbert Middaugh Residence

COLONIAL REVIVAL (1880–1955)

William C. Phillips residence, 1913. *University of Washington Libraries, Special Collections, UW13814*

William C. Phillips Residence (1909)

The William C. Phillips residence is a two-story, hipped-roof Colonial Revival building. The exterior of the structure is shingle clad, and while there is no front porch, a narrow, full-length concrete and brick stoop accentuates the entrance. The front door is the most heavily articulated design element of the house, with a transom and sidelights. The entrance is further articulated with a rounded pediment, supported by Doric columns. Block modillions, small rectangular brackets, are the primary design component on the pediment. French doors flank the front door, each with multipaned sidelights. The second floor of the house has a set of paired double-hung windows over each French door; the upper section of each window has nine lights. A smaller multi-lighted casement window is over the front entrance. Bracketed window boxes are beneath each window. The attic level has a single front-facing dormer, centered directly over the front door.

William C. Phillips residence, living room, 1913. *University of Washington Libraries, Special Collections, UW13857*

A historical photo of the living room shows simple plaster walls and a hardwood floor. A large Oriental rug covered the main section of the floor. Most furniture was placed against the walls, including an upright piano, a wingback chair, and several small chairs with cane seats. Bookcases were on the far wall. A simple fireplace was embellished with brass fire tools. An upholstered gentleman's chair was to the left of the fireplace, while a spinning wheel, a nostalgic Colonial touch, balanced the right side. The center of the room was open, with a round Empire Revival table resting on the carpet. Both the fireplace mirror and pictures were suspended from picture molding.

William Bell Phillips residence, in 1937. *Washington State Archives, Puget Sound Regional Branch*

William Bell Phillips Residence (1902)

The William Bell Phillips residence was designed as a two-family duplex. While the massing of the house is Victorian, the design elements indicate a stylized interpretation of Colonial Revival architecture. This hybrid is an excellent example of how buildings can slowly transition from one prevailing style to another. The front façade has an elevated ground floor, adding to the structure's imposing scale. The duplexes were originally accessed by a common porch with individual covered entries. On the right, a street-facing gable projects from the main structure toward the street. The main floor of the house has a curved bay (which extends up to the second floor), and an ornate entry door complete with sidelights. To the left of the entry door is a fixed oval window, accented with narrow keystones that divide the form into four quarters. To the right, a double-story bay has a cluster of three windows on each level. A truncated second floor Palladian window is centered above the entry. Dentil work is present on both the porch and the bays. The attic gable is accented with another truncated Palladian window. A tall, thin, two-story pilaster accentuates both front corners of the duplex.

The left front of the façade is boxier in shape, in part due to a hipped roof dormer. A double-story projecting bay is on the far left side, with three clustered windows on each floor, a larger transomed fixed window in the center, flanked by two narrower double-hung windows. The entry door design is similar to its neighbor. John M. Hester was the builder of the complex.

William Bell Phillips lived in one of the original duplexes. Born and educated in New York City, he moved to Seattle with his parents in 1888. His father, Michael Phillips, was a lawyer. After the completion of the duplex, both parents and son occupied the structure. William married in 1908, and lived with his wife, Annie, at 713 East Union until 1911. Mr. and Mrs. Michael Phillips resided in the structure until 1913. William Phillips was active in many Catholic organizations, including the Knights of Columbus and the Holy Names Society; the Knights' lodge was directly across the street from him. William spent his entire career with the John B. Agen Company, which was a butter, egg, and cheese wholesale business. Starting as a bookkeeper, he worked his way up and became secretary and treasurer of the company. In 1916 the company sold off its dairy interests, focusing instead on real estate.

Window detail, William Bell Phillips residence, in 2004.

Caroline Kline Gallard residence, in 2004.

Caroline Kline Galland Residence (1903)

The Caroline Kline Gallard residence is a two-story, wood-clad Colonial Revival structure. The rectangular form of the house is capped with a hipped roof, extending beyond the house on either side to form full-length, two-story side porches. Side chimneys are located on each end of the structure, with a smaller chimney on the rear of the house. Slender two-story pilasters, capped with Ionic capitals, articulate the main façade corners. A small gabled portico, supported by Doric columns, provides cover for the centered front door. Decorative elements include a fanlight and pilasters. A single one-over-one, double-hung window is on either side of the front door. The second floor has two smaller windows, each centered above the main ground floor bays and flanking a larger central window. The three gabled dormers have Classical detailing: the center one has a broken scroll pediment, and the side gables have triangular pediments. Colossal columns support full two-story porches on the sides of the house, creating an unusual effect that combines Neoclassicism with the Colonial Revival style. The interior of the home has undergone extensive remodeling.

Caroline Rosenberg Kline Galland was born in Bavaria, Germany in 1841. Her first husband, Louis Kline, owned a clothing firm in Seattle. After his death, she married Bonham Galland, a retired merchant. She gave thousands of dollars to the poor in food, clothing, medical care, and financial gifts during her lifetime, and left an estate in excess of $1 million to continue her charity work. One of the main recipients of her charity is the Galland Home for the Aged, established for Jews and members of the Society of Universal Religion.

Max Umbrecht designed the Galland residence in 1903. Umbrecht, born in Syracuse, New York, had personal ties to the building industry through his grandfather, a bridge builder, and his father, a building contractor. Umbrecht arrived in Seattle in 1900, and devoted a substantial amount of time to private residences. He returned to New York in 1922, spending the rest of his life there.

Reginald H. Parsons residence, in 2004.

Reginald H. Parsons Residence (1905)

The two-and-a-half-story Parons-Gerrard residence is a derivative of the Dutch Colonial style. The roof is gambreled, with the large front-facing gambrel intersecting a secondary gambrel to form the main body of the house. An addition to the right combines several roof types. The roofing material is slate, reminiscent of Colonial houses in the mid-Atlantic states. The brick foundation of the house extends to the base of the first-story windows, and stucco clads the rest of the structure. Window arrangement (fenestration) is highly irregular: lower stories contain a mix of casement windows, many with transoms, while second-story windows are predominantly double hung, with multiple lights. The eastern addition has several windows with leaded glass. The southeast corner porch was later converted into a greenhouse. The estate originally included a carriage house on the west side, which was replaced by town houses in 1968. The interior of the home had a large library and a conservatory with a tile floor, a large sunroom on the main floor, and a gymnasium originally on the third floor. The multiple chimneys were well used, with each bedroom having its own fireplace.

The house was designed by W. Marbury Somervell for businessman Reginald H. Parsons, who came to Seattle from Colorado to open a branch of the Bemis Bag Company in 1904. He was later involved with orchard management in Oregon, livestock, mining, and the Title Trust Company. His wife, Maude Parsons, was a patron of the arts and one of the founders of the Seattle Fine Arts Society, precursor to the Seattle Art Museum. The public park to the left of the house, Parsons Memorial Gardens, was given by the family to the city of Seattle in 1956.

David E. Skinner residence, period photograph. *University of Washington Libraries, Special Collections, UW2682*

David E. Skinner Residence (1905)

The David E. Skinner residence has a similar form to many other Colonial Revival houses found on Seattle's Capitol Hill. The structure, designed by architect W. W. Sabin, has a gabled roof, with the ridge line facing the street. The center bay is pulled out and is further accented by a front-facing gable and a second-story tripartite window design capped with an ornamental shell motif. A curved front porch, now replaced by a rectangular one, covered the front entry. Quoins, painted in a shade much lighter than the wood cladding, visually reinforce the corners while adding a vertical emphasis. Windows are double hung. Lower sashes have single lights, allowing the occupants to take full advantage of garden views, while the upper sashes have eight lights, in keeping with the Colonial Revival emphasis.

David Edward Skinner was a native of Michigan. Skinner's company, Skinner and Eddy Shipyards, established ship construction speed records during World War I. He also served as president of the Metro Building Company. Friends and business colleagues urged him to become involved in politics, hoping that he would run for mayor of Seattle, but he declined, focusing his attention on business interests.

Edwin G. Ames residence, period photograph. *University of Washington Libraries, Special Collections, UW23409*

Edwin G. Ames Residence (1906)

An abundance of timber in the Pacific Northwest ensured that wood was used for many Colonial and Neoclassical Revival homes. There were, however, some imposing masonry structures like the Edwin G. Ames residence, designed by the architecture firm of Bebb & Mendel. The two-story, hipped-roof, brick structure has a single-story entry portico on the front façade and a porte-cochere on one of the side elevations. The house has a remarkable amount of quoining: massive stone quions mark the four main corners of the structure and accentuate the center section of the front façade, which extends slightly beyond the main wall plane. Symmetry of the main façade is rigidly adhered to, with a central front door, flanked by one-over-one, double-hung windows on the lower level, mirrored by three one-over-one, double-hung windows on the second floor. A small single-story portico, supported by Ionic columns and detailed with Classical balustrades, shields the front door. The recessed front sections have a single one-over-one, double-hung window on each story, all with stone jack arches. A pair of arched windows with articulated stone keystones fill most of the dormer. The strong vertical lines of the columns and quoins compete with the horizontal lines of the jack arches and block modillion cornice, giving the building a busyness not found in most Colonial Revival structures.

The interior of the house was finished with Classical details. A period photo of the main entrance hall shows dark fir woodwork (supplied through Ames's lumber industry contacts), Classical columns, and exposed beams. Patterned wall-to-wall carpeting and small Oriental rugs covered the floors. Pocket doors may have been present, but are not visible through the ornate draperies that divide the living spaces from the front hallway. An upright piano occupied space in the outer vestibule, an unusual placement for the instrument. A small, upholstered sofa, a plant stand, and a grandfather clock filled the rest of space. The music room was paneled in Honduras mahogany.

Edwin Gardner Ames, a native of Maine, moved to San Francisco in 1879 to work for the Pope and Talbot lumber company. The Seattle-based Puget Mill Company offered

Front hallway of the Edwin G. Ames residence, in 1912. *University of Washington Libraries, Special Collections, UW2476*

him a position at their Port Gamble plant in 1881. Ames was broadly active in the lumber and timber industry, serving as president of the Pacific Lumber Inspection Bureau and director of the Pacific Coast Lumber Manufacturers Association. He was also director of the Douglas Fir Exploitation and Export Company and the Washington Forest Fire Association. Ames's business interests extended beyond lumber into banking. He served as vice president of the Seattle National Bank, director of the Metropolitan Bank of Seattle, and trustee of Washington Mutual Savings Bank. He was also active in a wide variety of social organizations, including the Rainier, Arctic, Athletic, and Metropolitan Clubs, in addition to belonging to the Masons and the Scottish Rite. He was purported to have owned one of the finest rare and old book collections in the Northwest. The Ameses had no children, and when they passed away, the house was given to the University of Washington for use as the president's residence.

Edgar H. Bucklin residence, in 1913. *University of Washington Libraries, Special Collections, UW13863*

Edgar H. Bucklin Residence (1908)

The Edgar H. Bucklin residence designed by English-born architect Frederick A. Sexton is a particularly elaborate example of the Colonial Revival style. The pyramidal roof, rectangular massing, and front gabled dormer are commonly found details in Seattle, but the large wraparound porch is an unusual feature. The ornamental woodwork on this house is elaborate, in keeping with Bucklin's profession in the lumber industry. The porch is supported with slender Ionic columns, and a pronounced Classical balustrade appears on the main level and along the balcony above. Another uncommon design detail is a delicate swag and wreath garland, which ornaments the entire frieze. First-floor windows have leaded glass in their upper sashes. Windows on the second floor are simpler, although leaded glass is used for sidelights located on either side of the balcony door and in a fanlight above the door. The center bay of the house projects slightly, adding greater emphasis to the front door. Two-story Ionic pilasters accent the corners, adding more Classical detail. The center dormer is quite large, with a Palladian window echoing the shapes of the fanlight and sidelights below.

Dr. Waldo Richardson residence, period photograph. *University of Washington Libraries, Special Collections, UW23664*

Dr. Waldo Richardson Residence (1912)

The Dr. Waldo Richardson residence is an excellent example of a brick Colonial Revival house. The structure has a side-facing gable with chimneys located at either end. The front elevation has a centrally located door, with a small entry portico supported by Doric columns. Dentil work is present at the top edge of the portico. Double multipaned casement windows, complete with shutters, are located on either side of the entry door. The brick pattern consists entirely of stretchers (horizontally laid bricks) for each row, although a row of "soldiers" (vertically laid bricks) accentuates the first row on the ground level and articulates the break between the first and second stories. Second-story windows are also shuttered; they are double hung, with six lights in both sections. They are smaller than the first-floor fenestration, but are centered on the façade as well. The center window of the second floor is taller and more narrow than its neighbors. All windows are articulated with jack arches, complete with centered keystones. Three evenly spaced dormers protrude from the roof. All three dormers have curved, double-hung windows, each with six-over-six lights. The center dormer is segmented, while the flanking dormers are gabled.

Raymond-Ogden residence, in 2004.

Raymond-Ogden Residence (1912–1913)

The Raymond-Ogden residence is another example of a brick Colonial Revival house. Its rectangular form is covered by a hipped roof. Three chimneys, one on each end and one in the center of the structure, anchor the home's symmetry. The central entry portico has slender Corinthian columns and a simple balustrade. The main entrance is unusually complex: the center door is capped with a fanlight, while a full-length window with matching fanlight is located on either side. The second-story windows are double hung, and are carefully centered above their first-floor counterparts.

The interior of the home is large, with almost two dozen rooms. A entry hall runs down the center of the house, and is flanked by the two formal living spaces, the dining room, and the drawing room. The hall is paneled, floor to ceiling, with mahogany. The central staircase balusters and handrail are of mahogany as well. Some of the fireplace mantles are marble. Other formal interior furnishings included crystal chandeliers and doorknobs.

The Raymond-Ogden mansion was built for Dr. Alfred Raymond, who moved to Seattle from Canada in the 1890s.

He was chief of brain surgery at Seattle General Hospital and also served as president of the King County Medical Society in 1892. Other professional honors included being named a fellow of the American College of Surgeons, and a senatorial representative to the Clinical Congress of the American College of Surgeons. Dr. Raymond was also active with local historical and cultural organizations, and had a large personal library and extensive art collection. The house remained in the family until the 1950s, when it was sold. During the 1960s the house served as Britain's consul-general's residence.

The architect of the house was Joseph Coté. Coté was born in Canada and educated at Columbia University, and originally worked for the New York architecture firm of Hines and LaFarge. He came to Seattle as supervising architect for the construction of Saint James Cathedral. Coté designed many prominent residences in Seattle, in addition to his commercial work. During the 1910s, several of his buildings were showcased in *Architectural Record*.

Nathan Eckstein residence, in 1915. *Museum of History and Industry, Seattle, 80.7166.1.46*

Nathan Eckstein Residence (1915)

The Nathan Eckstein residence is an elongated Colonial Revival house. The two-story brick dwelling has a side-facing gable, with three evenly spaced pedimented gabled dormers. A small, curved, entry porch is supported by Tuscan columns; the porch seems too small for the massive façade. The entry doorway is the most elaborate detail on the house: leaded glass fills the fanlight and sidelights. There are three evenly spaced one-over-one, double-hung windows on either side of the entry. The second-floor fenestration pattern mirrors that of the first. Jack arches ornament windows on the first and second floors. Delicate dentil molding runs along the underside of the cornice on all elevations.

Nathan Eckstein was born in Germany, and moved to New York where he worked in the grocery industry from 1888 to 1898. After his move to Seattle, he became president of Schwabacher Brothers, the largest wholesale grocery company in the region. Eckstein was a member of the Masons and the Elks fraternal orders and the Rainier and Arctic Clubs.

Dr. Albert S. Kerry residence, in 1957. *Werner Lenggenhager. Seattle Public Library, 22508*

Dr. Albert S. Kerry Residence (1917)

The Dr. Albert S. Kerry residence, designed by architect Joseph S. Coté, is a two-story, wood-frame house with an uncommon Colonial Revival detail, a hooded doorway. This small portico-like structure shields the front stoop from rain. The hood molding over the door is a feature many associate with Italianate architecture, but it is found on Colonial architecture in Old Salem, North Carolina. A very un-Colonial bank of casement windows, shielded by a narrow shed roof, flanks the main entry. Multiple lights keep the design somewhat period-appropriate. Four second-floor windows, two on either side of the door, are six over six, double hung. A small decorative window cluster is over the hooded doorway. The gable ridge runs parallel to the street, providing space for three eyebrow dormers.

Lloyd Tindall Residence (1913)

Lloyd Tindall residence, period photograph. Bungalow Magazine, January 1916, p. 21. Seattle Public Library

The Lloyd Tindall residence is an example of a Colonial Revival bungalow. Bungalow houses—small one-story or one-and-a-half-story structures—were advocated by the Craftsman movement and promoted by American Gustav Stickley. They were designed to be compact, affordable, and easy to maintain, with a number of built-in furniture pieces. This home, a stripped-down Colonial Revival, was featured in the *Bungalow Magazine*'s January 1916 issue. The exterior is described as distinctly Colonial with the decorative shutters, multi-lighted upper sashes, an arched multilight glass entry door (reminiscent of a Georgian window), a clipped corner on the front gable, and pronounced eave returns. The shingled exterior was painted gray-green, and the trim work was cream.

Master bedroom in Lloyd Tindall residence, with a built-in dressing table, period photograph. Bungalow Magazine, January 1916, p. 18. Seattle Public Library

The interior woodwork was painted ivory, and the living room walls were papered with a putty color and accented by a multicolored frieze. French doors divide the living and dining rooms. The dining room was painted "French gray." Although this house lacks the built-in pieces of furniture common in most bungalow designs, a vanity, complete with spindle legs, was built into the master bedroom wall. Woodwork in this room was painted French gray, while the wall was covered with a gray and pink paper.

A. Morris Atwood Residence (1915)

The A. Morris residence is another example of a Colonial Revival bungalow from the Craftsman era, showing how stylistic boundaries overlap each other. The simple rectangular structure has a gabled roof, with the ridge line facing the street. The Colonial detailing is sparse on this example as well, with the sole exterior Colonial elements being the symmetrical plan, simple pedimented door overhang, and multiglazed windows.

Built-in bookcases, with glass doors were to the right of the living room fireplace. The dining room was considered the main Colonial Revival attraction of the house, with built-in corner cupboards. The living room and dining room fireplaces had Classical mantles with Tuscan columns and a dentiled entablature. A period dining room photo shows Windsor chairs placed around the perimeter of the room. Interior colors were described as grayish buff, with white-painted enamel woodwork. This home was showcased in *Bungalow Magazine*'s May 1916 edition.

A. Morris Atwood residence, period photograph. Bungalow Magazine, *May 1916, p. 274. Seattle Public Library*

Living room fireplace, A. Morris Atwood residence, period photograph. Bungalow Magazine, *May 1916, p. 278. Seattle Public Library*

Dining room, A. Morris Atwood
residence, period photograph.
Bungalow Magazine, *May 1916, p. 279.*
Seattle Public Library

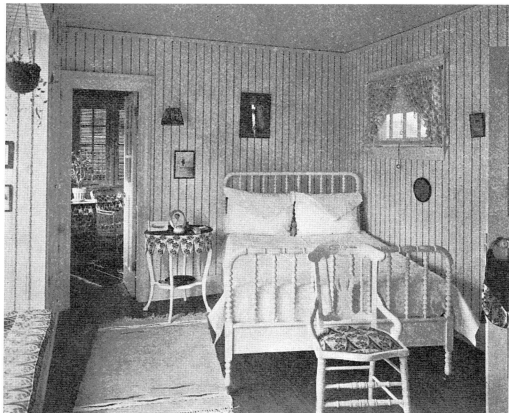

Bedroom, A. Morris Atwood
residence, period photograph.
Bungalow Magazine, *May 1916, p. 282.*
Seattle Public Library

NEOCLASSICAL REVIVAL (1895–1950)

Ballard-Howe residence, shortly after construction, period photograph. *Asahel Curtis. Washington State Historical Society, Tacoma, 2461*

Ballard-Howe Residence (1900–1901)

The Ballard-Howe residence has an imposing front façade. A small, centered, semicircular porch frames the main doorway. The porch is protected by a larger two-story entry portico, supported by colossal Ionic columns. Ionic pilasters accentuate the corners of the house. The front entry door has sidelights and a rectangular transom. Windows on the main floor have multilighted supersections, and are accentuated with block modillions. The second floor has a Palladian window-doorway combination, which opens out onto the small semicircular porch. Second floor windows have large single lights beneath multilighted upper sashes. Eaves on the original section of the house are articulated with additional block modillions. Dormers protrude from the attic. The central dormer is capped with a complex broken pediment, while smaller, simpler, flanking dormers have triangular pediments. During the 1930s, the house was remodeled to hold five apartments. Wings were added to either side of the structure and architectural embellishments, including the roof balustrade (now replaced), were removed.

The Ballard-Howe residence was built in 1901 for Martin D. Ballard, a native of Bridgeport, Indiana. Ballard traveled west with Oliver Meeker (brother of early

Ballard-Howe residence, in 2004.

Washington Territory pioneer Ezra Meeker), settling at various locations in Oregon, Montana, and Idaho. He arrived in Seattle in 1882 and worked in the hardware business. In 1885 he organized and served as president of the Seattle Hardware Company until his death in 1907. Ballard was also involved with finance, and helped organize the National Bank of Commerce (Rainier Bank) serving as their first vice president and later as president.

The next owner of the house was Judge George Donworth, who purchased the property in 1911. He undertook substantial redecorating, but ill health caused him to sell the house five months after its purchase. The house was then purchased by Donworth's former law partner, James B. Howe. Howe, a native of Charleston, South Carolina arrived in Seattle shortly before the 1889 fire. He set up a law office, becoming partners with Judge George Donworth and Samuel H. Piles, a future United States Senator. In 1907 Howe became a counsel for the Seattle Electric Company (later Puget Sound Power and Light Company). Interviews with the Howe family in the 1970s provide

interesting insights into family use of the large fifteen-room structure. The third-floor ballroom, designed for formal occasions, was converted by the couple's six children into a play space. The boys played basketball in the room, and the family Saint Bernard lived in the space as well. The Howe family occupied the house for almost two decades. The house was put on the market shortly after Howe's death, but the Great Depression made a sale difficult, and it sat on the market for two years. In 1932 the house sold, for $5,000, considerably less than the $25,000 the Howes had paid for it. It was then subdivided into apartments.

The Ballard-Howe house was designed by architect Emil DeNeuf, who came to Seattle shortly after the 1889 fire, and worked with commercial structures in the Pioneer Square district. He also designed a number of buildings for the Denny-Blaine Land Company, including the E. F Blaine home in Denny-Blaine Park. DeNeuf partnered with August F. Heide shortly after the construction of the Ballard-Howe house.

Dr. Adolph O. Loe residence, period photograph. *University of Washington Libraries, Special Collections, UW2883*

Dr. Adolph O. Loe Residence (1902)

Dr. Adolph O. Loe's residence is a compact, wood-sided Neoclassical Revival dwelling. The main roof is hipped, with cross-gable extensions, including a two-story entry portico. The large portico has an elaborate triangular pediment supported by colossal Corinthian columns. Corinthian pilasters decorate the front corners of the house and the back edges of the portico. Sidelights flank the central front door. The window treatment for this home is somewhat unusual: windows on the main floor are clustered in threes, with a central, fixed window flanked by narrower one-over-one, double-hung windows. A decorative transom, ornamented with triangular pieces of glass, runs the length of the three windows. Second-floor windows are centered directly above those on the main floor, and are eight over one, double hung. A set of French doors on the second story provides access to the balustraded porch. This house is also unusual in its use of multiple stringcourses. A narrow stringcourse runs below the windows on the first and second floors, while a thicker one runs above the first

floor windows. The numerous horizontal references serve to balance the strong vertical design elements. The house was designed by architect J. Harry Randall.

Dr. Adolph O. Loe, a native of Minnesota, received his medical training in surgery from the University of Minnesota, Minneapolis. He moved to Seattle in 1901, although he continued to return east periodically to keep up with current surgical practices. He held membership in a number of medical associations, including the King County Medical Society, the Washington State Medical Association, and the American Medical Association. He was also a fellow of the American College of Surgeons and a trustee of the State Medical Library. In addition to his extensive medical practice, he served briefly as director of the German American Bank, and was a member of Seattle's Chamber of Commerce. Dr. Loe was involved in a number of social organizations, and held membership in the Mystic Shriners, the Independent Order of Odd Fellows, and the Seattle Automobile Club. He was also a member of Holy Trinity English Lutheran Church.

The Harvard residence, in 1937. *Washington State Archives, Puget Sound Regional Branch*

Harvard Residence (1903–1909)

The Harvard residence (so named because it is on Harvard Avenue) is a two-story, wood-frame, hipped-roof structure. A full basement and usable attic space make this home large, in excess of 7000 square feet. Like many of the Neoclassical Revival houses discussed above, this home has a two-story portico supported by paired colossal Corinthian columns. The main level has a centered mahogany door with transom windows, and windows on the main floor have leaded glass transoms. A balustraded front porch wraps around the main level of the house. Square piers support the one-story porch. The roof of the porch is also balustraded, providing a large deck that is accessible from the second-story portico. Windows on the second floor also have transoms. The attic space of the house is accentuated above the portico with a large, imposing, gabled dormer. The top of the portico also has a balustrade, and is accessible from the dormer.

This house was built by Edward J. Duhamel, who was born in Buffalo, New York, moved west to Chicago, where he became an architect's apprentice, and eventually moved to Galveston, Texas, to open his own firm. In 1889 Duhamel moved to Seattle, where he shifted his professional focus to building construction more than building design. He received contracts from many of the city's well-known architects, including C. H. Bebb, A. Warren Gould, the firm of Saunders & Lawton, and Max Umbrecht. In 1900, Duhamel became partners with John Megrath and F. M. Gribble in the Washington Brick and Tile Company and the firm of Megrath and Duhamel. Duhamel sold the house to William H. Parsons in 1909.

Parsons came from Wisconsin, where he started a department store with his brother. In 1895, he moved to Seattle, eventually traveling north to become manager of the Ames Mercantile Company in Dawson City, Yukon Territory. By 1903 he had returned to Seattle, and a few years later was selected by the Washington Trust Company of Seattle to open the Washington-Alaska Bank of Fairbanks. The interior of Alaska had no banks at this time, and gold miners were anxious to trade their finds for federal currency. To get to Fairbanks, Parsons traveled 500 miles by dogsled with $100,000 in currency. He successfully started a credit company, and within a few months his bank had deposits of more than $2 million. Parsons purchased the residence upon his final return to Seattle. He continued to work in the banking industry, serving as vice-president and then president of Dexter Horton National Bank. He remained with the bank through its merger with First National Bank and Seattle National Bank.

John C. McMillan residence, 1903. *University of Washington Libraries, Special Collections, UW2468*

John C. McMillan Residence (1903)

Because of its corner lot location, the John C. McMillan residence has two impressive entries. The wood-sided house has a hipped roof with gabled dormers. Chimneys, while noticeable, are not nearly as ornate as those found on Tudor Revival or Queen Anne homes. A large balustraded portico, supported by colossal Corinthian columns, dominates the main elevation. Although the columns are paired on either side of the portico, there is only one pilaster for each set of columns along the back wall. The second-floor balcony does not extend across the entire portico, but instead, corbelled supports run along either side, an unusual element in Neoclassical Revival buildings. The front door is centered, with elaborate leaded glass sidelights. First-floor windows, one over one and double hung, are centered on either side of the entry door. The second floor is delineated by a narrow stringcourse, and a pair of double-hung windows is centered directly above those on the first floor. Quoins, a decorative embellishment more common in

masonry buildings, elaborate the corners but surprisingly do not extend beyond the first floor, making the structure look somewhat incomplete. The secondary entry for the house is marked by a one-story portico with paired Ionic columns.

The architecture firm Bebb & Mendel designed the John C. McMillan house. Charles H. Bebb was born and educated in England. He also attended the University of Lausanne, Switzerland. Upon his arrival in the United States, he joined the Chicago firm of Adler and Sullivan as a construction supervisor. By 1893, Bebb was residing in Seattle. Louis L. Mendel was a native of Germany, who eventually made his way to the Puget Sound region by 1889. The two architects formed a partnership in 1901, which lasted for over a decade, producing numerous residences, hotels, and business buildings, including the Washington State Building at the Alaska-Yukon-Pacific Exposition of 1909.

Arthur E. Lyon residence, photograph date unknown. *Museum of History and Industry, Seattle, 10816*

Arthur E. Lyon Residence (1907–1908)

A large portico graces the front of the two-story Arthur E. Lyon residence, while a one-story sunroom, located off to one side, breaks away from the typically symmetrical Neoclassical form. The home has a gabled roof, with the gable ridge running parallel to the road. The portico is rectangular, and covers much of the front façade, with an extended pedimented gable marking the entrance. The portico has six colossal Corinthian columns; those directly under the pediment are paired, a single column supports each corner, and a single pilaster shadows behind on the façade. The front of the residence is symmetrical, with side transoms and a fanlight surrounding the large front door. A small arched window is located on either side of the door, an unusual design detail. There are four evenly spaced windows on the ground floor. Each has ten lights on the upper sash, which helps add to the Colonial feeling of the structure, while the lower sash has a single pane, providing a clear, unobstructed view. The second floor mirrors window numbers and placement, the only variation being the set of French doors opening onto a small balcony above the main entrance. The house was designed by architect Ellsworth Storey.

Henry Owen Shuey residence, period photograph. *University of Washington Libraries, Special Collections, UW2484*

Henry Owen Shuey Residence (1908)

The Henry Owen Shuey residence, designed by architect E. S. Bell, is a large, two-story Neoclassical Revival house, rectangular in plan with a hipped roof. The projecting double-story portico covers more than a third of the front of the house and is supported with Corinthian columns. A more subtle interpretation of these columns is repeated in the two-story pilasters marking the corners of the house. The structure does not have a symmetrical façade, since the entry portico is off center. The front door is flanked by sidelights, and a prominent angled bay protrudes to the left. To the right of the front door is a single window. Many of the ground-floor windows have leaded glass in their upper sashes. A stringcourse of dentil work divides the first and second floors.

The second floor had a long balustrade that extended across the portico and crowned the top of the first-floor bay window. (This design element has since been removed.) Two double-hung windows are paired above the projecting first-floor bay. The section under the portico originally had a single one-over-one, double-hung window, but this area was enclosed in 1954. The extreme right portion of the second floor also has a single one-over-one, double-hung window. The house is recessed far beneath the eaves, and

the portico tympanum is deeply recessed as well, with a segmented, keystoned, bulls-eye window at the center. The interior of the home is well-preserved, with a large paneled entrance hall. The living room has box-beamed ceilings and a rusticated stone fireplace mantel. The stained glass windows illuminating the stair hall were ordered from a specialty glass company in Kokomo, Indiana.

Henry Owen Shuey was born in Bainbridge, Indiana, on April 29, 1861. After attending college, he married Lucina Sherrill and moved to Kansas. In 1888 Shuey relocated to Seattle. He sold insurance, but quickly expanded into loans, and by 1894 he was secretary and manager of the Equitable Building, Loan, and Investment Association. In 1897 he became president of the Home Builders Finance Company. He was also responsible for establishing the Bank of Ballard, Citizens National Bank of Seattle, and the H. O. Shuey and Company banking firm. Shuey was active in a number of philanthropic organizations. He served as director of the YMCA, and helped build several mission churches in Seattle and Washington state. He also served as a trustee for the Washington Children's Homefinding Society. Shuey retired to Los Angeles in the early 1920s.

Parker-Ferson residence, in 1937.
Washington State Archives,
Puget Sound Regional Branch

Parker-Ferson residence, in 2004.

Parker-Ferson Residence (1909)

The Parker-Ferson residence is a large Neoclassical Revival house with the characteristic two-story portico supported by colossal columns. The main entry doors and flanking windows are slightly recessed. A balustraded porch beneath the main portico extends across the entire front of the house. (The ballustrades have been removed.) This residence, quite spacious with more than thirty rooms, has interior mahogany woodwork. The main foyer has a large cornice molding that replicates the exterior cornice, and wainscoting covers the lower half of the wall. A Tiffany window lights the main interior staircase. The dining room has oak woodwork rather than the fine mahogany used in the other public rooms.

The Parker-Ferson mansion was built on "Millionaire's Row," a Capitol Hill neighborhood that was the place to live for Seattle's new rich during the early twentieth century. The house, with its lavish furnishings, was rumored to cost $150,000. George Parker earned the money for this house by unknowingly selling worthless stock shares for United Wireless, which claimed to represent "wireless" inventor Guglielmo Marconi. Parker moved into the house in 1909, but less than a year later the fraud was exposed, and Parker was sent to a federal prison in Atlanta.

Richard Dwight Merrill residence, in 1937. *Washington State Archives, Puget Sound Regional Branch*

Richard Dwight Merrill Residence (1909–1910)

The Richard Dwight Merrill residence is a two-story stuccoed structure. While most of the house has a flat roof, a massive cross-axial gable accents the three center bays. The gabled front section of the building projects slightly beyond the side bays. The front entrance is marked by a small Doric portico. A transom rests above the paneled front door. The interior of the home has a parquet hardwood floor, and wood paneling decorates formal areas.

Richard Dwight Merrill was an executive with the Michigan-based Merrill and Ring Lumber Company. He had settled in Seattle by 1903, the same time that company headquarters moved to the city. Merrill was elected president of the lumber company in 1907. He also served on the board of Polson Logging Company, in Hoquiam, Washington. His wife, Eula Lee Merrill, was a member of the Seattle Garden Club. She served on the board of directors for the University of Washington Arboretum, and was a committee member for the Garden Club of America, Western Zone. In 1930 she helped form the Washington State Council for Roadside Beauty.

The New York architect Charles A. Platt designed the house in part because of his work designing a Colonial Revival house for Merrill's sister and brother-in-law. Platt studied fine art at the National Academy of Design in New York. He designed a number of Colonial Revival homes in the Northeast, in addition to commercial buildings. One of his best known structures is the Freer Gallery in Washington, DC. Platt's broad interests led to numerous affiliations and honors, including membership in the American Institute of Architects, the Society of Landscape Architects, the National Institute of Arts and Letters, the Society of American Artists, the American Water Color Society, and the London Society of Painters and Etchers. He also served as president of the American Academy in Rome from 1928 to 1933.

Samuel Hyde residence, in 1937.
Washington State Archives,
Puget Sound Regional Branch

Samuel Hyde residence, in 2004.

Samuel Hyde Residence (1909–1910)

The Samuel Hyde residence is a two-story, wood-frame structure with brick veneer. The front elevation is symmetrical, with a large two-story portico supported by paired colossal columns. The main entrance is flanked by sidelights, while a massive entablature supports a second-story balcony with balustrade. A double door, also flanked by sidelights, accesses the balcony. Windows are double hung; those on the first story have elaborate terra-cotta surrounds, while second-story windows have less elaborate ornamentation. A porte-cochere is located on the left side of the structure.

Public rooms within the house were lavishly appointed. Trim woods are mahogany and oak. The main staircase had oak wainscoting and balustrades. The newel post was accented with an ornate candelabrum. The reception room's woodwork was painted, while the drawing room had mahogany trim, a large paneled overmantel accenting a marble fireplace, and gold leaf embellishing the ceiling. The dining room was paneled with oak and decorated by a canvas mural above the plate rail, believed to represent the Lake Washington shoreline. Several ceilings were decorated with frescos, and light fixtures were Tiffany style.

Samuel Hyde was a native of England. He moved to the United States in 1879, and was living in Seattle by 1888. He was involved in local coal mining as well as the alcohol business, serving as president of Hyde Liquor Company from 1899 until 1915. The architectural firm of Bebb & Mendel designed the house, and it is thought that the grounds were laid out by the Olmsted Brothers, the nationally recognized landscape architecture firm responsible for designing the Seattle parks system, Portland, Oregon's, park system, New York's Central Park, San Francisco's Golden Gate Park, and the central space of the Alaska-Yukon-Pacific Exposition (1909).

Horace Adelbert Middaugh
residence, 1913.
University of Washington Libraries,
Special Collections, UW2991

Horace Adelbert Middaugh Residence (1901)

The Horace Adelbert Middaugh residence, designed by the architect James E. Webster, is another fine example of a Neoclassical Revival house. A high foundation gives it pronounced stateliness. The two-story portico is supported by paired Ionic columns at the front, with single Ionic pilasters on the back wall. Dentil work over the entablature and the ornate balustrade along the top and on either side of the first level complete the portico. The front entry is reached by ascending an imposing staircase. Large multi-paned sidelights flank the front door. Windows on the first-floor façade are grouped in threes, with the center fixed window considerably larger than the two narrower double-hung windows on either side. Windows on the first and second floor have single lights. Instead of a stringcourse,

the space between the first and second floors is marked by ornate plasterwork reliefs. Second-floor windows are placed directly above their first-story counterparts; while those windows are in pairs, they are not joined together like those on the first floor. Also somewhat unusual for this style is the railing treatment on the second story of the portico: instead of the usual Classical balustrade, it has an argyle diamond-shaped pattern that looks rather Victorian.

Horace Adelbert Middaugh was a Civil War veteran originally from New York. He was the founder of Seattle's Pioneer Sand and Gravel Company. His interest in engineering led to his appointment as supervisor for Seattle Lakeshore and Eastside Rail Road. He also served as president of the German American Mercantile Bank.

DESIGNED AND BUILT BY PAGE CONSTRUCTION

3 CRAFTSMAN

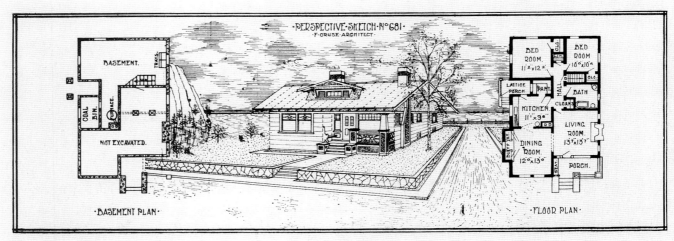

·PERSPECTIVE·SKETCH·N°681·
·F·CRUSE·ARCHITECT·

Plan No. 681.

A one story "bungalow" designed in the Craftsman style. This plan was published in the 1910s by the Seattle Building and Investment Company.
University of Washington Libraries, Special Collections, UW23615

CRAFTSMAN HOUSES, sometimes referred to as "bungalows," are a familiar sight in the Pacific Northwest. The term "bungalow" is architecturally imprecise, since it doesn't actually refer to a style. It describes scale, and it is used to describe small, one- or one-and-a-half story houses, regardless of style. The word "bungalow" originated in India, and evolved from the Bengali word *bangala*, which described a one-story British colonial structure. During the 1870s, the term was used in Great Britain to describe rustic one-story houses, and for the last thirty or so years of the nineteenth century, it referred to rural weekend or summer homes. Even in 1903, Gustav Stickley, a major proponent of the Craftsman movement, used "bungalow" to describe a type of simple living. Craftsman houses, and bungalows that are designed in the Craftsman style, emphasize function and simple materials. They generally have two bedrooms and one bathroom, with a main floor of less than 1000 square feet of space. While large, more ornamented examples of this design do exist, they are less common than the small structures that fill Seattle.

A major developer of the Craftsman style was the California-based architectural firm of Greene & Greene. The Greene brothers, influenced in part by the Japanese pavilion at Chicago's 1893 World's Columbian Exposition, developed an architectural vocabulary based on low-pitched rooflines, deep eaves, exposed or accented wood structural supports, and irregular floor plans. The Greene brothers designed numerous houses in the Pasadena area; the best known was the Gamble House of 1908. The Gamble house used a number of different woods, the varying tones and grains adding aesthetic interest.

While there were some high-style Craftsman homes built, most examples of this style are found in working-class neighborhoods, due to their major proponent, Gustav Stickley. Stickley was a furniture designer based in Syracuse, New York. During the 1890s he traveled to Europe and was inspired by the writings of Englishmen John Ruskin and William Morris. Ruskin was a critic who was interested in linking the daily lives of the working populace with art. Morris, a designer and social reformer, was interested in utilitarian art for the masses. In 1899, after Stickley returned to the states, he established the Gustav Stickley Company, which manufactured a wide variety of mass-produced, inexpensive furniture. From 1901 until 1916 he published the *Craftsman* magazine, which illustrated interiors filled with Stickley furniture and included house plans as well. Many of his designs, including prefabricated houses, were available from the Sears and Roebuck catalogue

Preceding pages: (far left) Craftsman house designed by Coles Construction Company (1916). *University of Washington Libraries, Special Collections, UW23562;* (chapter title page, upper left) Craftsman house, Mount Baker neighborhood; (upper right) Craftsman at 4222 Thackery Place. *Asahel Curtis. Washington State Historical Society, Tacoma, 55830;* (lower) Craftsman house, 909 Northeast 63rd Street (built 1917). *Asahel Curtis. Washington State Historical Society, Tacoma, 55829*

Plan No. 603.

A larger, one-and-a-half-story Craftsman-style house published in the 1910s by the Seattle Building and Investment Company.
University of Washington Libraries, Special Collections, UW23613

company, and as a result were shipped throughout the United States.

A major proponent of the Craftsman style in Seattle was Jud Yoho, who was active in the speculative housing market as owner of the Craftsman Bungalow Company. He was also president of the *Bungalow Magazine*, originally published in Los Angeles, and then in Seattle, 1912–1918. Unlike Stickley, Yoho didn't promote ideology, but instead focused on the design details. *Bungalow Magazine* showcased numerous Seattle-area homes, in addition to examples from other areas of the country. Although most the plans offered in the magazine are Craftsman in style, there were some examples of Colonial Revival "bungalows." Craftsman style home plans also received publicity in *Western Architect, House Beautiful, Good Housekeeping,* and *Ladies Home Journal.*

While some of the largest and most ornate variations of the Craftsman style, including the Gamble House, are irregular in floor plan, most Craftsman homes are rectilinear in plan, due to cheaper construction costs. In Seattle, the majority of Craftsman homes were built for working-class patrons, and were smaller than the grand multileveled dwellings associated with more formal styles. Construction costs were reduced by utilizing the area formerly reserved as attic space, thus providing a one-and-a-half story structure. Smaller one-story versions are also prevalent. Craftsman design elements typically include an asymmetrical façade and wide street-facing gables. When porches are

Japanese pagoda tower, Horyuji, Nara, Japan, in 1993. Parts of the temple complex date from the eighth century. The deep eaves and exposed structural supports influenced Craftsman designers.

A row of Craftsman houses on Northeast 34th Street in Fremont, in 2004.

present they commonly exhibit tapered or squared piers. Structural members are exposed, with rafter ends clearly visible. Vergeboards are proportionally large, and frequently extend beyond the roofline. Some have decorative detailing, and occasionally a Japanese accent is visible in upturned ends. The triangular knee braces and protruding beams so common on the gable ends are often decorative.

Craftsman houses use a variety of exterior wall treatments. In Seattle, wood exteriors are often found, due to an abundance of timber in the region. While wood shingles are the most common cladding material, clapboard and half-timbered elements are sometimes used, resulting in a variety of wall finishes, even on some of the smallest houses. Brick and stone accents appear as porch supports, articulated foundations, and chimney elements. Clinker brick, a rough, irregularly shaped brick with a dark, glossy surface, is often used for added texture. Living room and dining room windows are usually clustered in groups of three, with narrow double-hung windows flanking a larger fixed center window. Upper sashes have multiple lights, while lower sashes are single paned. Often the upper sashes are smaller than the lower counterparts, a style known as "cottage style windows." Framing elements tend to be more articulated, with large apron trim. Doors may have several small lights on the upper portion, underscored by a dentil course, and vertical panels on the lower section.

INTERIORS

Craftsman interiors, like the exteriors, use wood structural elements to accentuate spatial arrangements. Entry foyers, which were standard in most Victorian, Tudor Revival, and Neoclassical Revival houses, are generally missing in Craftsman houses, with the front door opening directly into a living room. This change in floor plan is due to a housing reform movement, which advocated small, affordable, working-class homes. Since Craftsman homes were designed for servantless occupants, special attention was given to eliminating cumbersome furniture. Numerous built-in furniture pieces shaped interior arrangements. Living room and dining room spaces are usually joined, and lack the pocket doors that were so common in the Victorian era. Room separation is achieved through half walls, usually connected to the ceiling by tapered wood piers. These half wall designs frequently house bookcases, thus adding extra storage space. Ceilings are often articulated with boxed beams, which, although they might look structural, in many cases are only decorative.

Window seats are common in both living and dining rooms, offering additional storage as well. Fireplaces may have built-in bookcases on either side, and particularly elaborate bookcases might have leaded glass doors. It is not uncommon for even small dining rooms to have built-in

Craftsman living room from a house built in 1914, with box-beamed ceilings, smaller throw rugs, and oak Mission style furniture. Period photograph.
University of Washington Libraries, Special Collections, UW23612

china cabinets, with buffet-type built-ins appearing in smaller houses, and elaborate floor-to-ceiling cabinets encompassing entire walls in larger residences. Although built-ins are more common in living and dining areas, they also appear in bedrooms and hallways. Decorative box-beamed ceilings and wainscoting are also common in living and dining areas. In some rooms, wainscoting runs from floor to plate rail height, the plate rail adding additional shelf space within the home. In the Puget Sound region, dark stained fir was commonly used for these wall treatments. Fireplaces occasionally have inglenooks, and clinker brick or decorative art tiles often accent the mantle area. While the accentuated fireplace designs might hearken to a more elemental time, the reality was that these features were primarily decorative, since coal-fired furnaces provided most of the household heat. Windows and doors were given added visual weight with the use of large apron trim. In many cases the upper and lower horizontal sec-

tions extend slightly beyond the vertical elements, adding an inexpensive design detail.

Craftsman furniture exhibits unadorned lines, making finished pieces less costly than the heavily carved pieces common during the Victorian period. The wood of choice for Craftsman furniture was oak, which was more readily available and less expensive than either cherry or mahogany. Stickley and other Craftsman furniture manufacturers designed furniture that was considerably more angular and rugged looking than its Victorian and Colonial Revival predecessors. Although Stickley encouraged the purchase of his Craftsman furniture, with clean lines and limited upholstery use, homeowners had other decorating options. Stickley himself designed Colonial Revival furniture, and spoke admirably of Windsor chairs. Although he personally felt that exact reproductions of old pieces were not desirable, he did advocate studying Colonial designs. Some furniture manufacturers of the period went even farther.

Details of period art tile surrounding Craftsman fireplaces.

A Craftsman style dining room, with wainscoting, plate rail, box-beamed ceilings, and tiled fireplace mantle, period photograph. *University of Washington Libraries, Special Collections, UW13848*

satin draperies were also discouraged, in favor of simpler curtains, drawn on metal rings, allowing a greater ease of use. Craftsman living rooms were described as "masculine," and homeowners were encouraged to decorate with Native American artifacts, military paraphernalia, and smoking accessories. The resulting style greatly contrasted with the layered draperies, swags, bric-a-brac, and curved, carved, upholstered pieces of the Victorian era.

Popular paint colors for main living spaces were rich earthy tones—ochre, greens, browns, and terracotta. Bedrooms were painted in lighter tones (a soft gray-blue was a typical choice), accented by white painted woodwork and wicker furniture. Bathrooms were common in house designs by 1900, although most homes usually had only one, located on the first floor of the house. White was still the color of choice, in part due to its connection with cleanliness. While plumbing was still generally exposed under sinks, porcelain water tanks began to replace wooden ones, and built-in towel racks, medicine

Sears routinely showed Colonial Revival furniture decorating the interior of its Craftsman style homes, thus allowing homeowners a considerable range of interior furnishings.

The large Brussels carpets preferred during the Victorian era were considered too time consuming to maintain, so smaller throw rugs became popular. Heavy velvet and

A built-in kitchen eating nook, in a 1921 Craftsman, in 1998. Bench seats lift up to provide additional storage space. Light fixture not original.

A built-in ironing board located in a kitchen cupboard of a 1915 Craftsman, in 1998.

cabinets, and soap dishes added additional storage space. By the early 1910s claw-foot tubs were less common. Tubs were boxed in, simplifying bathroom cleaning.

While a substantial part of Craftsman design, with its built-ins and easy to care for treatments, is directly related to middle-class buyers, there were other influencing factors. During the early twentieth century, public health officials worked tirelessly to educate Americans about the importance of domestic and personal cleanliness. Dark and poorly ventilated spaces were of particular concern, and the large window expanses in Craftsman homes, extensive use of built in furniture, and technologically improved bathroom and kitchen spaces were designed to allow more light and air circulation while eliminating areas for dirt and germs to collect. An article in the 1913 *Craftsman* magazine stated, "We all appreciate the 'home beautiful' but homemakers are coming more and more to think and plan for the 'home sanitary.' "

A bathroom in a 1914 Craftsman, circa 2000. Small, white, hexagonal tiles covered the floor, while larger rectangular "subway tiles" covered the bottom portion of the walls.

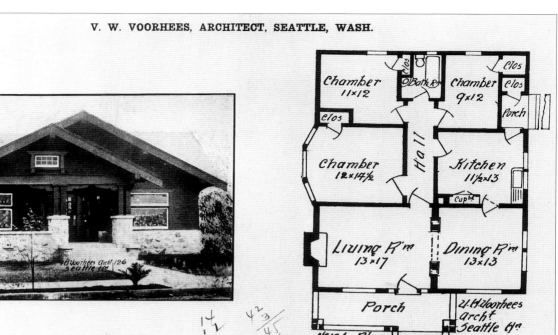

V. W. VOORHEES, ARCHITECT, SEATTLE, WASH.

DESIGN NO. 126.

Width of this six-room bungalow is 32 feet; length 38 feet; width of porch 7 feet; height of ceiling 9½ feet.

Porch chimney and fire places are constructed of cut stone.

Exterior is finished with shingles. Interior with slash grained fir, finished in Mission.

Approximate cost of construction, $1,700.00.

Cost of one set of plans, specifications and details, $12.00.

Cost of two sets of plans, specifications and details, $15.00.

(Any plan can be reversed to suit location.)

A Craftsman house plan featured in the V. W. Voorhees pattern book, *Western Home Builder*, circa 1910.

University of Washington Libraries, Special Collections, UW23598

CRAFTSMAN HOUSES (1905–1930)

1904–1905	Milnora de Beelen Roberts Residence	1913	G. S. Shirley Residence
1909	Brehm Brothers Residences	1914	Lars Larsen Residence
1910	George F. Cotterill Residence	1914	John H. Ogden Residence
1912	Charles B. Ernst Residence	1915	Harry W. Cullyford
1912	Mauss Residence	1915	Frederick E. Kreitle Residence
pre-1912	A. C. Schneider Residence	1915	Henry Larson Residence
pre-1913	E. Ryer Residence	1916	Belltown Cottages
1913	Bowen-Huston Residence		

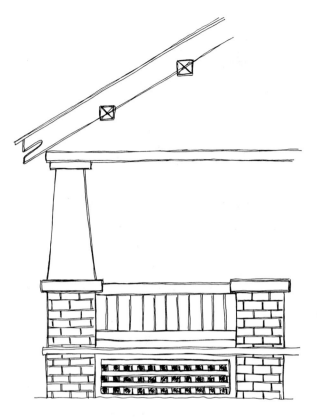

Craftsman porch detail with articulated brackets, decorative vergeboard, and tapered pier.

An interior Craftsman detail, showing how half walls between dining and living spaces were articulated.

An example of a clustered cottage window treatment on a Craftsman home.

CRAFTSMAN (1905–1930)

Milnora de Beelen Roberts residence, period photograph. *Museum of History and Industry, Seattle, 9732*

Milnora de Beelen Roberts Residence (1904–1905)

The Milnora de Beelen Roberts residence is an unusually large Craftsman house, with two main living floors in addition to a basement and attic space. The house is predominantly rectangular in plan, although there is an extended additional front and side gable, and a protruding front porch (since walled in). The main gable and a secondary cross gable are street facing, and are accented with wide vergeboards, and decorative trusses, reminiscent of the Victorian Stick style (late 1800s), which was ornamented by wood board patternwork in horizontal, vertical, and diagonal directions. A second cross gable protruding from the

side of the house is articulated in this manner as well. All rooflines extend well beyond the house, have exposed rafters, and are accented by large decorative brackets. Walls are clad with rough-hewn shingles, and an unusual paneled stringcourse separates the first floor from the second level, extending out to form a terrace above the front porch. While basement and ground-floor windows are simple one over one, double hung, second-floor windows sport multiple diamond-shaped lights in the upper sash and a single light in the lower sash.

The Brehm brothers residence at 219 36th Avenue North, in 2005.

Brehm Brothers Residences (1909)

The house at 219 36th Avenue North is one of a pair (the other is located at 221) on the street designed by noted Seattle architect Ellsworth Storey. The houses are now hidden under dense vegetation and are difficult to view from the street. They have classic Craftsman detailing—low-pitched, gable rooflines, enhanced by thick brackets, exposed rafter ends, and vergeboards. Building materials for the two homes include wood shingles, clinker brick, and river rock. Both homes share a front walkway. Brothers William R. and George O. Brehm operated a produce and grocery business in the Pike Place Market.

Ellsworth Storey, a Chicago native, traveled throughout Europe and the Middle East early in his career, and became particularly enamoured with vernacular Swiss chalets. Many of his houses are reminiscent of chalet designs, with wide gables, deep eaves, and sheltered porches. He was also quite adept with other styles, as evidenced in his design for the Arthur E. Lyon residence (see Chapter 2).

George F. Cotterill residence, in 2004.

George F. Cotterill Residence (1910)

The George F. Cotterill residence is a one-and-a-half story, side-gabled structure sided with rough-sawn cedar shakes. The full-length front porch is recessed under the main gable, and is supported by square piers. A large shed dormer houses two sets of triple windows on the second level of the front façade. Historic interior photos show plastered walls and ceilings. Hardwood floors were covered with a variety of rugs. The dining room housed an eclectic assortment of Victorian furniture in addition to a large built-in china cupboard. A variety of pieces, some Mission style, furnished the living room. The architect was the firm of Josenhaus & Allan; the builder was Ira S. Harding.

George Fletcher Cotterill, a native of Oxford, England, came to the United States in 1872. He graduated from high school in New Jersey and then studied civil engineering. He eventually made his way west, and by the 1880s he was employed as a civil engineer by several Northwest firms, including the Northern Pacific Railway and the Seattle Coal and Iron Company. By 1894 he worked in the City of Seattle's Engineer's Office, and the following year he served as the assistant city engineer. He remained in this position for five years until returning to private engineering practice. Cotterill was involved in regional and state affairs, and served on the state Irrigation Commission from 1903 to 1905. From 1907 to 1911, he was a state senator, and the following year was elected mayor of Seattle. He served as mayor until 1914, when he briefly returned to private practice. From 1916 to 1919 he was chief engineer of the Washington State Highway Department, and in 1922 was elected port commissioner for the Port of Seattle, serving the commission in a variety of positions, including secretary and president.

Cotterill was instrumental in developing civil engineering projects for the City of Seattle, including securing the Cedar River water supply, developing the original sewer system, designing and improving city plats, and extending street and park systems. He was also involved with irrigation projects for Yakima and Wenatchee. Cotterill started his own surveying and engineering business in 1888. He was responsible for over 100 square miles of platting, including the areas of Laurelhurst and Mount Baker, which do not follow a strict grid layout. In 1895 he was made chairman of the path committee for the Queen City Good Roads Club, which was responsible for laying out more than twenty-five miles of bike paths in the city. In addition to his professional interests, Cotterill and his wife Cora were both prominent temperance supporters. Cotterill was appointed as the American representative to the International Congress Against Alcoholism three times.

Living room of the George F. Cotterill residence, period photograph. *Museum of History and Industry, Seattle, 6524*

Dining room, George F. Cotterill residence, period photograph. *Museum of History and Industry, Seattle, 6398*

Charles B. Ernst residence, in 1913. Bungalow Magazine, *June 1913, p. 31. Seattle Public Library*

Charles B. Ernst Residence (1912)

The Charles B. Ernst residence was showcased in the June 1913 *Bungalow Magazine* and was described as "sufficiently quiet to be perfectly permissible in the more conservative East." The shingled, gabled structure was stained a natural wood color, and trim work was painted white. A piered front porch runs along the front of the house. The front door is on the left, while a large bank of four windows on the right side of the structure provides light to the interior. The windows are double hung, with twelve lights in the upper sash and a single light below. A low railing accentuates the porch, while an articulated cornice frames the recessed porch. Three smaller double-hung windows, each with six upper lights and one lower light, are located on the upper story. These windows have an unusual feature, a small railing that could double as a window-box holder.

All interior woodwork was dark stained fir, with oak flooring in the main rooms. A partial wall separated the living room from dining room. Craftsman built-in bookcases were omitted in this house, although a large built-in buffet with leaded glass doors was in the dining room. Although the pattern is not discernable in historic photos, the dining room walls were papered. The entire house cost $2350 to build. Charles Ernst served as secretary for the Rustad Heating and Plumbing Company and as treasurer for Christian Tait Manufacturing Company.

Mauss residence, period photograph. Bungalow Magazine, *November 1916, p. 681. Seattle Public Library*

Mauss Residence (1912)

The Mauss residence has the typical broad eaves and shingled exterior of a Seattle Craftsman. The front of the house is accentuated by a gabled entry portico. The portico is supported by clusters of three wooden beams resting on shingled, tapered piers. Windows are double hung, with four lights in the upper sash and a single light below. The front door is centered, with multipaned sidelights on either side. A grouping of three windows on each side of the entry provides light to the living room. A river stone chimney is located to the left, giving the house a rustic, rural appearance.

The living room has box-beamed ceilings, and a small, raised fireplace nook on the left wall. Built-in bookcases, complete with glazed doors, accent the stone mantle. Built-in seats line the walls in this area, and the floor is tiled. The entire room has a plate rail, with paneled wainscoting below. The living room floor is fir and is varnished the same golden color as the interior woodwork. The painted portion of the walls was tan, with a cream ceiling. An ornate built-in buffet completes the dining room, which is separated from the living room by an extended wainscoting. This house, published in the November 1916 *Bungalow Magazine*, was built by the Long Building Company. It is identical in plan and most interior details to one published in the March 1915 issue.

Mauss residence, in 2004.

Living room of the Mauss residence, in 1916. Bungalow Magazine, *November 1916, p. 688. Seattle Public Library*

A. C. Schneider Residence (pre-1912)

The A. C. Schneider residence is unusual in its extensive use of river rock for the foundation and chimney. A gabled roof covers the one-story structure, while a cross gable marks entry for the full-width recessed porch. Rafter ends are exposed, and the vergeboards have cut tails and ornamented bracing. The front door is slightly off center and flanked by diamond-paned sidelights. Clusters of three narrow windows on either end of the façade provide a well-lit interior. The origi-

A. C. Schneider residence, in 1916. Bungalow Magazine, *September 1916, p. 570. Seattle Public Library*

nal exterior paint colors were gray and white. Historic photos show a medium-toned paint on the clapboard siding, with a lighter tone used for windows. A very dark color appears to have been used in the side gables.

The front door accesses the box-beamed living room. The fireplace mantle is made of river stone, which continues to the ceiling, making a battered chimney. Like many Craftsman homes, living spaces are separated from each other by partial walls with tapered piers. Bookcases, with leaded glass doors, utilize the space provided by the partial walls in the living room and dining room. The main public spaces have fir wainscoting complete with plate rail. The dining room has a built-in buffet with brass hardware. The original interior colors were buff and brown. This house was featured in the September 1916 issue of *Bungalow Magazine.*

Living room of the A. C. Schneider residence, in 1916. Bungalow Magazine, *September 1916, p. 574. Seattle Public Library*

E. Ryer residence, in 1913. Bungalow Magazine, *June 1913, p. 16. Seattle Public Library*

The dining room of the E. Ryder residence, in 1913. Bungalow Magazine, *June 1913. Seattle Public Library*

E. Ryer Residence (pre-1913)

The E. Ryer residence is a wood-shingled bungalow. The roof is gabled, with a projecting gabled dormer and portico, both supported by brackets. A pergola accents a large bank of transomed casement windows. The interior floors are oak. The living room and dining room have a considerable amount of fir wainscoating, box-beams, built-in bookcases, and a large leaded glass china cupboard. The woodwork in the bedrooms was treated with aluminum bronze to create a gray color. The kitchen was painted a light gray. This residence was featured in the June 1913 issue of *Bungalow Magazine.* W. J. Jones was the architect, and G. C. Brandon from the Modern Bungalow Company served as contractor. The exact same design was also marketed as the "Corona," in Sears catalogues from 1916 until 1922.

Bowen-Huston residence, in 2004.

Bowen-Huston Residence (1913)

The Bowen-Huston residence is characterized by typical Craftsman horizontal design elements. The main gables are street facing, with shed roofs extending to cover a bay window at the entrance. A garage addition was completed in 1917, which introduced another front facing gable to the street façade. Vergeboards are raised at the gable peak, turning slightly upward at their ends, adding a faint Oriental accent to the design. Cedar shakes clad exterior wall surfaces. Windows have diamond panes on the street façade.

The Bowen-Huston residence was originally built for O. J. O'Callahan, using plans ordered from the firm Harris and Coles. Under the name The Bungalow Company, Inc., Harris and Coles designed and distributed plans for a number of Craftsman houses. This structure was the home of arts patron Betty Bowen (1919–1977), who was an original member of the Seattle Art Commission and was frequently referred to as "den mother of the city's arts." She promoted the careers of many regional artists, including Mark Tobey, Leo Kenny, Richard Gilkey, and Morris Graves. She was also a founding member of the Northwest Arts and

Detail of main gable, Bowen-Huston residence.

Crafts Center and the Allied Arts Historic Conservation Committee of Seattle. She also helped organize preservation efforts for the city's Pike Place Market. Two days before her death (February 16, 1977) Seattle Mayor Wes Uhlman named her "First Citizen of Seattle."

Exterior of the G. S. Shirley residence, in 1913. *Bungalow Magazine, October 1913, p. 14. Seattle Public Library*

G. S. Shirley Residence (1913)

The G. S. Shirley residence is a gabled bungalow, with a street-facing ridge line. The main gable of the house sweeps out with a curve toward to street. Eaves are exposed, and corbelled brackets provide visual support to the extended eaves. The house has shingle cladding, and a clinker brick front porch. Piers on the front porch draw upward into an arch. The cement porch floor and steps were colored red to match the clinker brick porch wall. The exterior was originally stained a reddish brown. Window trim was white, and sashes were black. A large oak entrance door (four feet in width) opened into a small entrance hall. The living room and dining room floors were oak, and most of the floors were covered with rugs.

Box-beamed ceilings completed the interior. Wainscoting was present only in the front hallway, with a plate rail appearing in the rest of the living spaces. Two white accent tiles, embossed with a tree design, offset the green tiled fireplace. Golden glass Tiffany light fixtures illuminated either end of the fireplace mantle. The living room and dining room were painted a warm tan, with a lighter cream ceiling. A light blue-gray was used below the plate rail in

Living room of the G. S. Shirley residence, in 1913. *Bungalow Magazine, October 1913, p. 22. Seattle Public Library*

the bedroom, and a rose color accented the upper portion of the wall. The woodwork in the bedroom and kitchen was stained gray. The bathroom had white woodwork on the lower portion of the walls, with a soft green above the rail line. The G. S. Shirley residence, designed by architect George J. Lockman, was featured in the October 1913 issue of *Bungalow Magazine.*

Lars Larsen Residence (1914)

The Lars Larsen residence is unusual, since the property has not one but two houses. A two-story Victorian framed house sits at the back of the lot, while a larger Craftsman occupies the front section. This Craftsman is two stories. Shingles clad the upper floor, and lumber sides the main level. The house has typical large Craftsman brackets under the extended gable roof. Vergeboards extend beyond rooflines, although gutters now hide the exposed rafter ends.

A small balcony extends from an upstairs bedroom, encompassing a pair of French doors flanked by narrow double-hung windows. This bay arrangement is visually

Lars Larsen residence, in 2004.

weighted to match the three-part window arrangement on the main floor. A large one-over-one, double-hung window occupies a significant portion of the remaining second-level façade. A small, thin, long window with multiple vertical lights illuminates the attic space.

The main floor has the typical Craftsman cluster of three windows, and a less common arrangement of two closely placed windows (not framed as one unit) to the right of the recessed front door. Square piers support the flat porch roof, and the main entry to the house is recessed, to the right. Cottage style windows are used throughout the house. Most windows are double hung, and numerous main floor windows have leaded glass details. The interior of the house retains much of its original woodwork. Both the living room and dining room have exposed box-beamed ceilings, and retain many of the original light fixtures. A massive built-in china cabinet occupies most of the dining room wall.

The older, Victorian house sits to the back of the main property. Sandborn maps from 1904, 1905, and 1915 indi-

cate that the Victorian structure may have once faced the main street, and was moved to the back of the lot when the larger Craftsman home was constructed. The one-and-a-half story structure is simple in form, with a front-facing gabled roof and clapboard siding. Large windows are simple one over one, double hung, and smaller, square, fixed-pane windows are used in some areas of the house.

The Lars Larsen residence is located in the second addition to the Queen Anne neighborhood, platted in the 1870s. The original frame Victorian house was constructed in 1898, by William and Mary R. Geddes, vocal and instrumental music teachers. Lars Larsen purchased the property in 1906, and was responsible for construction of the Craftsman style house on the property. The second house was rented out to tenants during this time. Larsen was a blacksmith, who partnered in Larsen and Weyandt, and then Columbus and Larsen, a metalworking business.

John H. Ogden residence, in 1916. Bungalow Magazine, *June 1916, p. 337. Seattle Public Library*

John H. Ogden Residence (1914)

The John H. Ogden residence is a street-gabled Craftsman with a concrete and brick porch. The porch is gabled, which repeats the decorative vergeboards and extended rafter tails. Paired posts with a centered decorative board support the portico instead of the more common tapered piers. The front door is to the left, and is flanked by a pair of double-hung windows. The upper sashes have small decorative lights on the perimeter. Four clustered windows to the right of the door light the living room, while a long narrow window at the top of the gable lights an upstairs bedroom.

The living room fireplace is brick, with built-in bookcases on either side that, like most Craftsman bookcases, have glazed doors. Box-beams accentuate the ceiling. The upper portion of the living room and dining room walls had a stenciled design that appears to be an abstracted floral. While the exact paint color is unknown, tonal differences in magazine photos indicate that the wall color was substantially darker than the ceiling paint. French doors separate the living room from the dining room. The dining room has a high plate rail supported by brackets. Woodwork in this room was painted ivory, with a darker color filling in the dado panels. A large built-in buffet dominates

Dining room of Ogden residence, in 1916. Bungalow Magazine, *June 1916, p. 344. Seattle Public Library*

most of one wall. The kitchen woodwork was white, while the walls and ceiling were cream. Woodwork in the downstairs bedrooms was painted white, while upstairs woodwork had a natural color applied. This home was featured in the June 1916 edition of *Bungalow Magazine*, which lists S. Swenson as the contractor. John Ogden was president of Ivy Press.

Harry W. Cullyford residence, in 1916. Bungalow Magazine, *April 1916, p. 210. Seattle Public Library*

Harry W. Cullyford Residence (1915)

The Harry W. Cullyford residence displays Japanese influences in its accented gable points and upswept gable ends. The gable ridge is parallel to the street and the curved brackets accent the flared roofline. Shingles cover most of the small structure, which has less than 1000 square feet. The front elevation is unusual, with the chimney facing the street. A brick-floored, Japanese-accented portico marks the front entry. The facade windows are small, although the rectangular, trimmed panes provide extra Craftsman detailing. Larger windows were used on the side of the house to maximize hillside views. The fireplace was rimmed by putty-colored tile and flanked by built-in bookcases. The living room and dining room had oak floors and a coved ceiling, a style usually reserved for smaller Tudors. Glass-paned pocket doors (an unusual feature) separated the living room from the dining room. The interior trim was painted a light color, and on the dining room wall a dado (that is plate rail in height) continued the Asian theme with Japanese grass cloth. *Bungalow Magazine* featured the Cullyford home in their April 1916 edition, and the Coles Construction Company was listed as builder.

Detail of the front entrance, Harry W. Cullyford residence.
Bungalow Magazine, *April 1916, p. 213. Seattle Public Library*

Front door of the Frederick E. Kreitle residence, in 2004.

Exterior of the Frederick E. Kreitle residence, in 2004.

Frederick E. Kreitle Residence (1915)

The Frederick Kreitle residence is a classic example of a small working-class Craftsman house. The structure is one story, with the gable facing the street. The small porch also utilizes a front-facing gable. Rafter ends are exposed, and large decorative brackets "support" the extended gable ends. The vergeboards sport a decorative slit cut into each protruding end. The front porch has two square piers (replacing the original paired tapered columns), joined by a cross brace. Exterior walls are clad with cedar shingles on the main level and with horizontal siding on the partially exposed basement level. In typical Craftsman fashion, large glazed expanses host multiple windows. Most windows on the main floor are double hung, with the smaller upper section containing ten square lights, in two rows of five. The exterior of the home was remodeled over the years, and the current owner is working diligently to bring the house back to its original appearance.

The interior of the house is remarkably intact, with almost all its original fir trim and built-ins. The living room has box-beamed ceilings and is separated from the dining room by a bookcase wall, complete with French doors. The dining room has a built-in window seat, box-beamed ceilings, high wainscoted walls, and the original swinging door that accesses the kitchen. The kitchen still retains many of its original cabinets and a built-in folding ironing board. The bathroom even retains its original medicine cabinet.

This house, in the Ballard neighborhood of Seattle, is representative of the working-class cottages that provided housing to workers in the lumber mills and fishing industries. Frederick E. Kreitle, a ship carpenter, bought an empty lot in 1915, and within the year built this house. The first long-term owners of the property were the Lundgren family, who occupied the house from the 1920s until 1950. Josephina Lundgren, a widow, purchased the house, which then passed to her son, Roy C. Lundgren, a welder with Pacific Huts Company. The dwelling has also been home to James Woolbert, a bridge carpenter for the Pacific Coast Railroad Company, Jack D. Blight, a driver for the Boeing Company, and Dayton R. Wintermute, a shipping handler for the United States Postal Service.

Henry Larson residence, in 1916. Bungalow Magazine, *November 1916, p. 693. Seattle Public Library*

Henry Larson Residence (1915)

The Henry Larson residence is a small, one-story Craftsman home, and typifies the building type at the smallest end of the Craftsman spectrum. The building has a gabled roof, with the ridge line facing the street. Vergeboards and brackets accentuate the gabled ends of the house, while the front and back of the dwelling have exposed rafter tails. The exterior of the house is shingled, including the partial porch wall. Large piers rise from the porch corners. Exterior woodwork was originally stained a Siena green with white painted trim. Interior colors were pale browns with cream ceilings. In an unusual move, the dining room, not the living room, was home to the fireplace. The brick for the fireplace was described as dark purple, with red hearth tiles. A coved ceiling design was used in the main living areas. Dark stained wainscoting with a plate rail finished the living and dining room walls. A built-in buffet occupies most of one dining room wall, and is accented by leaded art glass and a beveled plate mirror. This home, designed and

The dining room, Henry Larson residence, in 1916. Bungalow Magazine, *November 1916, p. 696. Seattle Public Library*

built by Emil Beck, was featured in the November 1916 edition of *Bungalow Magazine.*

Belltown Cottages shortly after construction, period photograph. *Courtesy of Myke J. Woodwell*

Belltown Cottages (1916)

The three Belltown Cottages, are indicative of the small Craftsman Bungalow commonly found in Seattle. The Belltown Cottages were built in 1916 by William Hainsworth, who was a well-known Seattle builder and developer from the late 1890s until the 1920s. Single-family houses were typical Hainsworth projects, although he constructed a hotel toward the end of his career and may have designed additional cottage clusters as well. He was active in promoting development above Alki Beach, and he left property to the City of Seattle for Fairmount Park.

The Belltown Cottages are examples of a multifamily housing, a detached bungalow court. These three houses were originally part of a six-unit grouping, representing a type referred to as "bungalow courts." The individual homes sat clustered around a courtyard. These particular bungalow courts were designed for working-class citizens, who most likely had professional ties to the nearby waterfront. Designed to help lower and middle-class workers achieve the American ideal of occupying a house, they were considered more conducive to family life than apartments. While some bungalow courts faced a common courtyard, after 1920 attached bungalow courts were more common. Many of these structures were constructed in transition areas, between commercial or multifamily buildings and single-family neighborhoods. Bungalow courts became less popular after the 1920s, due to more stringent zoning laws and better access to suburban land.

The Belltown Cottages were constructed in a part of the newly developed Denny Regrade. From 1900 until 1910, much of Denny Hill (located on the northern edge of Seattle's downtown) was sluiced into Elliott Bay. With the area now easily developed, commercial and apartment

Cottage at 2516 Elliott Avenue. The man in the hat is William Hainsworth, the builder, period photograph. *Courtesy of Myke J. Woodwell*

buildings began to appear where single-family dwellings once stood. William Hainsworth tore down an existing one-and-a-half-story house to construct the cottages, while at the same time renovating five other cottages built earlier, on a lot at Elliott Way and Vine Street. Advertising signs placed in the windows of the newly completed cottages read "Save Car Fare and Time, Modern Cottages, $16 to $18/month." During the 1920s occupants of the buildings included shipyard workers, fishermen, longshoremen, a telephone operator, and a waitress.

4 ECLECTIC REVIVALS

Tudor Revival and Exotic Revival

English farmhouse (1630), timber filled with wattle and daub, Worcestershire, England (moved to the Virginia Museum of Frontier Culture, Stanton, Virginia), circa 2000.

Germanic example of half-timbering from the medieval city of Rothenberg, in 1998. A northern climate required a steeper roof pitch.

TUDOR REVIVAL (1890–1940)

While many people may envision a Craftsman style house with broad overhanging eaves as the prototypical "Seattle house," the Tudor Revival style, marked by sharper roof pitches, decorated brickwork, and visually striking half-timbering was extraordinarily popular as well. The Tudor Revival style borrowed medieval European forms, and its design components were easily manipulated for both large-scale mansions and smaller speculative houses. Like the Queen Anne style, the Tudor style began in England, and was also employed by the British architect Richard Norman Shaw. Publications such as *Building News* and *American Architect and Building News* showcased Shaw's designs for Hopedene (1873) and Sunninghill (1879), which were large country homes with irregular massing, multiple gabled rooflines, extensive half timbering, and multiple articulated chimneys.

The Tudor Revival house was loosely based on English medieval structures, and could range considerably in scale and design elements, from thatched-roof vernacular structures to massive, elaborately detailed manor houses. The original Tudor style (developed during the reign of the Tudor monarchs, 1485–1603) came out of changing social and cultural trends in England. An increasingly wealthy merchant class combined with land redistribution from Henry VIII's monastic suppression allowed the opportunity for both nobility and merchants to construct grand homes and estates. As England became more politically stable, there was less need for the nobility to inhabit fortified castles. A major design element for newly constructed private residences was half-timbering, which was common in the forest districts of England. Oak framing was combined with wattle and daub infill to create intricate exterior design patterns. In regions where stone was plentiful, such as the Cotswolds or Dartmoor, a similar style utilizing masonry components instead of timber components developed; stone was varied in color and shape to create elaborate complex diamond and herringbone designs. Massive articulated chimney stacks are also a prominent style feature. While many associate the half-timbered design

Preceding pages: (far left) West Seattle Tudor Revival residence, in 1926. *Museum of History and Industry, Seattle, Pemco Webster and Stevens Collection, 83.10.3216.5*; (chapter title page, upper left) 3809 43rd Avenue Northeast. *Asahel Curtis. Washington State Historical Society, Tacoma, 55969*; (upper right) Dr. Johanson residence, Exotic (Swiss) Revival, 7315 34th Avenue Northwest, Capitol Hill (1909), in 2004; (below) Lenora Denny residence, in 1902. *Museum of History and Industry, Seattle, 15977*

The W. F. Foster residence, Seattle, 1913. *University of Washington Libraries, Special Collections, UW13881*

elements with England, other northern European countries employed similar construction techniques. German emigrants, long used to working with half-timber construction, brought this method with them to the New World, and half-timbered structures built during the 1700s still exist in Old Salem, North Carolina.

The Tudor Revival emerged in part from the English Arts and Crafts Movement, which favored Tudor architecture for its picturesque elements, much like the older (and also revived) Gothic style. John Ruskin, an important critic during the Victorian era, promoted the style, as did Richard Norman Shaw. In the United States, European-trained architect Henry Hobson Richardson included Tudor design elements in his residential designs. Other architects and the American public were introduced to the style at the 1876 Philadelphia Centennial International Exposition, where the British government constructed two Elizabethan style buildings. Both structures were favorably discussed in the journal *American Builder*.

A small, brick example of the Tudor Revival style, in 2004.

A detail of half-timbering and brickwork in a Tudor Revival gable.

A Tudor Revival detail showing a decorative brick design.

The revival style was spurred on by a growing interest in Colonial and pre-Colonial American history and America's architectural heritage. The Tudor Revival style was so pervasive that even Frank Lloyd Wright experimented with a Tudor Revival design for the Nathan G. Moore house of Chicago, in 1895. By the 1920s, the style was popular with middle and upper classes. It was associated with nobility yet it was less formal than a Colonial or Neoclassical Revival designs. While use of the Tudor Revival style declined in the United States during the 1930s, it has enjoyed renewed popularity in recent years, perhaps due to its sense of history overlaid with picturesque, fairy tale elements.

Early Tudor Revival style houses were commonly referred to as Queen Anne, especially in England, as was the case with Shaw's Leyswood of 1868. Use of this term is confusing, due to its associations with the Victorian spindlework houses. In many ways, Victorian Queen Anne and Tudor Revival houses share some of the same design elements, with their focus on irregular massing, prominent gables, articulated chimneys, and decorative façade treatments. However, the Tudor Revival style lacks the multi-leveled porches and the decorative gingerbreading found in Queen Anne houses. Tudor Revival design generally includes a steeply pitched roof, with front and side gables. Half timbering (decorative, not structural) can be present in stucco and brick examples. Tall, narrow, multipained windows appear, sometimes in a diamond pattern, or with small stained glass insets. Chimneys are large and articulated with decorative brickwork or chimney pots. While chimney stacks in the Victorian and Craftsman period are commonly contained inside the exterior walls so only the tops are seen, most Tudor Revival homes accentuate the

chimneys by pulling the entire brick structure outside the main wall, using it as a design feature. Brickwork is often patterned, either through the use of color or irregularly massed clinker bricks. Some homes even have crenelated brick or stone work, where pattern is added through repeated square indentations, much like those seen in medieval defense battlements.

An unusual and charming design feature of Tudor Revival homes is the frequent use of rounded top doors, reminiscent of fairy tale cottages. The doors often have small inset windows, allowing the homeowner to view visitors, and some are even designed to open, allowing discussion or the passing of letters. Large Tudor Revival residences are multistoried, with numerous dormers, overlapping gables, varied eave line heights, and crenelated battlements. These houses are more formal in character, and use carved plaster and dark stained woodwork extensively to further the illusion of an English country estate. In Seattle, most large Tudor Revival houses have half-timbering; however, smaller, middle-class versions of these houses are often brick. Smaller, one-and-a-half-story suburban versions, common during the speculative housing markets of the 1920s, are usually more regular in floor plan and have significantly fewer interior details. These houses are most commonly identified by a steeply pitched front gable with varied eave height over the main entrance. Their open plan and smaller scale makes them considerably less formal than their larger cousins. While superb individual examples of this style are found throughout the city, there are significant clusters of speculative Tudor Revival houses in Ballard. In Seattle, the foreign-born architectural team of Charles H. Bebb (English) and Louis L. Mendel (German) was often selected for Tudor Revival designs.

Dr. Johanson residence, Exotic (Swiss) Revival, 7315 34th Avenue Northwest, Capitol Hill (1909), in 2004.

EXOTIC REVIVALS (1890–1910)

Although Tudor Revival is one of the most common Eclectic Revival styles, there were other variations, most notably a Swiss Chalet Revival version. The Swiss Chalet Revival style was also introduced in design books like A. J. Downing's *The Architecture of Country Houses* (1850). The style was considered especially appropriate for heavily wooded or mountainous sites, so it is no surprise to find examples of this style in Seattle and the surrounding region, for the association with wooded mountainous areas and the abundance of freshly milled lumber made it an appealing choice. The original prototype for the design was the traditional Swiss Chalet, with its wood construction, rectangular massing, broad eaves with a front-facing gable, and abundant use of porches, balconies, and decorative vergeboards. The original Swiss Chalet prototypes frequently housed farm animals on the ground floor, and an exterior staircase allowed entry to the second-level of the house. American versions were entered from the main floor and usually did not have an exterior staircase. The Swiss Revival style was also popular in Scandinavian countries, which had an established folk tradition of log houses.

During the early twentieth century, Seattle had a large Scandinavian immigrant population. Thus it is not surprising to find an occasional house with Nordic design elements, including turned wood balusters, vertical wood siding, and painted rosemaling.

INTERIORS

Large Tudor Revival homes are filled with dark woodwork details, and have a significant front entry hall, complete with paneled walls and staircase. Massive fireplaces are commonly found in more than one room. Ground-floor rooms often continue the dark trim with beamed ceilings, with main-floor living rooms connecting via arched openings instead of the pocket doors so common in Victorian homes. Built-in bookcases (particularly around fireplaces), window seats, and occasionally built-in china closets are major interior details. Smaller middle-class examples of the Tudor Revival style also exhibit articulated fireplaces, and will have decorative art tile ornamenting the surround. Ceilings in these examples are less likely to have the ornamental boxed beams, and instead will have coved ceilings, evident by concave corner transitions between the walls and ceiling. Kitchens frequently have built-in eating areas, or perhaps a small alcove articulated with an arched opening, for benches and a small kitchen table.

Interior furnishings of Tudor Revivals could be rather eclectic, with an owner selecting between oak Craftsman furniture, mahogany Colonial Revival, or even some Spanish Colonial pieces. Wall colors, like furnishings, might mimic those found in Craftsman or Colonial Revival homes. White was still a standard for kitchens and bathrooms, since color did not start to appear in tile much beyond black or blue accents until the 1930s. Pedestal bathroom sinks were increasingly popular in the 1920s, and by 1930 they were fairly common. Claw-foot tubs remained common until the 1920s, at which time built-in tub-shower combinations became more frequent.

A Tudor Revival ogee arched entry door, in 1998.

A Tudor Revival coved, recessed ceiling, in 1998. This house has the original wall stenciling.

A Tudor Revival fireplace, in 1999.

A Tudor Revival fireplace detail, showing an art tile with a covered wagon design, in 1999.

A Tudor Revival living room with a Continental aesthetic, period photograph. *Asahel Curtis. Washington State Historical Society, Tacoma, 57786*

A Tudor Revival dining room, period photograph. The table and chairs are Restoration style, popular in England from 1660 until 1700. The sideboard, however, is Chinese.

Asahel Curtis. Washington State Historical Society, Tacoma, 57787

V. W. VOORHEES, ARCHITECT, SEATTLE, WASH.

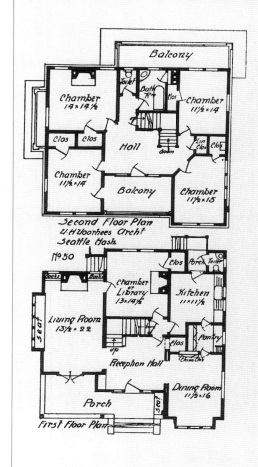

DESIGN NO. 50.

The width of this eight-room house is 40 feet; length, including porches, 40 feet; height of first story 9 feet; second story 8½ feet; basement 7 feet.

The foundation and porches are of clinker brick.

The gables are wood fiber plaster, finished with granite dash.

The outside walls are shingled. The interior is finished in Mission. Approximate cost of construction, $4,500.00.

Cost of one set of plans, specifications and details, $25.00.
Cost of two sets of plans, specifications and details, $30.00.

(Any plan can be reversed to suit location.)

A Tudor Revival house featured in the V. W. Voorhees pattern book, *Western Home Builder*, circa 1910. *University of Washington Libraries, Special Collections, UW23595*

ECLECTIC REVIVAL HOUSES

Tudor Revival (1890–1940)

1898–1901	Stimson-Green Residence	1909	M. Hardwood Young Residence
1903	Charles Henry Cobb Residence	1911	Joseph Kraus Residence
1905	Eliza Ferry Leary Residence	1919–1920	Perry B. Truax Residence
1907	William Hainsworth Residence	1925	Jesse C. Bowles Residence
1907–1909	Charles H. Black Residence	1925	*Times*-Stetson and Post Model House
1908–1909	Oliver David Fisher Residence	1927–1930	Anhalt Apartments, 1005 and 1014 East Roy Street
1909	McFee-Klockzien Residence	1900–1930	Various Tudor Revival Residences

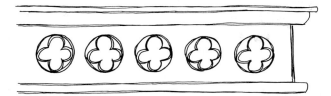

Tudor Revival quatrefoil details, usually found on porches or decorative masonry bands.

Diamond-paned windows, a common Tudor Revival design feature.

Tudor Revival articulated brick chimney stack.

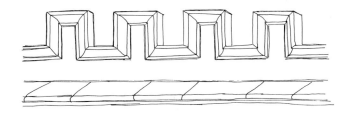

Crenelations on a Tudor Revival house.

Exotic Revivals (1890–1910)

1903–1905   Stimson-Griffiths Residence

1908   Norvell Residence

1933   Rosen Residence

TUDOR REVIVAL (1890–1940)

Stimpson-Green residence, in 1901. *Northwest Museum of Arts and Culture/Eastern Washington State Historical Society, Spokane, L91-161-39*

Stimson-Green Residence (1898–1901)

The Stimson-Green residence is a Seattle landmark that has hosted numerous social events through the years. This grand house is a lavish example of the Tudor Revival style, with multiple gables, different sized dormers, and large articulated chimneystacks. Exterior wall cladding is brick on the lower level, with a combination of stucco and half-timbering on the upper levels. The half-timbered detail work is elaborate, with curved and crossing pieces in addition to the more common grid elements. Many of the windows have diamond-paned leaded glass. The front entry is articulated by a small gable and a pointed arched doorway. The exceptional decorative detail on the house even extends to the vergeboards, which are scalloped.

The interior of the house is richly appointed and remarkably well preserved. The style is an eclectic mix of English Arts and Crafts, Romanesque Revival, and Moorish influences. Mantle pieces are ornate, and are designed to be the focal point of each room. Dark wood paneling and ornately carved columns are used extensively. The front door opens into a large central hallway, followed by a raised stair hall that accesses the formal dining room. The front hall has Romanesque design elements, including multiple clusters of dark wooden columnettes supporting a rounded archway. Painted details are in red and gold. The library is more Gothic in theme, with pointed arches framing the bookcases. The ladies' parlor is the only room in the house where the traditional dark Tudor Revival woodwork yields to a lighter design scheme: it was painted several shades of white and yellow, with delicate lines suggesting an Empire theme. The dining room has Renaissance detailing, including a large faux tapestry (painted corduroy) depicting a Renaissance king and his court. The fireplace has an impressive indigo glass surround. One of the most exotic rooms in the house is the billiard room, located in the basement. It has a Moorish theme, with a brick horseshoe arch accented by Near Eastern-inspired lighting and golden colored bottle-glass windows.

Entrance of the Stimson-Green residence, 1901. *Northwest Museum of Arts and Culture/Eastern Washington State Historical Society, Spokane, L91-161-29*

The Stimson-Green house is significant for its architect and original owner as well. The house was designed by the firm of Cutter and Malmgren. Kirtland K. Cutter, a native of Ohio, received his architectural training in London, Paris, and Rome. He arrived in Spokane by the late 1880s, where he quickly built a reputation by designing elaborate residences designed in a variety of period styles. He was also commissioned to design the Idaho State Building for the 1893 World's Columbian Exposition. The design of the Stimson-Green house was based on the A. B. Campbell house (1898) in Spokane.

The original owner of the house was Charles Douglas Stimson. A native of Michigan, he settled in Washington, where he organized the Stimson Land Company with his brothers. In 1890 they formed the Stimson Mill Company (in Ballard), which Charles headed for most of his professional career. Stimson was also director of the Metropolitan Bank and the General Insurance Company of America. His community involvement included active membership in the Seattle Chamber of Commerce and serving as director of the Alaska-Yukon-Pacific Exposition (1909). Harriet Stimson helped found the Seattle Symphony and the Children's Orthopedic Hospital. She also assisted Nellie Cornish in starting the Cornish School of the Arts. During World War I, Stimson managed the Northwestern Division of the American Red Cross. The family moved out of the house in 1908 to the Highlands, a community north of Seattle.

Joshua and Missy Green were the next long-term residents of the house, in 1914. In 1886 Joshua had arrived from Mississippi. He was involved in shipping, and soon purchased a steamer. Shortly thereafter he became president of the La Conner Trading and Transportation Company, which grew into the largest inland steamboat fleet on Puget Sound. Green held board positions with other businesses throughout the state, including People's Savings Bank, Dan Creek Placer Mines, Northern Life Insurance Company, Puget Sound Power and Light Company, and Bellingham Securities Syndicate. The Greens lived in the house until his death in 1975.

In 1986 the Stimson-Green mansion was purchased by Patsy Collins, granddaughter of the Stimsons. She used profits from her catering company to restore the family home, and in 2001 donated the house to the Washington Trust for Historic Preservation. The house serves as headquarters for the trust, which also rents out the house for special events. The Stimson-Green residence has become one of the most elegant entertainment venues in Seattle.

Library, Stimson-Green residence, 1901. *Northwest Museum of Arts and Culture/Eastern Washington State Historical Society, Spokane, L91-161-5*

Living room, fireplace detail, Stimson-Green residence, 1901. *Northwest Museum of Arts and Culture/Eastern Washington State Historical Society, Spokane, L91-161-4*

Billiard room, Stimson-Green residence, 1901. *Northwest Museum of Arts and Culture/Eastern Washington State Historical Society, Spokane, L 91-161-22*

Charles Henry Cobb residence, 1913. *University of Washington Libraries, Special Collections, UW2474*

Charles Henry Cobb Residence (1903)

The Charles Henry Cobb residence is another eclectic dwelling designed by the architecture firm of Bebb & Mendel. Large cross gables dominate the structure, which utilizes half-timbering on the upper floors, and stone for the main floor and the retaining wall around the property. The widely angled front eaves shelter a particularly elaborate half-timbered façade, which also includes unusual ornamental panels. The building's customized features—the ornamental panels on the main building and capping the portico, the flared width of horizontal beams, and the use of stone instead of brick—give this house an imposing presence, not an easy task in a neighborhood filled with numerous high-style examples.

Charles Henry Cobb was born in Lincoln, Maine. He came west as a young man and quickly became involved in the logging business. He eventually was a promoter and stockholder of the Metropolitan Building Company, and in his later life served as president of the International Timber Company. The scale of his house indicates his personal wealth, and indeed, a county history reports that he gave $600,000 to charity in 1937–1938.

Eliza Ferry Leary residence, in 2004.

Eliza Ferry Leary Residence (1905)

This large residence was originally part of a fifteen-acre tract styled after English country estates. Some of the estate land has been developed, and additional acreage has disappeared beneath widened streets. The rectangular massing of the house is broken up with multiple cross gables and a projecting front entrance. While stone is the predominant exterior cladding, there is extensive use of half-timbered stucco on the projecting cross gables. Windows have multiple lights, divided by lead muntins. The interior has dark paneling and multiple fireplaces.

The Eliza Ferry Leary residence was designed by Canadian architect Alfred Bodley, who arrived in Seattle in 1904. Bodley partnered briefly with John Graham Sr. but he practiced alone for this commission. Construction of the house took four years and had just started when the owner, Mr. Leary, died in 1905. A businessman and lawyer from the East Coast, in Seattle Leary promoted railroads and coal mining and eventually organized a gas company. Leary's wife, Eliza Ferry Leary, completed the house after her

Detail, leaded glass windows, Eliza Ferry Leary residence.

husband's death. She was a charter member of the Daughters of the American Revolution Rainier Chapter (1895), the Seattle Red Cross, and the Children's Orthopedic Hospital. She also served as vice-president of the Seattle YWCA, as building chairman. Nationally, she was vice-regent for the Mount Vernon Ladies Association of the Union, which was responsible for obtaining and preserving George Washington's estate.

Exterior of the William Hainsworth residence, side entrance, period photograph. *University of Washington Libraries, Special Collections, UW2971*

William Hainsworth Residence (1907)

The William Hainsworth residence is a massive Tudor Revival house. The first floor is clinker brick, while upper floors are stucco and half-timbered. The primary portion of the house has a side-facing gable, although cross gables, shed-roof dormers and a turret contribute to a complex roof treatment. A large cross gable dominates the façade, giving the residence a distinct English manor feeling.

William Hainsworth was an industrialist and real estate developer who came to Seattle in 1889. Although he owned and operated a Ballard steel foundry, he built his house in West Seattle. Hainsworth was active in developing West Seattle, and he donated Admiralty Point to the city of Seattle. The house was (and still is) impressively large for the area, and became a showpiece with its formal gardens, tennis courts, pools, summerhouse, and even a playhouse for his children.

John Graham Sr. and David Myers designed the house. British-born Graham arrived in Seattle around 1900 and designed the downtown Bon Marché building, the old Frederick & Nelson building (now Nordstrom), and the University Methodist Temple. Myers worked with Graham for a number of years before forming the partnership of Shack & Young.

Charles H. Black residence, in 1937. *Puget Sound Regional Archives*

Charles H. Black Residence (1907–1909)

The Charles H. Black residence epitomizes a Tudor Revival "country estate." The side-gabled roof has numerous cross-gable extensions, some in the form of dormers, and one that dominates the house's façade. Vergeboard ends are decoratively cut. The first floor and chimney are granite, while the second story and attic are stucco with half-timber design elements. The front entry is recessed: to the right is a bay window that creates space for a second-story balcony. The interior has a large oak-paneled and beamed reception room. The drawing room and dining room have mahogany paneling. The attic space provided servants' quarters while the basement level served as recreation space—plans originally called for a bowling alley, but it was used as a shooting gallery instead.

Charles H. Black founded Seattle Hardware Company. He also served as vice president of Black Manufacturing and as treasurer of the Alaska Fish Company. Black employed the architectural firm of Bebb & Mendel to design the house; the firm had designed several other homes in the neighborhood including the Kerry house (421 West Highland Drive, 1903), the Stimson house (405 Highland Drive, 1904), and the Treat residence (1 Highland Drive, 1905). The Olmsted Brothers, a Boston-based firm that helped lay out the 1909 Alaska-Yukon-Pacific Exposition in Seattle, designed the grounds, specifying a greenhouse, potting shed, tennis court, and playhouse that were never built.

Oliver David Fisher residence, period photograph. *Asahel Curtis. Washington State Historical Society, Tacoma, 55783*

Oliver David Fisher Residence (1908–1909)

The Oliver David Fisher residence, designed by the Beezer Brothers, architects, has a fairly symmetrical façade. The main roof is hipped. A single gabled dormer anchors the center of the front façade, and is flanked by extending cross gables that face the street. Massive chimney stacks break the symmetry of the house, with one located on the front of the structure and the other rising from the rear. While the main exterior wall treatment is brick, the gable ends and much of the second floor exterior are accented with half-timbering. Substantial brackets, some decorated with small shields, are used throughout the structure to add additional visual weight and to create associations with European

gentry. Third-floor windows have multiple lights; some are casement widows while others are double hung.

The main bay of the house is elaborate; a large leaded glass front door anchors the space, slightly recessed under a curved stone arch. Leaded glass windows, with colored glass and small coats of arms, flank the door. The front entry is set off from the yard by a small brick and stone wall that encloses a stone patio. Stained glass spans the main entry door and sidelights. The visual strength of the front bay, with the curved, stone-trimmed entry and the sparkling stained glass windows on two levels, dominates the structure. Located on the left side, a bank of three

Detail of the Oliver David Fisher residence. *Asahel Curtis. Washington State Historical Society, Tacoma, 55780*

curved windows, under a keystoned brick arch, occupies the main floor, echoing the shape of the front entrance. To the right of the front door, a single double-hung window is located directly under the main cross gable on that end of the structure.

Oliver David Fisher was co-founder of the Fisher Flouring Mills Company, one of the largest four mills in the world. Fisher was active in a number of businesses, serving as chairman for the Seattle-based General Insurance Company and as director of Weyerhaeuser. He also helped found KOMO radio and television stations.

McFee-Klockzien residence, in 2004.

McFee-Klockzien Residence (1909)

The McFee-Klockzien residence emphasizes Tudor Revival design through extensive half-timbering and accentuated chimneys. A front entry gable and gabled dormer windows also contribute to the style, and the exterior cladding has brick and stucco treatments, which convey the Tudor Revival style far more than the rectangular massing of the house. In fact, the strict rectilinear form, combined with the awkwardly attached sunroom, emphasizes a severe formality uncommon in most Tudor Revival houses. The residence was illustrated in the 1913 publication *Homes and Gardens of the Pacific Coast*, which noted that the unusual addition of the sun parlor was "an improvement on the usual English house." The interior of the house was somewhat formal, in part due to the plan, although the dark woodwork contributed to a restrained atmosphere as well.

John McFee, a native of Quebec, arrived in Seattle during 1890. His involvement with railroads was timely and helped him achieve considerable financial success. He hired the firm of Spalding & Umbrecht to design the residence. Spalding trained in the east and worked in the Midwest and Northwest before arriving in Seattle by 1901. Umbrecht practiced architecture in New York and moved to Seattle in 1900. Both architects designed commercial buildings in addition to residential work.

M. Hardwood Young residence, in 1913. *University of Washington Libraries, Special Collections, UW2788*

M. Hardwood Young Residence (1909)

Designed by the architect James H. Schack, the M. Hardwood Young residence, like so many of the large Tudor Revival houses on Capitol Hill, epitomized the ideal home of Seattle's newly wealthy industrialists. The main hipped roof gives the building a square massing that even the front accent gable and gabled dormers don't entirely counteract. Corbelled brickwork decorates the massive chimneys. The upper floors are stuccoed, with half-timbering. Most of the windows are casement, with multiple lights, and open out over the manicured lawn. The ground floor is primarily brick. Slightly curved arches accent the recessed entryway and window groupings on each side of the front door. Window clusters are also arched, with a center window flanked by smaller casement windows. The upper portions of the windows have multiple lights, while the lower sections have single lights, providing more expansive views from the home's interior.

Young was a native of Massachusetts. Although admitted to Harvard, he chose to fight in the Civil War. In 1868 he moved to Missouri, becoming an auditor for the Iowa-based Burlington and Missouri River Railroad. He returned to Boston to work as a cashier for the Boston Manufacturing Company. In 1889 he visited Seattle to help organize the New England–Northwestern Investment Company. He returned to Seattle two years later, as the company's western manager, and eventually sat on the board of directors for the Seattle Electric Company and for the Puget Sound Electric Company. He also served as director of the National Bank of Commerce and as manager of the Pacific Coast division of Boston's Planters Compress Company, which sold cotton and hay bale presses. Young bailed large amounts of hay and shipped it to the Philippines and Alaska, making a substantial return on his investment.

Joseph Kraus residence, in 1913. *University of Washington Libraries, Special Collections, UW13828*

Joseph Kraus Residence (1911)

The Joseph Kraus residence, designed by architect J. E. Douglas, is one of Seattle's finest examples of the Tudor Revival style, utilizing multiple cross gables and a mix of brick, half-timbering, and stucco cladding material. There are several different window treatments, the most common being double-hung windows with twenty-four small lights in the upper portion, and a single glazed sheet on the lower half. Also abundant are nine-over-nine, double-hung windows. Transoms above the first-story windows are filled with stained glass.

The interior of the house has a large foyer complete with central staircase. A stained glass window lights the stairwell. A parlor and dining room are to one side with a library located opposite. A kitchen and butler's pantry finish the ground floor. The majority of public spaces on the first floor have mahogany and fir trim, and hardwood floors have dark-stained inlay work. The second floor con-

tains bedrooms, as does the third, where the servants resided. Belgian glass was ordered for the stained glass windows and light fixtures, but was allegedly destroyed during the First World War before it could be shipped. The residence provided grand accommodations for sailors during the housing shortage of World War II.

Historic photos of the interior show an elegant home filled with Oriental rugs, furniture, books, and pictures. The main staircase has light fixtures attached to the newel posts, providing additional light to the interior. A living room, just off the front hallway has box-beamed ceilings, pendant lights, and decorated walls and ceilings. Although colors cannot be determined from the photographs, the various shades indicate that many different hues decorated the room. Portraits of George and Martha Washington grace the large table in the center of the room. Curtains provide privacy between rooms. The library continues the

Living room, Joseph Kraus residence, in 1913. *University of Washington Libraries, Special Collections, UW13852*

Library, Joseph Kraus residence,
in 1913. *University of Washington
Libraries, Special Collections, UW13853*

Dining room, Joseph Kraus residence, in 1913. *University of Washington Libraries, Special Collections, UW13855*

box-beamed ceiling treatment, with pendant lights. Large bookcases with glass doors flank the brick fireplace. The dining room continues use of box beams for the ceiling treatment. Drop light fixtures illuminate the space. A wall-papered frieze runs just below the ceiling molding while a large built-in china cupboard with ornately paneled doors occupies much of the far wall.

Peter B. Truax residence, in 1926. *Museum of History and Industry, Seattle, 7610*

Perry B. Truax Residence (1919–1920)

The Perry B. Truax residence, designed by architect David J. Myers, displays the Tudor Revival style through steeply pitched cross gables, an irregularly massed plan, and an articulated chimney. An ogee arch, reminiscent of Gothic architectural forms, marks the front entrance to the house. The brick exterior is given added visual weight and design interest through large light-colored quoins that surround the windows. This example of Tudor Revival is similar to a version known as Collegiate Gothic, which was common on university campuses during the early part of the twentieth century (the buildings of the University of Washington's liberal arts quadrangle exemplify this style). Truax served as vice-president of Seattle National Bank.

Detail of the Truax residence.

Jesse C. Bowles residence, in 2004.

Jesse C. Bowles Residence (1925)

The Jesse C. Bowles residence is rectangular in plan, with the predominant gable ridge running parallel with the street and the smaller cross gables and dormers accentuating the front of the house. The roofing material is flat clay tile. Exterior walls are treated with false half-timbering over brick. An accentuated brick chimney is pulled outside one of the cross gables, while another, smaller chimney rises from the house's roofline. The casement windows have multiple leaded lights, while a window near the stair landing is accentuated with colored art glass using a Gothic Revival quatrefoil. Bronze exterior hardware may have been custom made for the residence. The interior of the house continues the Tudor Revival aesthetic with paneled doors and wrought-iron fixtures. The library has the built-in bookcases and box-beamed ceiling that is common for the style, along with a carved wood mantelpiece.

The Bowles family was prominent in the region for their community activities and business interests in shipbuilding, manufacturing, real estate, and insurance. The family came to Washington Territory from Missouri, following the Oregon Trail. Charles Bowles, Jesse's father, was born in Vancouver, and practiced law in both Washington and Oregon. He moved to Seattle around 1900 and helped found the Bowles Company, a wholesale plumbing company, and the Northwest Steel Company based in

Front door, Jesse C. Bowles residence.

Exterior light fixture, Jesse C. Bowles residence.

Portland. The family divided their time between Seattle and Portland. Jesse C. Bowles, for whom this house was built, was born in Portland, and spent much of his youth in Seattle. After attending college back East he returned to Seattle, married, and by the 1920s was president of the Bowles Company, the Northwest Envelope Company, and the Bowles Realty Company.

As a child, Bowles lived in the Mount Baker neighborhood, and upon his return to Seattle he decided to reside in that area. He selected architect Arthur L. Loveless, a prominent residential designer, to build his house. Loveless had

arrived in Seattle in 1907, and briefly partnered with Daniel R. Huntington. In 1914 Loveless started his own architecture firm, focusing on single-family homes. Like many architects of his day, he produced designs in several different styles, including Craftsman, Colonial Revival, and Tudor Revival. The picturesque Tudor Revival style was a favorite of both the architect and his clients. The relatively informal style, with loose rules on both massing and planning, allowed placing the rooms, windows, and terraces to capitalize on picturesque views.

Times-Stetson & Post Model House under construction, in 1925. *Museum of History and Industry, Seattle, Pemco Webster and Stevens Collection, 83.10439.2*

The finished *Times*-Stetson & Post Model House, in 1925. *Museum of History and Industry, Seattle, Pemco Webster and Stevens Collection, 83.10516.1*

Times-Stetson & Post Model House (1925)

Constructed in 1925, this house is a modest wood-clad version of a Tudor Revival residence. The irregular massing of the house is created by two cross gables, the smallest with a rounded archway that leads to the rounded-top entry door. The larger gable to the right covers nearly half the façade. Decorative half-timber elements are in the uppermost portion, centered over a pair of casement windows. On the first floor, two narrow windows flank a large picture window, the entire assemblage capped with a leaded glass transom. To the left of the door, a pair of six-over-one, double-hung windows are accented by a window box. A small gabled dormer with a six-over-one window is aligned directly above the double-hung pair. The left corner of the main gable is clipped, making an easier visual transition from the main roof down to the small projecting section of the dining room below.

This residence, designed by architect Edward L. Merritt, was the *Times*-Stetson & Post Model House in 1925. It was part of a number of festivities that centered around Better Homes Week in June of that year. Merritt had worked with Jud Yoho and the Craftsman Bungalow Company from the 1910s through 1920. Stetson & Post Lumber Company provided the lumber for the structure. Malmo and Company provided the landscaping services. The contractor in charge of the project was Herman Neubert. Grote-Rankin Company provided decorating services for the project and displayed a miniature landscaped replica of the home in their store windows. The city of Seattle was even involved with the endeavor, and erected large floodlights so the home could be viewed in the evening hours.

The interior of the house had hardwood flooring. A slender picture railing was just a few inches below the living room ceiling, and dark paint color accented this area. The living room fireplace was tiled in several different colors and sizes, providing visual interest, and a minimal mantelpiece. An overhead lighting fixture and four sconces provided bare-bulb lighting to the room. The upholstered pieces of furniture were placed at an angle, and allowed flow through the room while maintaining fireplace views.

The living room wall color was described in the Seattle *Daily Times* as having "a warm neutral shade . . . with a Tiffany finish." The Wilton rug had a Persian design in shades of deep rose, green, blue, and black. The draperies were silk damask, in shades of sage green, rose, and gold. In an era before television, a radio and phonograph were placed against the inside wall. The dining room furniture was described as "walnut in the Italian Renaissance style that is being used in many of the newer homes." A Chinese rug in colors of sand, mulberry, blue, and copper covered most of the floor, while windows were treated with sheer golden gauze below and overpanels of "heavy blue" with copper stripes. The kitchen had linoleum floors and the latest in domestic appliances, including a combination Westinghouse oven and stove. Newspaper articles describing this house offer unique documentation of an early twentieth-century middle-class residence and the construction trades in Seattle. Those who worked on the project would be proud to know that the house is in excellent condition, and looks almost identical to the pictures taken more than seventy-five years ago.

The newly installed hardwood floors, *Times*-Stetson & Post Model House, in 1925. *Museum of History and Industry, Seattle, Pemco Webster and Stevens Collection, 83.10513.2*

The fully furnished living room, *Times*-Stetson & Post Model House, in 1925. *Museum of History and Industry, Seattle, Pemco Webster and Stevens Collection, 83.10516.10*

The bathroom, complete with pedestal sink and built-in medicine cabinet, *Times*-Stetson & Post Model House, in 1925. *Museum of History and Industry, Seattle, Pemco Webster and Stevens Collection, 83.10516.4*

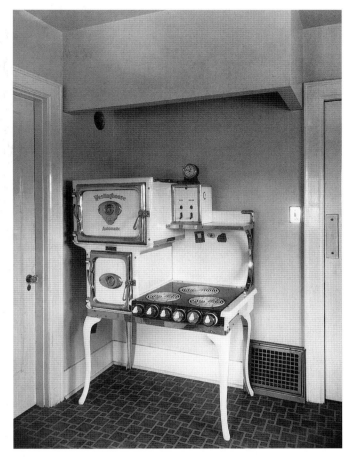

The kitchen, *Times*-Stetson & Post Model House, in 1925. *Museum of History and Industry, Seattle, Pemco Webster and Stevens Collection, 83.10.516.5*

The *Times*-Stetson & Post Model House, in 2004.

Anhalt Apartments, 1005 East Roy Street, in 2004.

Anhalt Apartments, 1005 and 1014 East Roy Street (1927–1930)

While this book focuses on single-family houses in Seattle, the "apartment home" complexes designed by Fred Anhalt are so unique that two are included here. Both of the buildings have Tudor Revival design elements, including rough clinker brick, cedar shakes, wrought iron, and leaded glass windows. Entrance to the 1005 East Roy Street compound is marked by a small, rounded guard tower. The main structure has three stair towers, with small clusters of apartments opening into each tower. The ground floor is brick, and the second floor, which projects slightly beyond the main level, is faced with half-timbering. Cast stone provides detail work.

The three-story unit contains twenty-five apartments, although the horizontal nature of the building, combined with the lush landscaping, gives the appearance of a smaller, intimate structure. A three-story, free-standing staircase is one of the most striking interior features of the building. This apartment complex had the city's first underground apartment parking garage. Apartment interiors have oak flooring, beamed ceilings, and fireplaces. Some of the upper units have fifteen-foot-high ceilings. The building at 1014 East Roy Street has a less elaborate exterior, and uses brick as the main cladding material. It is smaller, housing twelve units. There are numerous other Anhalt design apartments in the city, including 730 and 750 Belmont Avenue.

Fred Anhalt was born in Minnesota, and moved as a young child to North Dakota. Not enjoying the life of a rural farmer, he eventually moved to Montana where he briefly worked as a butcher. By 1926 Anhalt opened an appliance store in Seattle. He soon became involved with building and leasing small retail markets, and enjoyed the design process so much he began studying architectural books, including *Tudor Homes of England* by Samuel Chamberlain and *American Country Houses of Today* by Arthur Holden. He soon undertook apartment house design and served as designer, developer, and promoter for his apartment buildings. From 1926 to 1929 he constructed more than two dozen buildings.

Anhalt's buildings are distinctive. He avoided long public hallways, and added design elements such as fireplaces, front and rear entries and balconies, which were uncommon in apartment buildings at the time. He had a large workforce, almost 135

Anhalt Apartments, 1005 East Roy Street, detail.

people, who served as draftsmen, bricklayers, carpenters, metal workers, and landscapers. This allowed tight control over projects and helped him maintain a rapid construction schedule—most buildings took only three months from start to occupancy. The interesting design of the apartments, their small scale, period details, and lush landscaping continue to make his residences some of the most desired units in the city.

Prosser residence, in 1913. *University of Washington Libraries, Special Collections, UW2346*

Various Tudor Revival Residences (1900–1930)

Three selected Tudor Revival residences suggest the range of Tudor Revival styles in Seattle. The first example is the Prosser residence, which is a large house, although more restrained than many of the high-end examples in this chapter. Although it has the multiple gabled eaves, and the mixed use of brick, half-timbering, and stucco of the style, it has considerably less half-timbering then many of its Capitol Hill neighbors. The front of the house is articulated by two large cross gables, each facing the street, giving the front facade a symmetrical appearance. A small gabled dormer anchors the center of the roof. Casement windows with multiple lights are located in the third floor attic space and the gable ends. The half-timbering under each cross gable is slightly curved, an infrequent, striking detail. The gable vergeboards and the stringcourse between the first and second floors have small, carved wooden brackets. The second floor is predominantly stucco. Gable windows on

the second floor of the façade are placed in clusters of three, each double hung with multiple upper lights. The main floor is brick, with a gabled entry portico sheltering the front door. Windows on either side of the entry are similar to those found on the upper story: double hung, with multiple lights in the upper sash, a single pane in the lower sash, and placed in groups of three.

The second example, a stuccoed Tudor Revival house, was built at 1740 Interlaken Boulevard. The main entrance of the house was later moved to the rear, giving the residence its current address of 1859 Boyer Avenue East. Unlike many of the larger houses of the style, this one does not have multiple front-facing gables. The dominant visual accent is the extended roofline on the left, which ends with a small arched opening that provides access to the front door. The chimney is front facing. Tudor Revival houses are unusual in having street-facing chimneys, and this one is accented with brick work that provides some of the only texture and color changes on the house's exterior. The casement windows have eight lights, with leaded muntins.

The smallest example is a brick structure, representative of Tudor Revival houses in the Ballard neighborhood. The massing of the house is simple, and the usual steeply pitched roofline is absent. Instead, brickwork is the main design element of the home. While many small brick Tudor Revivals utilize multiple brick patterns or clinker brick, this one uses two contrasting colors of bricks for visual interest. A lighter shade forms quoins around all structure, window, and door edges. Crenelations also appear over the small front portico. The extended front-facing gable to the right has a small, arched, casement window in the attic.

Tudor Revival residence, 1740 Interlaken Boulevard, period photograph. *Asahel Curtis. Washington State Historical Society, Tacoma, 55785*

Small brick Tudor Revival house at 7523 33rd Avenue Northwest, in 2004.

EXOTIC REVIVAL (1890–1910)

Stimson-Griffiths residence, period photograph. *Museum of History and Industry, Seattle, 12202*

Stimson-Griffiths Residence (1903–1905)

The Stimson-Griffiths residence (originally owned by Frederick Spencer Stimson, a brother of C. D. Stimson), designed by the architecture firm of Bebb & Mendel, has elements of a Swiss Chalet mixed with the Tudor Revival style. The broadness of the gable angle, combined with the decorative trussing and articulated third-floor balcony spaces, would seem to indicate the Chalet style. However, the irregularity of the plan and interior details support the classification of Tudor Revival. Exterior walls are clad with both stone and half-timbered treatments, with the stone covering most of the ground-floor elevation. The windows are predominantly double hung, with the upper sash consisting of leaded diamond-shaped lights.

The main floor interior was dominated by a formal entryway with a monumental staircase. Walls were finished with oak paneling and the ceiling has exposed box beams. Pocket doors connect the formal hallway with the drawing room. Ornate molded plaster decorates the drawing room and was also used in the dining room. Decorative wood paneling and exposed beams were also utilized on the bedroom level of the house, which was an elaborate treatment for private residential spaces at this time.

The Stimson-Griffiths residence is significant due to the prominence of its owners and architects, in addition to the architectural integrity of the structure. Frederick Stimson was a member of the prominent Stimson family that developed land and timber businesses in the late

Stimson-Griffiths residence, detail of main façade gable with half-timbering and leaded glass windows, in 2004.

1800s. The family had been involved with lumber businesses in the Great Lakes region, but as timber resources in that area became depleted, the family sought more profitable holdings.

Frederick Stimson was born in Michigan and joined his father in the lumber business. He traveled to Puget Sound in the late 1880s to study lumber conditions, and decided to return to Seattle in 1891 to start his own lumber company. He eventually sold his interest in the lumber operation and a subsidiary railroad to invest in timber, real estate, banking, cannery operations, and farming. He was particularly interested in dairy cattle, and maintained one of the largest Holstein herds in the country at his Hollywood Farm, near Woodinville. Although he was offered directorship of the National Holstein-Fresian Association, he refused, preferring to work at the local level, serving as director and president of the Pacific International Livestock Exposition and director of the Washington Holstein Association. His activities in agriculture led to a regent position at Washington State College, Pullman.

Stimson was a member of numerous clubs and organizations, including the Anti-Tuberculosis League, which led to his interest in sanitary farming practices, particularly milk production. He was a member of the Rainier Club, Seattle Golf and Country Club, and the Arctic Club. He also started the Hollywood Fresh Air Farm for undernourished children. Stimson maintained his residence on Queen Anne Hill until 1918 when he relocated to Hollywood Farm.

Captain James Griffiths, originally from Liverpool, England, acquired the house in 1928. Griffiths arrived in Tacoma in 1885 and opened a ship brokerage firm, later expanding with a branch office in Port Townsend. He was involved in numerous shipping enterprises. Griffiths played an important role in establishing trans-Pacific steamship service with Japan. James J. Hill, president of the Great Northern Railroad, selected Griffiths in 1896 as his personal representative to negotiate with officials from Nippon Yusen Kaisha, a Japanese steamship company. Griffiths traveled to Japan to persuade the Japanese company to partner with the Great Northern Railroad's terminus in Seattle. This business arrangement provided a major link to the Orient for ports in the Puget Sound region. In addition to his involvement with steamship shipping to and from Asia, Griffiths was the first admiral of the Pacific International Yachting Association and president of the Coastwise Steamship and Barge Company. He also founded the shipping company of James Griffiths and Sons.

Norvell residence, in 2004.

Norvell Residence (1908)

The Norvell residence is an exceptional example of a Swiss Chalet Revival. It is an unorthodox interpretation of the style, since the usual horizontal rectangular plan is broken by turreted projections on the second floor. The broad, pitched roof provides overhanging eaves supported by patterned brackets. Window lintels and porch posts extend beyond their supports, giving the ornately detailed house a rustic appearance. This house also had a stable (now a garage) that is stylistically similar to the rest of the residence.

The ornate projecting porches make this house look considerably larger than it actually is, since all three upstairs bedrooms have porches. The original owner of the house was the manager of the Stimson Lumber Mill, and the house was entirely constructed from fir milled at the Ballard-based business. Ballard, incorporated in 1890, was one of the largest cities in Washington State before it was annexed to Seattle in 1907. Lumber milling, particularly shingle manufacturing was a primary business in the city, and Ballard was home to one of the largest shingle-manufacturing centers in the world. The combination of lumber activities, boat building, and fleet fishing attracted a large number of Scandinavian immigrants to the Ballard area.

Norvell residence, detail of corner tower.

Rosen residence, in the 1930s. *Walter Miller Photography Studios, courtesy of Carol Neiman*

Rosen Residence (1933)

Eclectic Revival houses have numerous stylistic influences. In addition to Tudor Revival and Swiss Chalet Revival, one can also find French and Mediterranean style homes although these styles are infrequent in Seattle. The Rosen residence is an unusual example of a Scandinavian Revival house, specifically a Norwegian revival, and is an anomaly among Seattle's Eclectic Revival dwellings as it was built after the popularity of that style trend had ended. At the turn of the twentieth century, Seattle had a large Scandinavian population. Immigrants from Norway, Sweden, Finland, and Denmark were drawn to this region's fishing, shipbuilding, and lumber industries. By 1910, Scandinavians were the largest ethnic group in the state, making up 31 percent of Seattle's foreign born. Social clubs, churches, and newspapers all formed to serve the large immigrant groups. The *Washington Posten*, a Norwegian-Danish newspaper, was established in 1889 and continued circulation until 1961, when it was sold to the *Western Viking*, which is still in publication. Although many immigrants adopted building styles in their new region, some brought design preferences from their homeland. The Rosen residence shows the distinctive Norwegian influence of its original owner, Capt. Ole E. Nilsen.

At first glance the exterior of this house looks similar to a Tudor Revival, or a Minimal Traditional, a stripped-down version of a Colonial Revival or Tudor Revival (discussed further in Chapter 7). The main house is predominantly rectangular with large front gables, one on the ground floor sheltering the attached garage, and another projecting beyond the main entrance. The bent timber brackets around the front entrance and garage (later remodeled) could easily be at home on a Tudor Revival or Craftsman structure. The house was built in 1933 by Capt. Nilsen, and was supposedly a copy of his childhood home in Bergen, Norway. While houses in Bergen didn't entirely look like this on the exterior, the three clustered windows over the main entry door are similar in styling, with the transoms at the top of each window. Another design feature that looks Norwegian in influence is the partially balustraded entryway. The screen formed by the turned wood balusters on top and enclosed with vertical wooden siding on the bottom is almost identical to those found on the exterior of Norwegian stave churches. Stave churches, constructed during the twelfth and thirteenth centuries, were steep-roofed buildings made entirely of wood and ornamented with ancient Norwegian symbols.

The interior of the home is striking, and shows a clear Norwegian influence. The living room has a vaulted ceiling, with a small loft. The balcony is similar to those found in Swiss Chalet architecture and prevalent in Norwegian houses in the mid nineteenth century. Similar balconies are found in stave churches as well. Rosemaling appears in the living room and breakfast room. It is a Norwegian style of folk painting that came into being when high-style Baroque and Rococo décor was introduced to rural areas in Norway. Travelers to the United States often packed trunks decorated with rosemaling. Smaller portable goods, mugs, or boxes were decorated as well. Although rosemaling went out of style around 1870, it experienced an American revival in the early twentieth century. The rosemaling examples in the Rosen house are of the Hallingdal variation—Baroque scrolls and acanthus leaves wrap around a central flower. Rosemaling floral designs are symmetrical, and most commonly painted on a red, black-green, dark green, or lighter blue-green background.

Breakfast room, Rosen residence, in the 1930s; the cupboards have rosemaled details. *Walter Miller Photography Studios, courtesy of Carol Neiman*

Living room, Rosen residence, with the loft balcony and large rosemaled beam in the background, in the 1930s. *Walter Miller Photography Studios, courtesy of Carol Neiman*

5 FOUR-SQUARE

THE FOUR-SQUARE, or "box" as it is sometimes called, has a simple, square plan, with a room in each corner, and a low-pitched, pyramidal roof. Dormers are common, as are full-width front porches. Interior details on the homes can vary; those built closer to 1900 will have more Victorian interiors, while those built in the 1920s may appear more Craftsman in style, with a range of box-beams and built-in furniture. Some versions even display Mission Revival styling, with stucco exteriors, tile roofs, and a shaped roof parapet. The Four-Square design was spread nationally by pattern books, and there were several variations sold by Sears, Roebuck and Company. Larger versions of the style have a center hall, with four rooms on each floor. Smaller renditions may have an offset floor plan with the front door off-center, and only three rooms per floor with the staircase occupying the fourth quadrant. Because many Colonial Revival houses have a similar floor plan, (which is Georgian in origin), there can be confusion distinguishing the two styles. Generally a Colonial Revival house will favor symmetry with a front entry, while columns support the front porch (if there is one), and Classical moldings and detail work will be evident. A side-facing gabled roof is also more common in Colonial Revival homes. In Seattle, wood is the primary cladding material for this style, which is clearly a regional variation, since brick is considerably more common in other areas of the country.

The Pacific Northwest has a particular variation of the Four-Square design, often called the "Seattle Box," where the front porch, which typically projects out from the plan, is recessed under the second level (reducing the square footage of the house interior). Sometimes the front porch may take up the entire width of the house, but more commonly it covers a portion of the front. Many of these houses have large, elaborate, decorative brackets at the top of the porch piers. Projecting square corner windows are also found in the Seattle variation, located on each end of the front façade, and protruding slightly from the main plan of the house on both the front and side elevations. These projecting spaces are usually in bedrooms and provide dramatic views. The center of the second story is also commonly accented with a small window or two. Roof eaves are often open with exposed, rounded end, rafter tails. While the origin of this substyle is uncertain, it is illustrated in 1903 newspaper advertisements for designer Fred Fehrens's work and in Victor W. Voorhees's *Western Home Builder*, first published circa 1907 and in its seventh edition by 1911. Victor Voorhees was partner in the Ballard firm of Fisher & Voorhees, and designed buildings in a number of Eclectic Revival styles. By 1911 a Four-Square variation with projecting corner windows was featured in Sears and Roebuck house catalogues, which sold basic Four-Square designs between 1908 and 1922.

INTERIORS

Four-Square interiors are not easily identified like those of the Victorian or Craftsman eras. There is no such thing as "Four-Square style" furniture, or "Four-Square" textile patterns. Design elements for a Four-Square might include Colonial Revival or Craftsman furnishings, or perhaps Victorian pieces brought from an earlier home. Much like Colonial Revival, Tudor Revival, and Craftsman houses, wood floors were prevalent. In part, this was due to space planning: fewer divisions between rooms meant a uniform floor treatment was desirable. During the early twentieth century, hardwood floors, like oak, were common in public rooms, while softwoods, like fir, appeared in private spaces. Painted softwood floors were popular; the perimeter of the room might be finished in this manner, while a colorful rug usually occupied the center. A 1900 trade catalogue encouraged homeowners to paint the floor border one color and use an analogous shade for baseboards. Printed and inlaid linoleum were still popular, particularly for service spaces and even bedrooms. Floor tiles were most commonly used in bathrooms; small, white hexagonal or octagonal tiles were still used for bathroom floors, and blue or black tiles were used as accents. By the 1920s, square tiles were becoming more popular for kitchen and bathroom walls.

Wall treatments during the early twentieth century changed little from those of the late nineteenth century. Critics denounced wallpaper, considering it inferior to painted treatments, but the general public didn't follow their advice. In 1905 a homeowner could purchase wallpaper for an entire room, including the borders and ceiling, from Sears, Roebuck and Company for 26 cents. Floral borders and scenic papers also gained popularity during this time period.

Foyer staircase in a 1904 Four-Square house, in 2001.

Preceding pages: Four-Square houses (far left and chapter title page, upper right) in the Mount Baker neighborhood; (chapter title page, upper left) in the Madison Park–Madrona neighborhood; and (below) on Capitol Hill.

V. W. VOORHEES, ARCHITECT, SEATTLE, WASH.

DESIGN NO. 91.

The width of this eight-room house is 28 feet; length 36 feet; height of first story 9 feet 6 inches; height of second story 8 feet 6 inches; basement 7 feet.

Approximate cost of construction, including cement basement and cement floors, $2,400.00.

Additional cost for hot air heating plant, $150.00.

Cost of one set of plans, specifications and details, $18.00.

Cost of two sets of plans, specifications and details, $22.00.

(Any plan can be reversed to suit location.)

A Four-Square design featured in the V. W. Voorhees pattern book, *Western Home Builder*, circa 1910. *University of Washington Libraries, Special Collections, UW14785*

A Seattle Four-Square house, projecting corner window.

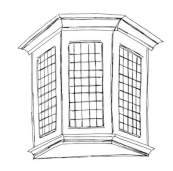

Ornamented center window, on second floor of a Seattle Four-Square house.

Four-Square house at 431 12th Avenue East (1906), in 2004.

FOUR-SQUARE HOUSES (1900–1925)

1906	Clara Fraychineaud Residence
1907	W. Williamson Residence
1909	Thomas J. King Residence
1906	Patrick W. McCoy Residence
1904	Martin J. Heneham Residence
1904	307 and 309 Boylston Avenue East Residences
1905–1906	Satterlee Residence
1906–1908	Robert C. Saunders Residence
1902	William D. Hofius Residence
1907	2403 and 2407 7th Avenue West Residences
1907	N. M. Wardall Residence
1906	1205 16th Ave East Residence

FOUR-SQUARE (1900–1925)

Clara Fraychineaud residence, period photograph. *Asahel Curtis. Washington State Historical Society, Tacoma, 47785*

Clara Fraychineaud Residence (1906)

This wood-clad Four-Square house has a hipped roof and an unusually small front porch. Wide eaves and exposed rafter tails give the structure a horizontal look, particularly with the narrow stringcourse directly below the second-floor windows. The first floor of the house has an off-center door, flanked by leaded glass sidelights. A small porch with tapered piers emphasizes the front entry. There are two windows on the first floor, both one over one, double hung. The second floor has three one-over-one, double-hung windows. The front elevation windows are handled in an unusual manner: they are different widths and heights, giving the façade a haphazard appearance. The tapered, squared columns and the exposed rafter ends are a Crafts-man influence.

W. Williamson residence, in 1913. *University of Washington Libraries, Special Collections, UW13816*

W. Williamson Residence (1907)

The W. Williamson residence has a brick-clad first story and a stucco-clad second story. The full-length front porch is supported by square wooden piers. A small pedimented cross gable accents the stair entry to the porch. While Craftsman influence is suggested in porch supports, the pedimented cross gable appears more Classical. The front door, to the right, is flanked by wide sidelights; to the left is a large window. The porch roof provides a balcony for the second floor which is enclosed by a balustrade. The balcony area is accessed by a small centered door, flanked by one-over-one, double-hung windows. A large pyramid dormer faces the street, and several windows, surrounded by a balustrade, take advantage of territorial views offered by the hillside location of the house.

Thomas J. King residence, period photograph. *Museum of History and Industry, Seattle, 9522*

Thomas J. King Residence (1909)

Like the W. Williamson residence, this Capitol Hill Four-Square has a brick first story and a stucco-clad second story. The Thomas J. King residence has an unusual element—a two-tiered portico. The portico is on the left side, and follows the exterior ornamentation with brick appearing on the first floor, and stucco above. Massive brick piers support the pyramidal roof, and a balustrade encloses the second-story porch perimeter. The front door has a cluster of casement windows on the left, and a similar cluster of windows to the right, flanking a larger, fixed-pane window in the center. Both sets of windows have fixed transoms. The second story follows a similar fenestration pattern. A door opens onto the patio on the left, while a cluster of transomed casement windows (all the same proportion) are above. Two distinct cladding materials, the stringcourse, and the extended eaves give the structure strong horizontal lines, while the portico on the left and chimney on the right add a vertical emphasis.

Patrick W. McCoy residence, in 1913. *University of Washington, Special Collections, UW13809*

Patrick W. McCoy Residence (1906)

The Patrick W. McCoy residence, built by contractor W. A. Perk, also utilized multiple cladding materials. Narrow clapboard sheaths the first floor, while textured stucco is on the second level. This house has a large, full-length front porch. While part of the porch projects out from the house, a substantial portion of it is recessed under the second floor. The porch wraps around to the right, and the arched openings over squared piers give the structure a Mediterranean nuance. The second floor of the building is irregular in plan as well, with the far right portion being a recessed balcony. All windows are one over one, double hung, although there is some variation in width. The prototypical pyramidal dormer faces the street. Other elevations also have dormers.

Martin J. Heneham residence, in 1913. *University of Washington, Special Collections, UW13864*

Martin J. Heneham Residence (1904)

The Martin J. Heneham residence shows traces of the Seattle Four-Square variation, with its exotic windows centered on the second floor. Cladding treatment varies by level, with the ground floor utilizing clapboard, and stucco appearing on the second level. The front entry is marked by a pyramidal roofed portico, with massive square piers. The large front door is flanked by double-hung windows that have a single lower light, with leaded glass lights on the upper sash. One stringcourse divides the first and second floors, while a second stringcourse runs below the first-floor windows, giving additional horizontal emphasis. Fenestration changes on the second floor: paired, arched windows add an Oriental detail. Large windows on either end of the floor are double hung, with a single pane in the lower sash. The upper sash has leaded glass that differs in design from the first floor windows. A small pyramid-shaped gable brings light to the attic space. Heneham served as president and treasurer of the Seattle Frog and Switch Company.

307 and 309 Boylston Avenue East residences, in 1917. *Calvin F. Todd. University of Washington Libraries, Special Collections, Todd 12219*

307 and 309 Boylston Avenue East Residences (1904)

The two Four-Square houses on Boylston Avenue East are unusual in that they are essentially small, one-story versions of the classic "Seattle Box." The front doors are recessed, and the entry porches are supported by large, square piers, accented with scroll-shaped brackets. The pier designs are repeated as a pilaster on the left side of the house facade. The single ground-floor windows have a curvilinear lattice pattern in the upper sash. The attic spaces have a large, hipped-roof dormer and broadly projecting eaves. Smaller versions of the first-floor windows are centered, flanked by two elaborately ornamented circular windows. Dentil work runs just beneath the attic eave.

Satterlee residence, period photograph. *Southwest Seattle Historical Society, 21.02*

Detail of the projecting corner windows, Satterlee residence.

Satterlee Residence (1905–1906)

The Satterlee residence is a grand example of a Four-Square that dominates the landscape from its hillside perch. The house has a high basement, which raises the first floor considerably, providing sweeping views from all levels. This variation of the Four-Square has strong symmetry. A centered front door is flanked by transoms and then clustered double-hung windows. While the center window of each grouping is larger, a matching fenestration pattern of decorative upper lights serves to unify the arrangement. The large, full-length front porch, supported by squared piers, provides outdoor living space. Detailing at the top of each pier includes massive scroll-shaped brackets, a Classical Revival design feature that appears often in Seattle variations of the Four-Square plan. The second floor has a smaller porch, centered directly over the front door. Smaller versions of the first floor pier treatment support this level as well. Windows on each end of the second floor project, creating corner bays. These windows also have a curvilinear lattice pattern on the upper sashes. The attic space of the house has several dormers. The front dormer is the largest, and utilizes three clustered windows to light the top floor. These windows follow the same design pattern.

The Satterlee residence emphasizes both horizontal and vertical lines. The projecting corner windows and the low, extended roofline draw the eye horizontally, while the tiered effect added by the porches and center dormer gives the dwelling a distinctly vertical direction. The centered front door gives this house a formal interior, with a large staircase occupying the middle portion of the home.

George Baker, a mortgage banker, built the house with his wife Carrie to serve as a summer home and provide space for a vacation Bible school. The home's landmark name comes from David and Margita Satterlee, who acquired the structure in 1971.

Robert C. Saunders residence, period photograph. *University of Washington Libraries, Special Collections, UW5981*

Robert C. Saunders Residence (1906–1908)

Robert C. Saunders was a lawyer with Saunders and Nelson. His exotic clapboard residence, designed by architect Frederick A. Sexton, is another variation of the Four-Square style. The two-story house has a bell-cast hipped roof, with bracketed eaves that flair out as they extend beyond the exterior walls. The main elevation is almost completely symmetrical, with a one-story portico marking the center portion of the first floor. The portico has unusual detailing, with a broad flat roof, supported by paired wooden piers. Each pair of piers is joined by wooden scroll-work, creating a Moorish-inspired horseshoe arch on the upper portion. The front entry door is flanked by multi-paned sidelights with Tuscan pilasters on either side. On the right side of the house, a large single-paned window is accented by a transom. On the left side of the building, clustered windows are one over one, double hung. The second story, unlike the first, is symmetrical. Three main bays stretch across the façade, and each window is one over one, double hung. The central bay is flanked by two smaller single-lights. A hipped gable, extending from the attic space, is an unusual design, with windows recessed and flanked by bulging columns. All three attic windows are one over one, double hung.

RESIDENCE MR. W. D. HOFIUS

Drawing of the William D. Hofius residence, published in *Seattle Architecturally* in 1902. *University of Washington Libraries, Special Collections, UW23631*

William D. Hofius Residence (1902)

The William D. Hofius residence is a Gothic style Four-Square house with elaborate interior and exterior detailing. A period illustration of the house shows an intricately screened recessed porch on the second floor, although when the house was built this second-story loggia was never constructed and thus this area projects slightly beyond the main walls. The front portico is supported by ogee arches in varying widths, which (in the illustration) appeared on the upper floor as well, serving as a decorative screen for the recessed second-level porch. Quatrefoil decorations embellished the spaces between the arches. The second floor has two oriel windows, one on either side. Most windows are double hung. A historic photograph shows that the interior of the house was even more elaborately ornamented than the exterior, with painted ceilings, pierced screens, and multiple layers of ornamental woodwork.

William D. Hofius started working in the iron and steel industry at a young age, for the Geddis Foundry in Sharpsville, Pennsylvania. He became owner of several steel operations in New York, Pennsylvania, and Ohio, before eventually traveling west. In Seattle he was president of Hofius Steel and Equipment Company. He also served as president of the Seattle Dock Company, director of Superior Portland Cement Company, and director of the Seattle First National Bank. The firm of Gribble & Skene were general contractors for this residence.

Foyer of the William D. Hofius residence, period photograph. *Asahel Curtis. Washington State Historical Society, Tacoma, 5519*

Detail of the William D. Hofius residence, in 2004.

2403 7th Avenue West residence, in 2004.

2403 and 2407 7th Avenue West Residences (1907)

The residences at 2403 and 2407 7th Avenue West were constructed in 1907, probably by the same builder. They share the basic massing, hipped roof, pulled out corner windows, ornamental center window, and off-center entrance that are features of the Seattle Box. As these two structures show, the different types and styles of hardware available to builders made customizing homes quite easy. The house at 2403 has open eaves with exposed rafter tails, and the upper floor is clad with shingles. The center decorative window is a small oriel, and multiple lights appear in the upper sash of the corner windows. The front porch piers have the scroll-shaped brackets that are typical in Seattle. The residence at 2407 utilizes different stylistic variations. Although color treatment varies, both levels are sided with clapboard. The corner windows are double hung, but the upper sash has a curvilinear lattice treatment. The center window is round, and ornamented with elaborate scrollwork. Even the porch treatment is varied; in this case the porch is recessed under the second floor, and is marked by a pedimented gable.

2407 7th Avenue West residence, in 2004.

Detail of corner windows,
2407 7th Avenue West residence.

N. M. Wardall residence, in 2004.

N. M. Wardall Residence (1907)

The N. M. Wardall residence is almost a textbook example of the Four-Square style. This clapboard house was featured in the 1910 booster publication for West Seattle. The structure has a pyramidal roof, hipped front gable, projecting corner windows, and smaller center windows on the second floor. The front porch, however, projects from the front of the house instead of being recessed under the second level, which has the advantage of giving finished building more interior square footage. Square piers accented with large, scrolled brackets support the front porch. Wardall was the King County auditor.

Detail of porch bracket, N. M. Wardall residence.

1205 16th Avenue North residence, period photograph. *Asahel Curtis. Washington State Historical Society, Tacoma, 42714*

1205 16th Avenue North Residence (1906)

This Four-Square house represents the Seattle variation with the recessed front porch, projecting corner windows, and the small central windows on the second floor. The wood-clad structure has a pyramidal roof, complete with broad overhanging eaves. Simple columns support the porch. The front door is off center, with a small decorative window to the left and a cluster of three larger windows to the right. The projecting corner bays on the upper floor have one-over-one, double-hung windows. Small decorative brackets accentuate the corner windows, adding additional depth to the façade. A pair of small multilighted windows placed directly under the eaves occupies the central bay of the second floor

6 SPANISH REVIVALS

Mission Revival and Spanish Eclectic

Carmel Mission Basilica (1793), in 1996.

but striking styles. The Mission Revival style, nationally favored from 1890 until the 1920s, had a local following during the 1910s and '20s. While the East Coast was building Colonial Revivals based on English and Dutch architectural styles native to the area, the western states turned to their native colonial forms, Spanish missions. The Mission Revival style originated in California, and is thought to be the first style that diffused from the west to the east. The Santa Fe and Southern Pacific Railroads selected Mission Revival designs for their stations and resort hotels, to create a unified theme, and the popularity of the style spread.

Mission Revival style buildings can utilize either symmetrical or asymmetrical façades. The basic massing of the structure is usually square or rectangular, with porches and towers providing asymmetry. Wall surfaces are stuccoed. Roofs can be either pyramidal or gabled, and are commonly covered with tile. Like Craftsman homes, eaves project over the exterior walls, and have exposed rafter tails. Porches are common, and are supported by square piers, sometimes arching into the wall. Dormers and roof parapets are usually shaped with curving undulating lines and coping.

Detail of a Santa Barbara Mission (1815), in 1996.

MISSION REVIVAL (1900–1920)

At first glance, stucco-covered, southwestern forms seem out of place in the misty evergreen Pacific Northwest. Mission Revival and Spanish Eclectic are infrequently seen

SPANISH ECLECTIC (1915–1940)

The Spanish Eclectic style grew out of the Mission Revival style. It can be more varied in form, drawing design elements from different periods of Spanish history, including Moorish, Gothic, or even Renaissance. While large, elaborate examples exist in this style, those found in Seattle are generally small, one-story builder's houses, rectangular in plan, but with asymmetrical window and door placement.

Preceding pages: (far left and chapter title page, below) Mission Revival L'Amourita Apartments (1925), 2901–2915 Franklin Avenue East, in 2004; (chapter title page, upper left and upper right) Spanish Eclectic houses on 77th Street North in Greenlake.

Mission Revival residence in Seattle, period photograph. *Asahel Curtis. Washington State Historical Society, Seattle 17697*

Roofs can be gabled or flat, and are generally tiled. Eaves for this style have a minimal overhang. Wall surfaces are stuccoed, and arches above main doors and windows are common. Leaded glass windows are often used to accent primary windows. Because of its prevalence in with Southern California, the style reminds many of Hollywood's glamour days.

INTERIORS

Mission Revival and Spanish Eclectic interiors are usually quite similar to Craftsman, with built-in bookcases and art tiled fireplaces. Ceilings occasionally have box beams, but are more often coved, similar to those found in Tudor Revival homes. Staircases in the smaller examples are usually hidden, while larger homes with more elaborate entry halls might showcase elaborately carved banisters. This style also makes use of decorative iron sconces and door hardware that are similar to those found in Tudor Revival or Craftsman style homes. Furnishings could vary

Spanish Eclectic house, 77th Street North, in 2004.

considerably, with homeowners selecting between Craftsman style furniture or more traditional Colonial Revival furniture.

Parapet and windows on a Mission Revival building.

Rustic Mission Revival–Spanish Eclectic door.

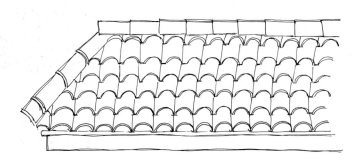

Tile roofing commonly found on Mission Revival and Spanish Eclectic houses.

SPANISH REVIVAL HOUSES

Mission Revival (1900–1920)

1905	Flora Allen Residence
1904	Brace-Moriarty Residence
1907	Rolland H. Denny Residence
1909	James Clemmer Residence

Spanish Eclectic (1915–1940)

1929	John Hamrick Residence
1925	B. C. Keeler Residence
1926	Stanley S. Sayres Residence
late 1920s	North 77th Street Residences

MISSION REVIVAL (1910–1920)

Flora Allen residence, period photograph. *University of Washington, Seattle, Special Collections, UW13812*

Flora Allen Residence (1905)

The Flora Allen residence is a smaller Mission Revival style structure, which could also be classified as a Four-Square. Instead of the more common stucco treatment, this dwelling has wood cladding, so the style is articulated almost exclusively by the parapeted roofline. A full-length porch runs along the front of the house and is supported by square piers. The balustrade along the top of the porch is unusual, with the trimwork and tapered design faintly reminiscent of a Classical pediment. The second floor projects slightly over the main level, and on the right end there is a projecting corner window, commonly found with Four-Square designs. A pair of diamond-paned casement windows occupies the upper most level of the parapet, pro-

viding light into the attic level. A similarly designed parapet is on the left side of the structure.

A large sleeping porch appears to extend off the back of the house. Sleeping porches were common at the turn of the century; they allowed homeowners to practically sleep outside. A solid lower wall provided privacy for cots or beds, while an open or screened upper section allowed ventilation. These porches were used in summer months, before electric fans and air conditioning provided a cool sleeping environment. They were so popular that even some Craftsman bungalows had them, although few remain in their original condition. Over time many have been boarded up and turned into primary living spaces.

Brace-Moriarty residence, in 2004.

Brace-Moriarty Residence (1904)

The Brace-Moriarty residence, like many other Mission Revival houses in Seattle, has a Four-Square plan, with a symmetrical façade, recessed front porch, and projecting corner windows. The architecture firm of Kerr & Rogers used a variety of wall treatments: river rock for the foundation, wood (designed to imitate masonry), and stucco. Porch arches are ornately decorated in carved wood reliefs, reminiscent of the organic forms decorating the works of famed Midwestern architect Louis H. Sullivan. The projecting corner windows are an unusual variation, with the extension occurring on both floors. The corner windows are accented by bracketed boxes, which echo the form under the center oriel window. The only parapet shape on the structure is the attic gable. The interior has box-beamed ceilings, wainscoting, built-in bookcases, and pocket doors. In the dining room a plate rack runs along the wainscoting, while additional china storage is provided by a built-in buffet.

John Stuart Brace was a lumberman who started a business in Spokane, and moved to Seattle in 1888. He owned the Brace and Hergert Mill, which provided the materials used for the home's construction. Brace was active in Seattle's business community, serving as president of the Lake Washington Ship Canal Association and as a Seattle alderman from 1892 to 1894.

Detail of the corner bay, Brace-Moriarty residence.

Rolland H. Denny residence, as seen from the water, period photograph. *Museum of History and Industry, Seattle, Pemco Webster and Stevens Collection, 83.10.7891*

Rolland H. Denny Residence (1907)

The Seattle architecture firm of Bebb & Mendel designed the massive Mission Revival style Rolland H. Denny residence. Sited on a knoll above Lake Washington, the building is predominantly rectangular in plan, with a gabled tiled roof extended by cross gables on the left and right ends of the façade. Extended Mission Revival parapets on either end flank the central section, which has a recessed second-level loggia designed to take advantage of the sweeping lakefront view. The interior of the house was decorated with Craftsman elements. A period photograph of the living room shows box-beamed ceilings, a copper fire-place hood, wainscoting with plate rail, and numerous pieces of Craftsman furniture.

Rolland Denny was the son of Seattle founder Arthur A. Denny. He attended the Territorial University, graduating in 1869. Denny became involved in the banking industry, and worked with Dexter Horton. He eventually became director of the Seattle First National Bank. Rolland and his wife Alice M. Denny named their Lake Washington home Lochkelden ("loch" for lake, "kel" for Alice's maiden name Kellogg, and "den" for Denny).

Rolland H. Denny residence, circa 1926. *Museum of History and Industry, Seattle, Pemco Webster and Stevens Collection, 83.10.3340*

Living room, Rolland H. Denny residence, circa 1910. *Museum of History and Industry, Seattle, Pemco Webster and Stevens Collection, 83.10.7888*

James Q. Clemmer Residence (1909)

The James Q. Clemmer residence is a Mission Revival Four-Square design. Classifying this house demonstrates some of the difficulties encountered in building typology. The house is clearly a Four-Square, not only in plan but also because of the projecting corner windows at either end of the second story. In this particular case, though, there is the unmistakable mark of another architectural style, that of Mission Revival. So in what category does one place such a structure, Four-Square or Mission Revival? If you look at your home and find that it seems to fit more than one style, you may very well be right—hybrid styles do exist.

James Q. Clemmer residence, period photograph. *Museum of History and Industry, Seattle, SHS9521*

The residence has a massive front porch, defined by a wooden railing and stuccoed arches. The top design element is undulating, reminiscent of a Mission adobe church. The front door is on the left, with a large bank of double-hung windows occupying the right end of the façade. The windows have an unusual glazing pattern: the lower sash has a single light, but the upper sash is square with an X-shaped muntin dividing the sash into four triangular panes. The second story of the house has the typical pulled corners, each with a bank of three windows. A door on the central portion of the floor provides access to the patio created by the porch below. There is no highly articulated attic space, which is unusual with Four-Squares. Roof tiles add Mission style detailing, as do the parapets extending up from the corners. A second parapet with accented coping defines the upper edge of the top story. The interior of the home was lavishly appointed with Craftsman style furniture and fixtures.

James Q. Clemmer was owner of Seattle's Clemmer Theater, located at 1414 Second Avenue. The theater, constructed in 1912, was among the first in the United States built specifically to show motion pictures.

Interior of the James Q. Clemmer residence, period photograph.
Museum of History and Industry, Seattle, SHS9525

Exterior, John Hamrick residence, circa 1930. *University of Washington Libraries, Special Collections, UW23575*

John Hamrick Residence (1929)

With its irregular massing, arched opening port cochere, rounded tower, detailed chimneys, stucco wall covering, and tile roof, the John Hamrick residence designed by architect Lionel Pries is a textbook example of the Spanish Eclectic style. The rooflines are complex, with different treatments unified only by tile cladding and a limited overhang. The main elevation has few windows, which is not unusual, since this style emphasized interior courtyards. An arched loggia, behind the rectangular entry bay, provides access to the front door. The interior of the house was designed in the Spanish Eclectic style as well, with exposed beams, arched openings, and thick interior walls. Tiled steps descend to the sunken living room. The decorative carving and the painted details on the beams are reminis-cent of folk art, as are the hammered metal light fixtures. The pointed arch details indicate a blending of Gothic forms. Spanish Eclectic houses often blended Moorish, Gothic, or Byzantine details into their designs.

During the early twentieth century, Lionel Pries practiced architecture in California. He created a number of Spanish Eclectic buildings in Santa Barbara, where local building codes require this style in the historic core of the town. This residence was one of his earliest houses in Seattle, since he moved here in 1928. This style may well have been selected for its connotations with the Hollywood film industry, since Hamrick was a vice-president of Cascade Theaters Corporation.

Living room, John Hamrick residence, in 1930. *University of Washington Libraries, Special Collections, UW23611*

B. C. Keeler Residence (1925)

The B. C. Keeler residence is an example of a builder's Spanish Eclectic. This small structure is symmetrical, with a centered front doorway flanked by plate glass windows. The gabled entry portico, although centered on the façade, is accessed from the side, and is the building's most notable architectural feature. The parapeted roof is flat and not visible from the ground. Terra-cotta roof tiles were used only to accentuate the picture windows and on the gabled porch. Massive stucco piers support the porch and curve inward creating a Mission style arch.

The main public spaces in this house have recessed plaster ceilings, which have an outer border while the main portion of the ceiling recesses slightly. The living room contains the original fireplace, flanked by large beveled, leaded glass bookcases. The small windows on either side of the fireplace are beveled as well.

Keeler residence, in 2004.

Keeler residence fireplace, in the late 1990s.

Stanley S. Sayres residence, in 2004.

Stanley S. Sayres Residence (1926)

The Stanley S. Sayres residence is typical of a larger Spanish Eclectic dwelling. The stuccoed exterior has a simple, smooth form and like most homes of this style, and there is no front porch. The entryway is recessed, marked by a rectangular tiled panel. The tiles, in shades of blue and turquoise with a few floral accent squares, provide a sharp contrast to the creamy beige stucco. The left section of the house projects slightly, emphasizing the entryway and the small metal balcony directly above the front door. French doors access the balcony. The right section of the house has a large expanse of clustered windows on the first floor, shielded by a fabric canopy supported by metal rods, which adds an exotic flair to the exterior. There are two sets of casement windows on the second floor. One is stained glass, while the other has three horizontal lights in each sash.

One of the first residents of this home was Stanley S. Sayres, president of the American Automobile Corporation. Sayres is known for his involvement with hydroplane racing in Seattle. His boat, Slo-Mo-Shun IV, set a world record for the mile straightaway. In 1950, he won the American Power Boat Association's Gold Cup, and defended it against challenges for the next four years.

Exterior, 1146 North 77th Street residence, period photograph. *Asahel Curtis. Washington State Historical Society, Tacoma, 47757*

North 77th Street Residences (late 1920s)

This house is a builder's version of the Spanish Eclectic style, and is small enough to be classified as a bungalow. Houses like this were often built in clusters by developers, who chose a particular style and then built variations of the design. This residence is part of a large builder's cluster by Greenlake. The front porch is accessed from the side, a common design feature for the vernacular version of Spanish Eclectic. The front parapet design is repeated on the porch, the smooth stucco structure having little other ornamentation. Windows have the same tripartite arrangement found in Craftsman homes. During the late twentieth century, the house underwent a substantial exterior remodel.

Remodeled exterior of 1146 North 77th Street residence, in 2004.

The interior images appear to be from another house in the development. The living room fireplace is surrounded with art tile. Smaller accent tiles in varying shades were used in the upper portion of the surround. Coved plaster ceilings, a frequent interior detail in this style, appear in the main living spaces. Although the black-and-white photograph can't reveal the owner's color choices, tonal variations indicate that the lower walls were painted a darker color. Window treatments were elaborate: an Austrian valance overlays a two-way draw. Sheers and roll blinds also provided privacy. A kitchen photograph shows a linoleum floor and a simpler wall treatment, with no coved ceiling. White hexagonal tile formed the counter top, while a rectangular subway tile covered part of the backsplash. Half-moon drawer pulls and a built-in sliding cutting board completed the kitchen. Kitchen furniture provided additional storage space.

Living room, a North 77th Street
Spanish Eclectic residence, period
photograph. *Asahel Curtis. Washington
State Historical Society, Tacoma, 47758*

Kitchen, a North 77th Street
Spanish Eclectic residence, period
photograph. *Asahel Curtis. Washington
State Historical Society, Tacoma, 47760*

7 MODERN

International Style, Minimal Traditional, and Contemporary

Mies van der Rohe's Barcelona Pavilion (1929), reconstructed, photographed in 2001.

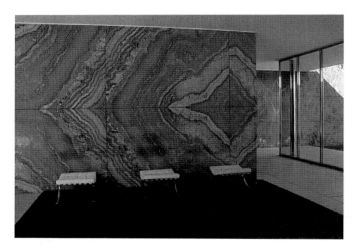

Interior of the Barcelona Pavilion (1929), in 2001.

IN SHARP CONTRAST to Craftsman and Four-Square styles, the Modern movement had its design roots firmly in European soil. The Modern styles developed after World War I and continued to evolve throughout World War II. The Dutch design movement of Rationalism, led in part by architect Gerrit Rietveld, emphasized simple geometric architecture devoted to utilitarian needs avoiding applied ornamentation. Le Corbusier in France and Walter Gropius in Germany also developed modern architectural forms with a similar vocabulary. The term "International Style" gained widespread use after the 1937 exhibit at the Museum of Modern Art in New York, entitled "The International Style: Architecture since 1922." To one degree or another, proponents of the new style embraced an almost utopian pursuit of universal order and harmony. This in part was a response to the chaotic conditions in Europe following World War I.

A Modernist icon, the Barcelona Pavilion, designed for the 1929 Barcelona World's Fair by German architect Ludwig Mies van der Rohe, is a pure example of International Style form in both building design and interior furnishings. The building has a metal frame and thus an open

Preceding pages: (far left) Dusanne residence, Contemporary, Tucker, Shields & Terry, architects, in 1949. *Dearborn-Massar. University of Washington, Special Collections, DM05356*; (chapter title page, upper left and right) Minimal Traditional houses on 30th Avenue Northwest between 75th and 76th, in Ballard; (below) William F. Paddock Contemporary residence, 1830 Broadmoor Drive (1948). *Museum of History and Industry, Seattle, 11.600*

interior plan. The structure is one story, horizontal, with a flat roof. Exterior walls are smooth stone, alternating with expansive sheets of glass. The interior is ornamented primarily by rich materials, especially cut and butterflied slabs of travertine marble, green marble, and onyx. Dividing walls of colored and etched glass were also used. The furniture was chrome and leather—low-slung, understated pieces that emphasized Modern production and materials.

In Germany, the Bauhaus design movement led the way, under the direction of Gropius, who worked to reunite Modern art and design through synthesizing architecture, art, and craft. A result of his work was a revised interest in interior design as an integral part of the architectural process. Since applied decoration was almost nonexistent in this movement, emphasis was placed on material quality and design. Chrome, leather, glass, and even Bakelite (an early form of plastic) were used in innovative ways. After the Nazi regime closed the Bauhaus in 1933, more European Modernists, artists and architects, fled Europe and came to the United States. Walter Gropius emigrated to the United States in 1937, and took a teaching position at Harvard University.

Seattle architect Paul Thiry was instrumental in introducing the International Style in Seattle. After graduating from the University of Washington's architecture school in 1928, Thiry traveled to Europe, where he eventually met with Le Corbusier. Upon his return to Seattle in 1935, Thiry designed his own house in a Modern style. Architects J. Lister Holmes and John R. Sproule were among those who followed Thiry's lead.

Percival K. Nichols Jr. residence, International Style, in 1937. *Museum of History and Industry, Seattle, Seattle* Post-Intelligencer *Collection, PI22265*

INTERNATIONAL STYLE (1925–1940)

The International Style utilizes a flat roof, smooth stuccoed wall surface, an asymmetrical façade, ribbon windows (long banks of glazing that wrap around the building), and large expanses of plate glass. Windows, instead of being set in slightly from the exterior wall surrounded by the frame and moldings, are set flush, adding to the exterior flatness. The roof usually lacks coping or eaves, contributing to a smooth wall treatment. A true International Style building does not have a wood frame like most houses, but is constructed with steel. The steel skeleton is structurally much stronger, and allowed great flexibility in providing an open floor plan since interior support walls are not needed. The use of steel also allows for significant cantilevers, areas where the roof or floor sections may project out substantially beyond lower sections. This style of building was generally architect-designed, and is fairly uncommon. In Seattle low hipped roofs occasionally appear, or flat roofs with projecting eaves. Glass block is used at times as well. Regardless of the variations, these buildings are a clear break with revivalist architectural forms and the Craftsman style.

New houses under construction in Seattle's Arbor Heights neighborhood, 1948. *Museum of History and Industry, Seattle, Seattle Post-Intelligencer Collection, PI23752*

world war housing market. By 1950 Levitt calculated that his firm started a new house every sixteen minutes, and *Time* magazine estimated that the Levitt firm built one out of every eight houses in the United States. In Seattle, hundreds of Minimal Traditional houses were built. Almost 200 were constructed in the Columbia Ridge housing development on Beacon Hill during the early 1940s. The Seattle *Post-Intelligencer* advertised Minimal Traditional designs for several model home projects, further exposing the style to their readers.

MINIMAL TRADITIONAL (1935–1950)

Although Modernist architecture became increasingly popular, a number of homeowners felt more comfortable living in traditional designs. The Minimal Traditional house is a simplified, stripped-down version of a Colonial Revival or Tudor Revival style. It is a transitional style, which introduces some elements of Modernism, such as a more open floor plan. These small houses often have a dominant front gable, but decorative detailing was severely restrained. Other versions have a cross gable only on the garage, which projects beyond the house. Building eaves are close to the house and boxed in, with no broad Craftsman or Tudor Revival overhangs. Porches are almost nonexistent. In part, this minimalist direction was a product of the Depression, the period in which many of these houses were built. The style continued after World War II, and provided quick and inexpensive housing to returning veterans. While two-story versions of the style exist, one-story versions are far more frequent. For G.I.s returning home, these "modern" houses epitomized contemporary living at its best, as did living in the suburbs.

Many of the country's largest builders (William Levitt and John LaPlan) developed their skills with military units. Levitt's firm won a government contract in 1941 to construct more than 200 units of defense housing units in Norfolk, Virginia. In 1947 the first Levittown was built on Long Island. Levitt became a major force in the post-

CONTEMPORARY (1935–1980)

The Contemporary style, favored by architects during the 1940s and 1950s, was the outgrowth of the academic International Style mixing with vernacular materials and building forms. There are two basic subtypes: the flat-roofed version, called "Miesian" by some (after Mies van der Rohe), clearly shows European roots, and the gabled version. The Miesian subtype lacks decorative embellishments. Wall surfaces employ a variety of materials, including wood, brick, and occasionally stone. The gabled version has broad, overhanging eaves reminiscent of the Craftsman style or the work of Frank Lloyd Wright. While one-story versions were common nationally, two-story variations are more frequent in Seattle, particularly with the city's hilly ground and small building lots.

The Contemporary style placed a new emphasis on the house interior and its relationship to the external world. The room compartmentalization found in Colonial Revival and Tudor Revival houses gave way to an open interior. The use of nonload-bearing interior walls made this type of design possible. The relationship between indoor space and outdoor space was also a consideration: extensive use of glass allowed building interiors to visually expand into nature. This intense interest in utilizing exterior space is evident in a design consultation given by Seattle architect Bert A. Tucker in the spring 1949 issue of *Popular Home* magazine. A monthly column, called "My Idea of a House," allowed potential architects to critique homeowner's plans. A young couple, Mr. and Mrs. W. E. Warren, sent in designs for their first house, a small one-bedroom structure. Tucker commented on the couple's needs, representing any number of young couples and veterans searching for "good housing." He revised the plan to make a one-bedroom addition possible in the future, and specifically commented on how a home should visually be open to its outdoor environment: "Whether or not one wants to live outdoors is immaterial. A minimum size house can achieve a feeling of spaciousness through relating inside living areas to outside terraces."

William F. Paddock Contemporary residence (1948), Broadmoor. *Museum of History and Industry, Seattle, 11.600*

INTERIORS

The 1920s were a glamorous time for interior designers. International Style buildings were known for their lack of color: shades of pale blue, green, buff, beige, coffee, or classic combinations of black and white were most common. Lighting was mass produced from industrial materials, and simple globe or tube forms showcased streamlined chrome and glass designs. Glass was rarely colored, and etching provided decorative treatments. Walls were kept relatively bare; complex wood paneling and coved plaster ceilings were a thing of the past. Furniture shapes were streamlined—no more elaborately carved mahogany, or Stickley oak designs—and the fussy floral wall papers and fabrics of the late nineteenth century gave way to geometric patterns. Houses gradually began to shrink in size, as modern technologies provided enough labor saving devices to dispense with servants in all but the most elaborate households.

During the late 1930s and through the 1940s, designers emphasized the use of exterior materials—natural stone, wood, and brick—to decorate interior spaces. The idea was not entirely new: Craftsman houses had employed similar materials, with the focus on contrasting textures and patterns, and had emphasized a new way of employing the materials. Instead of bringing the rustic qualities of the outside into the home, Contemporary houses sought to expand into the environment, and visually gain square footage with large plate-glass windows and with patios.

During the 1930s, furniture with a bent steel or laminated wood frame (instead of the traditional wooden legs) was popular. But for the smaller multipurpose spaces found in 1920s houses, this type of furniture was too bulky. Contemporary living required smaller, lighter pieces of furniture that could be easily moved from room to room. Furniture was not only light in terms of weight, but it was designed to be visually light was well. Technology became increasingly important as kitchens utilized more electric appliances. Although wood cabinets were still popular, metal cabinetry was increasingly shown in design magazines. By the late 1940s, Formica counter tops were becoming a standard as well, replacing the tiled counters of the 1930s and the wooden counters of previous eras. Kitchen appliances were also increasingly built into rooms. Refrigerators and oven-ranges seamlessly flowed into kitchen cabinets. Kitchens and bathrooms became more colorful during this time period: bright red, yellow, and maroon countertops and paint were paired with white cabinetry, giving these rooms strong visual appeal. Sherwin Williams paint cards from 1938 show lots of creams, buffs, mid-tone yellow-greens, and pale institutional greens.

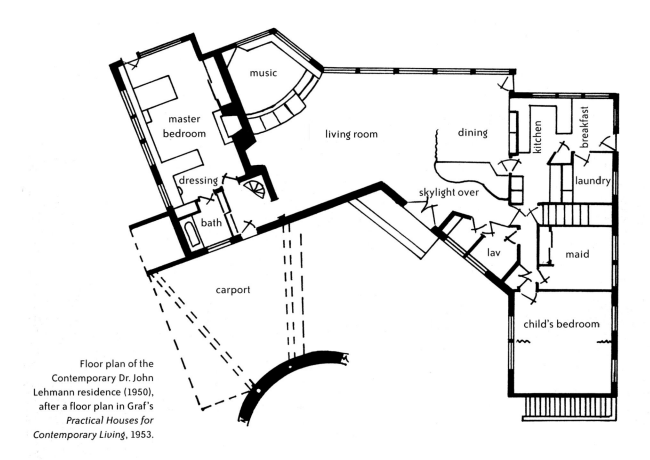

Floor plan of the Contemporary Dr. John Lehmann residence (1950), after a floor plan in Graf's *Practical Houses for Contemporary Living*, 1953.

MODERN HOUSES

International Style (1925–1940)

1936	Edwin C. Edwards Residence
1936	Percival K. Nichols Residence
1937	Frank J. Barrett Residence

Minimal Traditional (1935–1950)

1935	Seattle *Post-Intelligencer* Model Home—Lake Forest Park
1940	Arthur French Residence
1948	Seattle *Post-Intelligencer* Model Home—Arbor Heights

Contemporary (1935–1980)

1936	Smith Residence
1944	Paul Hayden Kirk Residence
1946	Walter P. Coulon Residence
1947	Phillip A. Stewart Residence
1947	Sam Rubinstein Residence
1948	Harold Mayer Residence
1948	Rader-Revere Residence
1950	Dr. John Lehmann Residence

INTERNATIONAL STYLE (1925–1940)

Edwin C. Edwards residence, in 1960. *Werner Lenggenhager. Seattle Public Library, 22447*

Edwin C. Edwards Residence (1936)

The Edwin C. Edwards residence has wide eave overhangs that add a horizontal thrust to a predominantly vertical structure. Although broad overhangs are uncommon in International Style houses, the smooth wall treatment, flush-set windows, and corner wrapping windows are standard International Style elements. The interior of the structure is split-level, a design feature made clear by the off-level location of windows and doors. The front door lacks any kind or ornamentation or additional fenestration. Directly above the front door, a small balcony breaks the wall's smoothness by projecting out beyond a recessed bay. The garage treatment indicates the growing prominence of the automobile. Edwards was a building contractor.

Percival K. Nichols Jr. residence, in 1937. *Museum of History and Industry, Seattle, Seattle* Post-Intelligencer *Collection, PI22265*

Percival K. Nichols Jr. Residence (1936)

The Percival K. Nichols Jr. house, with the exception of its unusual hipped roof, is an almost picture-perfect example of the International Style. The building, designed by Thiry & Shay, is primarily rectangular in form, with a projecting two-car garage. The unusual window treatment—tall narrow banks of glazing on both front corners—indicates nonload-bearing walls. A covered rain stoop and hipped roof are concessions to Seattle's rainy climate. Nichols served as a manager for an industrial company.

Frank J. Barrett residence, period photograph. *University of Washington Libraries, Special Collections, UW23633*

Frank J. Barrett Residence (1937)

Architect Paul Thiry helped introduce Modern European architecture to the Northwest. Although many of his clients were resistant to stark Modernist forms, Frank J. Barrett welcomed an International Style design for his residence. Barrett managed the Seattle office of Portland Cement, so it is not surprising to find a cement-based stucco on the exterior of his International Style house. Like the Edwards house, this residence is unusual, with its slightly extended eaves. This modification to the style may, in part, be an adjustment for the region's rainy climate. Typical of International Style buildings, the smooth, undecorated exterior is punctuated only by flush windows and door openings. The steel windows were painted a blue-green, creating a strong contrast with the smooth, white stucco. Glass brick was used around the entry to admit light while preserving privacy.

The house is formed by two major rectangles—the garage that projects toward the street, and the long primary block that ran parallel with the street. A massive chimney anchors the right end of the structure. The garage, unusually decorative with a chevron pattern, projects in front of the house, emphasizing the automobile's importance. A grade-level basement provides sweeping lake views from the back of the house. On this split-level house, large front doors opened into a small entry hallway, which provided access to the upper, private rooms of the house, or down, to the public areas. Extensive glass block helped preserve privacy in the living room, which was partially below grade. This house was showcased in *The Modern House in America*, published in 1940.

Interior foyer, Frank J. Barrett residence, period photograph. *University of Washington Libraries, Special Collections, UW23632*

MINIMAL TRADITIONAL (1935–1950)

Seattle *Post-Intelligencer* Model Home—Lake Forest Park, 1935. *Museum of History and Industry, Seattle, Seattle* Post-Intelligencer *Collection, PI22290*

Lake Forest Park (1935)

This Lake Forest Park residence clearly shows the transition from Tudor Revival to the Minimal Traditional style. The steep roof pitch, cross gables, and casement windows are retained, but other details are eliminated. Large, twelve-light, fixed-pane windows create a brightly lit interior. The building has one-and-a-half stories, with a simple shed-roof dormer and a projecting gabled dormer providing extra living space on the upper floor. The chimney is accented with a small band of corbelling along the rim, the only decorative detail on the building.

This project, lauded as "the highlight of Better Housing Day in the Northwest," was jointly sponsored by the Puget Mill Company, the Seattle Real Estate Board, and the Federal Housing Administration. Paul Thiry and Alban A. Shay were responsible for the plan, although the original version was far more modern in design, with a flat roof and flexible interior plan. A "French Norman" plan (as it was advertised) was selected with hopes that it would appeal to a broader market.

Arthur French residence, in 1943. *Museum of History and Industry, Seattle, Seattle* Post-Intelligencer *Collection, PI22260*

Arthur French Residence (1940)

The Arthur French residence represents the most austere interpretation of the Minimal Traditional style and is representative of the housing stock available to Seattle's working class in the early 1940s. It is L-shaped in plan, providing an underground garage, still the most basic of requirements, even for the most basic of houses. Eave projections and window trim are nonexistent. The large multipaned windows provide plenty of interior light, but do not provide ventilation, since they are fixed. Small one-over-one, double-hung windows are used on the rest of the house. Although the chimney is still large, it is devoid of decorative elements. An alternative term sometimes used to describe diminutive, austere houses of this style is "World War II era cottage." Arthur French was a photographer for the Seattle *Post-Intelligencer.*

Seattle *Post-Intelligencer* Model Home—Arbor Heights (1948). *Museum of History and Industry, Seattle, Seattle* Post-Intelligencer *Collection, PI22297*

Seattle *Post-Intelligencer* Model Home—
Arbor Heights (1948)

A quick comparison of this model home to the Seattle *Post-Intelligencer* 1935 model home shows how much smaller middle-class houses became immediately after World War II. Even so, this simple masonry dwelling has a garage, proudly extending from the front of the house. The house is side gabled, and the only decorative detailing occurs on the gable ends, where faint articulation by vertical boards with decoratively cut ends creates accentuated pediments.

CONTEMPORARY (1935–1980)

Smith residence, exterior, 1947. *Dearborn-Massar. University of Washington Libraries, Special Collections, DM04147*

Smith Residence (1936)

The Smith residence has the standard gabled roof found in most Minimal Traditional houses, but the fenestration pattern clearly indicates a Contemporary dwelling. Most of the windows are fixed, with a few sliding windows or transom windows providing ventilation. The balcony partially rests on the extended garage. There are no applied ornaments like those found on Victorian, Tudor Revival, Craftsman, or Colonial Revival houses. The wood siding and roofline give the building a horizontal feeling. From the exterior, windows and doors appear to be located for utility, not fashion.

The interior is also minimalist, with high ceilings in the living room, which accesses the front balcony. The crossed braces and massive brick fireplace are the only design features in the room. A metal railing along the far back wall is indicative of how quickly styles changed from the predominantly wood ornamented interiors of Craftsman, Tudor Revival, and Colonial Revival homes, to Modern styles. Hardwood floors are partially covered with Oriental rugs. Unlike the house, most of the furniture is quite traditional in design, and a bit out of place. A kitchen photograph shows built-in cabinets and a laminate counter

top. Sleek, chrome drawer pulls replace the cup pulls and cabinet latches found on early twentieth-century cabinetry. Cabinet doors are no longer set inside the frame, they now rest on the outside, which is a cheaper and faster construction method.

The architect of this house, John R. Sproule, moved to Washington as a child. He attended the University of Washington and then worked with a number of architects before becoming an instructor of architecture at the University of Washington.

Smith residence, living room, 1947. *Dearborn-Massar. University of Washington Libraries, Special Collections, DM04149*

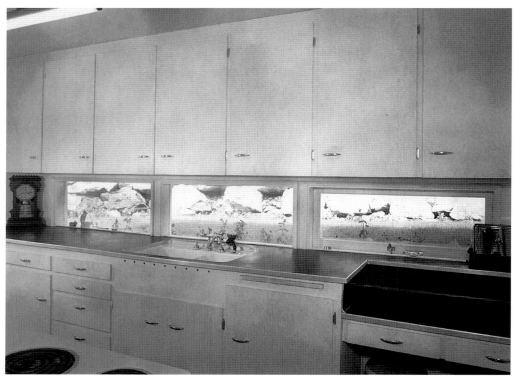

Smith residence, kitchen, 1947. *Dearborn-Massar. University of Washington Libraries, Special Collections, DM04155*

Paul Hayden Kirk residence, exterior, in 1944. *Dearborn-Massar. University of Washington Libraries, Special Collections, DM02425*

Paul Hayden Kirk Residence (1944)

The Paul Hayden Kirk residence is small, just over 1000 square feet. A traditional street-facing gable form is used but in an innovative way. Two large recesses are carved out of the front facade, one providing shelter for the car, the other serving as an entry porch. There are no windows on the front of the dwelling, emphasizing the importance of privacy, and the automobile. The small square footage required careful space planning. A photo from the right of the property shows the large floor-to-ceiling plate-glass windows that helped visually enlarge the living room and take advantage of the landscaped garden.

The architect and client for this house were the same, Paul Hayden Kirk. Kirk arrived in Seattle in the early 1920s, and received a degree in architecture from the University of Washington in 1937. He worked in a number of different historical styles, but was increasingly drawn to Contemporary architecture and designed a number of religious and public buildings in addition to residential structures. Kirk was well known nationally, and his work was frequently published in architecture journals.

Paul Hayden Kirk residence, exterior from front, in 1944. *Dearborn-Massar. University of Washington Libraries, Special Collections, DM02415*

Walter P. Coulon residence, exterior, 1946. *Dearborn-Massar. University of Washington Libraries, Special Collections, DM01768*

Walter P. Coulon residence, living room, 1946. *Dearborn-Massar. University of Washington Libraries, Special Collections, DM01774*

Walter P. Coulon Residence (1946)

The two-story Walter P. Coulon residence uses traditional residential design elements—the rectangular massing, and long, side-gable roofline—but augments them with strips of casement windows and an elevated balcony entry. Roof eaves project widely on the front and back, but are nearly flush on the sides. The interior is more dramatic, with a soaring cathedral living room. Interior details are minimal; there are no ceiling moldings or ornate paneling. The fireplace end wall with a built-in bookcase is the only design element. Furniture, while contemporary, reflects conservative choices, including a wingback style armchair.

This house was designed by J. Lister Holmes. Holmes started his architecture practice working with Neoclassical Revival and Tudor Revival forms. Although born in Seattle, he studied architecture at the University of Pennsylvania, returning to Seattle in 1920. He worked briefly for the firm of Bebb & Gould. Holmes also participated in the Yesler Terrace project.

Phillip A. Stewart residence, exterior, in 1949. *Dearborn-Massar. University of Washington Libraries, Special Collections, DM04273*

Phillip A. Stewart Residence (1947)

The Phillip A. Stewart residence is small, just over 1000 square feet. Horizontal lines dominate most of the structure, from its one-story grade elevation to the projecting boxed eaves. Windows are also horizontal, and even the chimney has more width than height. Large banks of glass windows overlook Lake Washington from the living room. The kitchen, dining, and living areas have an open plan, with furniture and floor treatments providing spatial division. Vertical paneling is used in the living room, and creates a strong contrast with the massive Roman brick fireplace surround. The living room furniture was quite contemporary: the soft molded chairs on the right lack arms and were lifted up off the ground on small legs, creating a floating appearance. The chair was also made smaller without arms, a designer's technique that helped furniture fit into increasingly tight spaces.

Phillip A. Stewart residence, living room, in 1949. *Dearborn-Massar. University of Washington Libraries, Special Collections, DM04280*

Sam Rubinstein residence, exterior, in 1950. *Dearborn-Massar. University of Washington Libraries, Special Collections, DM01818*

Sam Rubinstein residence, bar. *Dearborn-Massar. University of Washington Libraries, Special Collections, DM01833*

Sam Rubinstein Residence (1947)

The Sam Rubinstein residence was another project by J. Lister Homes. The horizontal emphasis of the ashlar masonry, extended-eave roof, and broad chimney stack was balanced by the tall narrow glazing, giving this house a Miesian appearance. The interior of the plan was predominantly open, with partial walls and glazed surfaces dividing many of the open spaces. Linoleum was the primary floor covering in the breakfast room and kitchen. Spatial definition was gained through the use of alternating shades. The backless stools and armless chairs to the right were streamlined with tapered legs. A sitting room in the house used ashlar masonry for one interior wall, a large expanse of glass opened the space up to exterior views, and a built-in wooden screen provided privacy from other public spaces.

Harold Mayer residence, exterior, in 1950. *Dearborn-Massar. University of Washington Libraries, Special Collections, DM05400*

Harold Mayer Residence (1948)

The Harold Mayer residence utilizes the same tension between horizontal and vertical elements as many of the other Contemporary structures in this chapter. This house, built into a bank, has a partially elevated basement. The structure is horizontal in massing with rows of horizontal awning windows to the left of the entry, countered by a tall perpendicular wall, supporting the broad eave overhang. Although the front door is wood, the entry is primarily glass. In keeping with the Contemporary style, public spaces have an open plan. A cathedral ceiling adds much needed height to the large living room, which would feel tunnel-like and cramped with a traditional-height ceiling.

Furniture is kept simple with angular forms. The arms of the chairs are not upholstered, and so the chairs take up minimal space. The back wall is entirely glass, and provides a stunning view into the courtyard. A view from the back of the house shows a small yard, mostly paved over to create additional living space.

The architectural firm of Tucker, Shields, & Terry, practicing from 1946 to 1951, designed this house and a number of other custom residences in the Seattle area. They also designed Canlis restaurant. Terry was known for his integration of architecture, interior design, and landscape architecture.

Harold Mayer residence, living room, in 1950. *Dearborn-Massar. University of Washington Libraries, Special Collections, DM05411*

Harold Mayer residence, patio, in 1950. *Dearborn-Massar. University of Washington Libraries, Special Collections, DM05405*

Rader-Revere residence, exterior, in 1950. *Dearborn-Massar. University of Washington Libraries, Special Collections, DM01168a*

Rader-Revere Residence (1948)

The Rader-Revere residence is compact, with less than 1500 square feet of living space. The skillful design by Chiarelli & Kirk led to this house's inclusion in House and Garden's 1952 *Book of Building*. Automobile storage is at basement level in a partially open carport. The roof has wide boxed eaves, which emphasize the horizontal structure of the house. Although the chimney's vertical form pulls the eye upward, its large width and Roman bricks accentuate the horizontal massing. The small interior has an open floor plan for the main public spaces. Wood floors are used in the living room and dining room, a throw rug providing the only division between the two spaces.

The most striking piece of modern furniture in the living room is the butterfly chair. The butterfly chair, a classic example of 1930s furniture, was designed by Argen-tine architects Ferrari-Hardoy, Kurchan, and Bonet. Inspired by British officer chairs from the nineteenth century, the chair is visually and physically light and was manufactured in a variety of colors. A quick comparison between the butterfly chair and the heavy Chinese dining room chairs to the right indicates how Contemporary design furniture allows the small space to appear open and flowing. A compact kitchen, behind the dining room, has its own small seating area. Linoleum defines the kitchen area; a small door and sliding panels could completely close the space off from the rest of the house. Inexpensive mate-rials, including pegboard, were used for the cabinetry. Although the front of the house has very little glazing, massive windows on the rear provided views into the forest. The first owner of the house was Melvin M. Rader.

Rader-Revere residence, living room and dining area, in 1950. *Dearborn-Massar. University of Washington Libraries, Special Collections, DM01173c*

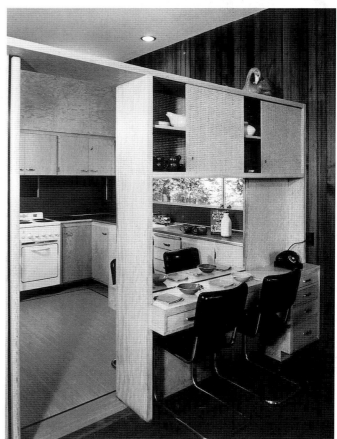

Rader-Revere residence, kitchen, in 1950. *Dearborn-Massar. University of Washington Libraries, Special Collections, DM01173b*

Dr. John Lehmann residence, exterior, in 1951. *Dearborn-Massar. University of Washington Libraries, Special Collections, DM01616*

Dr. John Lehmann Residence (1950)

John and Thelma Lehmann's narrow parcel of land overlooking Puget Sound required a carefully planned residence design. Their house is angular in plan, created to fit the landscape and take advantage of views, with most windows on the water side. Brick is the primary cladding material for the lower level, while vertical wood boards delineate the artist's studio, perched over the carport. This house is larger than most; the family employed a live-in maid. The interior has few walls; the music room, living room and dining room are combined into one large space. Even the children's bedroom has a dividing partition, which can be opened during the day, creating a large playroom. The main living room wall is a stacked bond brick, which adds a linear texture to the room.

Furniture is sparse and, in the typical Contemporary style, primarily armless. The adjoining dining room uses a partial wall faced with cork and a tracked curtain to separate the space as needed. The far wall, which separates the dining room from the kitchen, is covered with floor-to-ceiling cabinetry, giving the room a sleek appearance. A cutout section opens to a passageway between the kitchen and dining area.

This house was designed to meet specific client needs. Dr. Lehmann's profession often demanded irregular hours, so the master bedroom has direct access to the carport. Thelma Lehmann was a painter, so her studio was placed above the garage, allowing additional natural light. The studio has direct access to the master bedroom as well.

Architect Roger Gotteland graduated in 1936 with an architecture degree from the University of Washington. In 1952, this house won a Washington State American Institute of Architects Award. It was also featured in a 1953 book of Contemporary architecture, *Practical Houses for Contemporary Living*, by Jean and Don Graf.

John Lehmann residence, living area, in 1951. *Dearborn-Massar.* *University of Washington Libraries, Special Collections, DM01624*

John Lehmann residence, dining area, in 1951. *Dearborn-Massar.* *University of Washington Libraries, Special Collections, DM01627*

HOUSE TALES

Researching Your Home's History

EVER WONDER when your house was built? Who first lived in it? How it originally looked? Every house has a story to tell, regardless of age. Researching a building's history takes a bit of detective work and can be time consuming, but there are so many interesting things to discover. Maybe your "Tudor Revival" home was really Victorian that was drastically remodeled in the 1930s. Perhaps it was owned by someone locally prominent, or even nationally significant. Houses can change considerably over time. Two Craftsman houses, located on the same street in Fremont, illustrate the types of changes that can occur. Although clearly built from the same plan, the one at 1710 has undergone alterations that mask its original features. Windows, doors, and brackets have been removed, and the original siding has been covered as well. Even the front step design was changed. A "house genealogy" can help track physical changes to the structure and uncover past owners. This information is crucial for establishing property significance, if you are interested in local, state, or national register status.

There are several different ways to research a building's history. The three main steps are inspection of the building site, gathering oral history, and searching for documents. Site inspection can help quickly identify the basic style and presumed period of a house. This involves looking at the building site, any additional outbuildings (garages, carriage houses, chicken coops), and a close exterior and interior investigation of the main building. Such detective work can alert the researcher to additions, remodeling projects, and other alterations. Gathering oral history involves discussing the property with past owners, long-time neighbors, and possibly local historians, who can often provide clues not readily accessible through building or document examinations. A house in the Fremont neighborhood was set back from the street much farther than its neighbors. Conversation with a previous owner explained the setback. The house was one of a pair, on neighboring lots, owned by a single family. A small fruit orchard, long gone, had originally been planted on the front of the second lot, explaining why the second home was built on the back of its lot. This type of information is not usually documented in official city or state records, so taking the extra

Craftsman houses at 1702 and 1710 North 34th street in Fremont, just a few doors from each other, in 2004.

Preceding page: Photographic clues: Catholic Sisters, instructors at St. John's Parochial School, stand in front of a Craftsman dwelling at Northwest 79th Street. The house served as their convent from 1926 to 1948. Period photograph. *Museum of History and Industry, Seattle, Pemco Webster and Stevens Collection, 83.10.3013.2*

time to find oral history sources can be rewarding. The document search takes one into local repositories for deeds and wills, where past owners can be determined. Once you have their names, you can examine family histories, obituaries, and other records to determine more specific owner history.

BUILDING SITE RESEARCH

Exterior Investigation

An important step in researching the history of a house is to examine the building site. This task allows you to see not only what is there currently, but also to search for signs of previous buildings. How close is your property to neighbors? If most of the lots on your street are a standard size, with similarly proportioned and decorated buildings, set back at roughly the same distance from the street, then it is possible your home was part of a contractor's development. Is your house considerably larger or does it appear older than neighboring properties? This may indicate that your dwelling was part of a larger tract of land, which was later subdivided and sold as urban areas encroached. Does it look more contemporary than surrounding residences? It may have undergone a massive remodeling, or it might be a newer house, built on property that was split off of a larger estate. A grounds investigation at one site found the remains of three brick entry stairs half buried under a large bush toward the side of the property. Further research showed that a small rental house, destroyed in the 1960s, had once occupied part of the lot. Other things to look for, even with urban houses, are traces of outbuildings, such as chicken houses or sheds. Owners of one late nineteenth-century home discovered that the "playhouse" used by children for more than fifty years had originally been a chicken coop.

Massing and Roofing

After examining the site, detailed attention should be given to the main house. Houses can be categorized, in part, by their proportions. Queen Anne style houses generally have irregular massing, with porches, bay windows, or towers. Colonial Revival houses are almost always rectangular in plan, so from the exterior, certain additions and alterations are usually evident. Changes in foundation material may mark an addition. Also look for changes in rooflines. Shed roofs are commonly used on additions, even if the rest of the house has a gable or a gambreled roof. Roofing material is usually not useful for dating a house, since it is replaced frequently. However, slate and tile roofs can last a century or more, so if your home has either of these roofing materials, a closer investigation might be in order.

If roof eaves project considerably beyond the walls, or are "supported" with large brackets, then your home might well be Craftsman in style. Steep, sharply pitched, gabled rooflines, particularly those over main entries, usually indicate Tudor Revival design. How many chimneys does your property have? Multiple chimneys usually indicate older houses, where fireplace heat was essential for warming the structure. Houses with a single chimney were usually built later, at a time when oil or coal was the main heat source for the dwelling. The number of stories a house has is more indicative of status than the actual style of the dwelling. Victorians can range from small one-story structures to three story mansions. Tudor Revivals are usually one and a half stories to three stories. One-and-a-half story structures are common for Craftsman dwellings, but one-story and occasionally two-story Craftsman structures are found.

Wall Cladding

Exterior wall cladding can also help identify the period in which a house was built. Vinyl and aluminum siding have been added to many houses over the years, so it may take a bit of detective work to discover which type of exterior cladding your home originally had.

Queen Anne house covered with faux brickwork, after the gable ornaments and the decorative brackets over the canted corners were removed, photographed in 2004.

Then again, sometimes it is easier than you might expect. A Craftsman home I lived in for a number of years was sided, but a portion of the wall under the entry staircase was not covered. As a result, rows of beautifully laid shingles were still intact, and easily accessed. Patterned shingles are commonly found in Queen Anne and Folk Victorian structures, and usually covered only a portion of the building. These shingles might be rounded on the end like fish scales, angled, or even sawtoothed. Plain rectangular shingles were more commonly used on Colonial Revival or Craftsman houses, often laid in a common bond, where each row is off-centered above the preceding one. Staggered butts, where shingle length varies, was commonly found with Craftsman homes.

Tudor Revival houses, and some Craftsman houses as well, have applied half-timber details for exterior accent. The decorative gingerbreading found on Victorian houses was often one of the first things removed when a house was modernized. Keep in mind that the decorative trim you see might not be original to the house. Currently, with an interest in all things Craftsman, faux Craftsman details are being added to Victorian houses, whereas a decade or so ago, Craftsman houses were sometimes remodeled with faux Victorian details. An example of such remodeling is evident in a Ballard residence, which was probably built during the Victorian era. At some point, an owner remodeled it using a Colonial Revival theme. Windows have multiple lights, shutters were added, and a new front door with a broken pediment surround was added. The steeply pitched, street-facing gable and decorative scrollwork suggest the home's original style.

A Ballard Victorian house, with added Colonial Revival elements, in 1999.

Doors and Windows

Doors and windows are usually among the least helpful components in dating a house, since they are frequently replaced during remodels. My own house, a Craftsman, has a faux Victorian front door that dates from the 1990s, period double-hung windows on the main façade, an ill-fitting aluminum replacement window in one bedroom, and vinyl replacement windows in another. Doors and windows on the front of a house usually showcase more elaborate examples of the style than those on the side or back. Typically, a Victorian house would have a main entry door with a large pane of glass. While modern homeowners may bemoan the lack of privacy or security, the glass allowed light into dim center hallways. Paneled entry doors, particularly if coupled with sidelights and transoms, can indicate a Colonial Revival or Neoclassical design. Doors with rounded tops, or with unique small inset doors (which allow the occupant to see and talk with people on the other side) are commonly found in Tudor Revival houses. Craftsman doors typically contain multiple lights on the upper section, with thick muntins. Dentiled shelves are also frequent. Window placement is also more prone to movement than doors. Some older houses had windows lighting closets, and it is not uncommon to find these sided over during home remodels. Houses may have had a second level added, thus removing original dormers. Craftsman homes would usually have three or four windows run together in a living room or dining room, but in a remodel these may have all been replaced with a single, fixed window. Contemporary houses often have large expanses of plate glass windows, and plain, unpaneled doors.

A cluster of Craftsman windows, in 2004.

A Queen Anne sash, commonly found on Victorian houses, in 2004.

Interior Investigation

Once you have thoroughly reviewed the exterior of a property, it is time to move inside. Floors, walls, interior doors, and wall coverings can all help determine a building's age. Hardwood and softwood floors are found in most of Seattle's historic homes. In this region it is not uncommon to find oak, a more durable wood, used in major public areas, like the dining room and living room, while fir, a softer material that is more easily scarred, was relegated to hallways and bedrooms. Sometimes looking at the floor can give clues to additions or removals. Additions might have floorboards of varying widths, or the boards might run in a different direction from the rest of the house. Sometimes partial screen walls or built-in furniture were removed from Craftsman houses years after they were built. Ghost patterns on the floor will show slightly different finish colors, and often the original rectangular shape of a partial wall can be seen. If built-in furniture was removed, likely the space underneath it was subflooring or subwall, and differences in the replacement flooring or wall surfaces might alert you to their removal.

Walls

The back of a lath and plaster wall, showing the keys, in 2004.

A picture suspended from a picture rail on a wire sheathed in velvet, in this Victorian interior, in the late 1990s.

Walls can be defined both by their construction and their covering. Plaster was commonly used for most interior wall construction in Seattle before World Word II. A combination of lime, sand, water, and gypsum plaster (with an occasional addition of horsehair or straw) was mixed and spread over wooden lath in layers, with the finest and whitest coats applied last. Plaster needs a framework to adhere to, and lath provided that framework. Wooden lath, in boards about an inch and a half wide and about one-third-inch thick, was nailed horizontally to studs, leaving spaces between the lath. When wet plaster was applied, it would squeeze into the gaps, forming "keys" that hold the plaster in place, creating the surface of the wall. If too many keys break from age or mechanical pounding, a plaster surface can delaminate, requiring an expensive repair project. Sometimes one will find mesh-like metal lath, which provided lots of small, open spaces for plaster to adhere.

During the Victorian era many types of molding were made of plaster. Larger houses may have ornate plaster finishes, while more modest dwellings may have a simple treatment. Moldings could be elaborate, and either painted or papered. Craftsman and Tudor Revival houses rarely have elaborate plasterwork. Wall surfaces in Tudor Revival homes may be smooth, but some were given a wavy troweled finish designed to look more "historical." Plaster walls are durable, but they have a tendency to crack as a house settles and shifts with age. Sometimes these surface cracks are patched, but it is not uncommon to find later owners either placing drywall over the plaster, or simply spraying on a new textured finish coat. These later steps can make detecting original plaster finishes difficult. Sometimes in closets or under stairs, a little detective work can help uncover original lath.

Because a plaster wall is only as strong as its keys, pictures were not hung directly from the walls. A picture railing, usually found at the top of the ceiling, was used. Small metal S-shaped hooks could support a picture, while distributing the weight across the molding. If the original hooks have long since disappeared from your home, replacement hooks are available from restoration companies. Tudor Revival houses frequently have unusual plasterwork at the wall and ceiling junctures. Instead of 90-degree corners, the ceilings are coved, a technique achieved by running a pattern board into the plaster while wet. Coved ceilings can be expensive to create; if your home has one, it is most likely an original feature.

Paint Most houses have been repainted many times. Weathering may allow you to break off a paint chip and discover an original color. Removing long-term fixtures (like a radiator) also might help you discover the paint color, although keep in mind that pigments can discolor over time. Another way to discover original colors is to take a small piece of sandpaper and rub it in a circular motion over the same area for a while. The result will be a bulls-eye of sorts, with the oldest colors being closest to the center. A wide range of colors was available to homeowners in the late nineteenth and early twentieth centuries. Don't be surprised if the colors you find are brighter than expected. Paint chips from a 1915 catalog show vivid carmine red, royal blue, and bright carnation pink, in addition to more subdued creams, beiges, and soft blues. Stenciling interiors was a common and inexpensive decorating technique. Designs were usually inspired by wallpaper. Sears, Roebuck and Company stocked stencil patterns and tools. Craftsman interiors favored the cleanness of stenciled designs, which were often based on organic Art Nouveau motifs.

Wallpaper and Wood Paneling Many older houses have been wallpapered at least once. In many cases, new layers were added directly on top of existing paper. Even ceilings were papered. A wallpapered room may occasionally hold clues regarding door and window additions. Windows and doors may have been added later if removal of their wood molding uncovers wallpaper. If all you see is plaster, the window and door locations are likely original. Other popular wall treatments during the late nineteenth century were Lincrusta and Anaglypta, which are embossed papers with raised designs; these were applied in a similar manner to wallpaper, then painted over. Sometimes the raised areas were accented with different colors.

Some walls have large expanses of wood paneling. The amount of wood paneling is correlated more to the economic status of the owner than the architectural style. Large Victorian, Colonial Revival, and Tudor Revival houses may have floor-to-ceiling paneling in the major public areas of the house. Smaller, less high-style examples are more likely simply to have wainscoting, or only baseboards. One exception to this trend is Craftsman style houses. Many of these dwellings have wainscoting that extends up to a plate rail, about two-thirds up the wall. Box-beamed ceilings are also common in even the simplest examples of Craftsman style.

Staircases and Fireplaces Staircase location and design can sometimes be stylistic clues. Victorian houses usually had central staircases ending in the main foyer. Stair banisters were often elaborate, even in smaller examples. Some large two-story Colonial Revival or Neoclassical Revival houses also have articulated center staircases. In contrast, vernacular examples of Tudor Revival and Craftsman houses are more likely to have small, steep, narrow staircases, hidden toward the back of the house. These smaller spaces are more functional, without the ornamentation of their predecessors. Both of the Craftsman houses that I have lived in have narrow staircases with almost no ornamentation.

Fireplaces can also give clues to the original period of a house. During the Victorian era, mantelpieces were often ornate, particularly in public rooms. Fireplaces also were used to heat some bedrooms during this era, so you may find them in these rooms as well. In periods after the Victorian era, the number of fireplaces is usually based on the scale of the house. Larger houses might have fireplaces in bedrooms and studies, mainly for aesthetic reasons. Smaller houses might have a token fireplace in the main living area. Colonial Revival and Neoclassical Revival houses treat fireplace mantels in different ways. Larger houses may have ornate marble mantelpieces, while smaller middle-class homes are more likely to have simple wooden surrounds with minimal Classical molding. Craftsman houses frequently have interesting art tile surrounding fireplaces, with reliefs of land-scapes, plants, or even covered wagons represented. Clinker bricks are also commonly found around Craftsman and Tudor Revival fireplaces. Modern houses often have simple, mantel-free fireplaces made from proportionately longer Roman bricks.

Basement and Attic

Visiting your house's basement or attic will also help you identify additions or remodels. Does a basement extend only under a potion of the house? It is not uncommon for only the original section of the house to have a basement. Can you see the subflooring? Are there any breaks, with a different width of wood being used? This may indicate an addition. Is there a row of nail marks along a break in the boards? This probably indicates that an interior wall was removed. While basement spaces can indicate changes in floor plan or horizontal additions, attic spaces can give clues about adding additional floors. Splices on corner posts might indicate that they were made higher. Breaks in gable end boards can suggest a change in roof pitch.

DOCUMENT SEARCH

Government Records

The next step in your search is the paper trail. This pursuit is important not only because a physical inspection rarely gives concrete dating information, but also because you will need to know who the previous owners were to further research the history of the house. There are various research tools, some taking longer to use than others and yeilding different kinds of information. There are two main categories of information: the first deals with the house and physical changes to the house, and the second deals with the owners, who lived in the property, and what their lives were like.

One of the quickest sources of information about homes built in Seattle before 1937 are the house photographs located on the Property Record Cards. In 1937, Seattle houses were photographed for the King County Assessor's Office. Each residence has a card that lists the address, information regarding plumbing, construction, dimensions, a small map, and a photo of the structure. The cards also listed current owners, and sometimes later owners, even giving a possession date, starting in 1937 until the 1972. This source can be useful to cross-reference with records from the grantor-grantee indexes (discussed below). The cards provide excellent documentation, particularly the photographs. If you suspect that your house has undergone modifications since its construction, the photograph may help you determine the original appearance of the structure, if the changes were made after 1937.

To access records on your home, you will need the tax parcel number. This information is on your property taxes, although you can also access it from the King County Assessor's Office or from a link to the real property finder, located on the Puget Sound Regional Archives Web site. The property record cards are kept at the Washington State Archives, Puget Sound Regional Branch, in Bellevue. Previous property owners can also be accessed by looking at the King County Assessment Rolls. Seattle property was assessed every five years. The Washington State Archives, Puget Sound Regional Branch, holds the records from 1892 through 1941. Assessment Rolls are filed by legal description.

If holes are left in your ownership history, you can always research a full "chain of title," which is time consuming but will generally yield all owner names. Start with deeds to discover the names of previous property owners. Deeds are indexed by the property owner's name and will list the seller and buyer of the property, how much they paid for it, and a legal description. Sometimes a deed will even indicate if the property was transferred through a will. On rare occasion older documents even list houses and outbuildings. The property seller or giver is called the "grantor," and the buyer, or receiver, is called a "grantee."

Real estate is usually transferred through purchase, but sometimes it is transferred due to inheritance, a gift, or even a mortgage or property tax default. Deed descriptions will not necessarily tell whether there was a house on the property, but there are other ways to establish this. You can trace each deed back to its predecessor, creating what is called a "chain of title." You may be fortunate enough to have a copy of the report created for your home purchase. If so, you may be able to eliminate some of the next steps, and instead of tracing ownership back from your purchase, you can start several decades back. Another option that will save time but costs more money is to pay a title company to compile the ownership history, which includes creating the chain of title and gathering copies of all the property deeds.

Property owners from 1972 up to the present are located in the King County Assessor's Office. Changes in ownership are organized by tax parcel number. Grantor-Grantee (seller-buyer) Indexes from 1853 until 1972 are located at the Puget Sound Regional Archives in Bellevue or on microfilm at the King County Recorders Office. Begin the process by looking up the deed that shows the transfer of your current property from the previous owners. Deeds are indexed by the first three letters of the last name, in two sets of volumes—one for the grantors, and another for the grantees—in chronological order by filing date. Deeds are not always alphabetized beyond that, so don't be surprised if you find "Anderson" after "Andrews." Each entry will list the date that the deed was filed at the Recorders Office, the seller, the buyer, the citation for where the deed is filed (volume and page) and, occasionally the legal description of the property. You then continue back in time by looking up each previous individual deed.

If the people you bought your house from a decade ago were named John and Susan Doe, then you need to discover who they bought the property from. Look up the name "Doe" in the grantee book, until you find when they acquired the property and from whom. Then proceed, using the grantee index to find the grantors and the grantors to find the grantees. Occasionally, the purchasing paperwork for your home will have a partial chain of title, saving you time. In theory, if all records are still intact, you can trace property back to the settlement of Washington Territory, long before there was a house on your parcel of land. (To go this far back, you will need to access Federal Archives on Sand Point Way. This repository holds early records for the state.)

Deeds that were recorded after 1910 are usually typed; most records before that time were handwritten. It is not always easy to read the documents, since the writing style may be unfamiliar or the ink faded. Also, many deed books are no longer accessible directly, and you work with microfilm instead of the original document. Be prepared for this to be a time-consuming process. You can make photocopies of the deeds, but the quality may be weak, so it is best to make sure you clarify any unclear passages with the original document. There are specific pieces of information that you are looking for with the deed—namely, the date, grantors and grantees, amount of sale, and the property description. The last piece of information is particularly important. It is not uncommon to find that at some point the property that your house sits on was merely one parcel of many that were owned by a single individual. If you do not continue to check the legal description of the property, you might end up tracing the wrong parcel of land.

Also be aware that not all deeds were recorded. Some were filed long after the property sold, most commonly with transfers from one family member to another. Sometimes you can find who owned the property by another method (city directories) and reconnect the chain of title. In other cases a missing deed or an unclear legal description may end that part of your search. Once the deed research is completed, you can create a chain of title for the house. It should list each property owner and the exact dates they held possession.

The chain of title can be used to locate tax assessments, mortgages, wills, and other helpful documents. Tax assessments after 1972 are located at the King County Assessor's Office. Those from 1973 to 1983 are located on microfiche, and from 1983 until the present they are in a computer database. Records before that date are located at Puget Sound Regional Archives. From 1891 until 1941 assessments are in the Tax Assessment Rolls, and from 1937 until 1972 they are recorded on the Property Record Cards. These documents usually list acreage, the assessed value of the land, and the assessed value of the property. These records were updated periodically, so don't expect to necessarily find them for consecutive years. They will sometimes have additional information, referring perhaps to late tax payments.

Mortgages are usually more specific about houses and other buildings on the property, and will sometimes address fire insurance (in urban areas). Be aware that you will not always find mortgages, particularly in older chain of titles, since homes were not always financed in this manner. Since your title chain lists all owners of the property, simply go to the mortgage index and look up the grantee (who usually held the mortgage) in the year the home was purchased. The information that mortgages provide can be spotty, and may not be of substantial help to your research.

Wills are another legal document that can indicate how your home was furnished or used. Deeds can usually be used to determine if property was transferred due to a death. Probates from the 1850s until 1972 are located at the Puget Sound Regional Archives. Those from 1973 on are located at the clerk's office, King County Superior Court, King County Court House. Records from the 1850s until 1917 are indexed by name, and starting in 1918 they are indexed by the first letter of the last name and by filing date. The filing date is usually weeks or months after the death. I have seen wills from the nineteenth century stating that the spouse of the deceased will retain right to live in portions of the house, furnished with specific pieces of furniture. Sometimes an estate sale might be filed with a will, listing interior furnishings and any livestock the deceased may have owned. These can be particularly helpful in determining how interiors were furnished. Usually the deceased's death date is listed, which can help locate an obituary.

For additional information regarding building construction, check building permits for your property, which are located at the Department of Planning and Development and are organized by address. The permits will give the owner's name, architect, builder, and date of issue. Most pre-1974 residential building plans are no longer available.

Library Records

There are several other sources of information for both the property and owner history. Sanborn maps are excellent for building footprints, materials, and changes over time. These maps helped fire insurance agents determine fire hazards for specific properties by showing streets, property boundaries, house numbers, and the size, shape, and construction material (wood, brick, or stone) of each building. These maps were periodically updated, so compare earlier versions of a map with a later rendition, to establish when a building might have been constructed. For example, you suspect your home was built between 1900 and 1930. You examine the 1905 Sanborn map and see that there was no dwelling on your property yet. But a check of the 1917 Sanborn shows a dwelling on the lot with the same footprint as your home. So it is probable that your house was built sometime between 1905 and 1917.

Depending on how altered your home is, past Sanborns may help you determine the home's original footprint. Baist maps and Kroll maps didn't appear until the early twentieth century, and they give approximate legal descriptions and note the existence of a building. The University of Washington Library and the downtown Seattle Public Library have various editions of these maps. The first Sanborn map of Seattle was printed in 1884, and publication continued until the 1960s. The maps were not updated every year, so you will need to contact a reference librarian for help locating maps that cover your neighborhood and the date of interest.

Since you now have the names of your home's previous owners, you can do a more detailed investigation into their lives. Polk Seattle city directories list residents alphabetically. These directories usually give the spouse's name, in addition to the resident's occupation. Be aware, it is indeed the resident that they list, not the owner. So if the property owner was a landlord, you will perhaps find his name paired with a different address. Starting in 1938, Polk included a reverse directory, listing buildings by address. At this point in the search you should have a list of every owner and occupant of your property, matched with corresponding dates.

Now you can examine other types of resources to find more detailed personal information. If your property was built around the turn of the century, particularly if it is a larger, more elaborate building, there is a chance that someone important in the early history of Seattle may have been associated with it. A quick check through the Pacific Northwest Periodical and Newspaper Index at the University of Washington's Special Collections division might turn up a marriage announcement or obituary. The downtown Seattle Public Library also has a newspaper index. Obituaries are very good sources of information, since they often list which organizations people belonged to, in addition to information about their professional careers. Books that offer information on earlier property owners are Clarence B. Bagley's *Pioneer Seattle and Its Founders* and *History of King County, Washington*, Frederic Grant's *History of Seattle, Washington*, and C. H. Hanford's *Seattle and Environs*. Photos of your house may exist in the photo collections at the University of Washington, Special Collections, the Museum of History and Industry, and, if you live in Ballard, the Ballard Historical Society.

Pattern Books   If your house was built between 1908 and 1940 it might be worth your time to examine catalogues of Sears, Roebuck and Company. During this period they sold almost 100,000 houses in kits. They offered several hundred different styles, small and large. Building parts were shipped by rail. Every piece of lumber in a Sears house had a stamped number, aiding in assembly on site. You may even find a shipping label still attached to a beam in the attic or basement. Dover Press has reprinted several Sears home catalogues, *Houses by Mail*, by Katherine C. Stevenson and H. Ward Jandl, has a comprehensive list of Sears model homes. In addition to Sears, Montgomery Ward, Aladdin and Lewis Manufacturing, and Gordon Van-Time offered precut houses by mail. If you are interested in examining the catalogues, many have been reprinted and can be found at local libraries or ordered from a bookstore. Some of the titles available include *117 House Designs of the Twenties*, Dover Publications, and *Aladdin "Built in a Day" House Catalogue*, 1917, Dover Publications.

A local designer, Jud Yoho, specialized in Craftsman houses. He was editor of *Bungalow Magazine*, published from 1912 until 1918, which showcased Craftsman homes built in

Plan No. 692.

A Dutch Colonial house plan, from a Seattle pattern book by the Seattle Building and Investment Company, 1910s.
University of Washington Libraries, Special Collections, UW23614

the Seattle area and in California. The Seattle Public Library has a collection of the magazines, and the University of Washington Library system has a few issues as well. Addresses are given for some of the illustrated houses, while others merely give the name of the owner or indicate that the house is in Seattle. For her Master's thesis from the University of Washington, *Jud Yoho and the Craftsman Bungalow Company* (1997), Erin Doherty located the addresses and 1937 assessor's photographs for many Seattle houses featured in *Bungalow Magazine*. The houses are located throughout the city, with the largest concentrations in the Wallingford and Fremont neighborhoods.

A FEW HOUSE RESEARCH CASE STUDIES

By examining all the information you have uncovered, a fairly cohesive history of your home can be compiled. What type of information can you expect to have? Below are two case studies which reveal the process and the types of information that were available.

Charles McInnis Residence (circa 1895)

The Charles McInnis residence intrigued me when I first saw it a number of years ago. While from the exterior it appeared to be a Craftsman, with tapered piers supporting the front porch and stucco work in the street-facing gable, but the irregular massing of the structure seemed more Victorian, as did the angles of the cross gables. The front door knob's backplate was curvaceous and ornate, more Victorian looking than Craftsman. Gaining entry, I discovered that the front door opened onto a small formal hallway, with a highly visible front staircase. Wood floors in the living and dining areas had elaborate inlay. Something about the house didn't look quite right; it presented an odd stylistic mishmash of different periods. Indeed, the property owner indicated that the house had been built in the late 1800s. I found the tax assessor's photo of the home, but in it the house looked identical to its current state, so any changes had occurred before the photo was taken. A chain of title on the property and an evaluation of Baist and Sanborn maps provided the following information.

During the 1880s, J. W. Graff purchased land that later was named Graff's Salmon Bay Addition. On February 19, 1892, the property in Block 18, lot 9, was sold for $100 to Charles

Charles McInnis residence, in 2004.

Front doorknob and backplate, in 1998.

Front hall floor, inlaid wood pattern, in 1998.

and Elizabeth McInnis. In 1895 the couple purchased lot 8, next door, and constructed a house that covered parts of both lots. (The tax card for this property from Puget Sound Regional Archives' 1938 survey lists the construction date as 1892, but tax records for 1892 show no land improvements. The next available tax record, from 1895, shows an improvement of $200.) On March 23, 1901, the McInnises transferred the property to Sarah F. Smith, of Milwaukee, Wisconsin, for $1. This unusual price could perhaps indicate that the house was transferred by a gift or was financed by a mortgage. On May 12, 1903, A. H. Green purchased the property, and on March 30, 1907, the property was purchased by Hilda M. Smith. The property stayed in the Smith family until May 20, 1957. It was sold several times during the next several decades, until the current owners purchased it in 1996.

The 1895 Polk Seattle city directory lists Charles McInnis as a shingle cutter, and the 1898 Polk directory gives his occupation as a lumber cutter. The purchaser in 1907 was Hilda M. Smith, wife of Charles (or Carl) Jorgen Smith. The deed was placed in the wife's name, a common practice at that time to avoid claims by the husband's creditors. A review of the 1910 U.S. census shows that Smith emigrated from Norway in 1882, and Hilda came from Sweden in 1898. Bagley's *History of King County* and Charles Smith's obituaries give a considerable amount of information about his life. His parents had both died in Norway before he was ten. He graduated from Norway's Astronomical and Nautical College by the time he was seventeen, and he became second captain on an English sailing ship that brought him to the United States. In the mid 1880s he settled in Chicago to study architecture and building construction. He came to Seattle just before 1889, immediately becoming involved with real estate.

In Seattle, Smith worked with a number of Seattle businesses, including the Alaska-Yukon Transportation Company, and went back to school for a law degree. In 1903 he married Hilda. The couple soon had two children, Hjordis in 1905 and Charles Jr. in 1907. (Charles Jr. died the next year.) In 1909 the couple had another son, Kiert Servie. Smith was admitted to the Washington State Bar that year. Shortly thereafter, the couple had their final son, Thorgny Hjorvard. Charles became a manager and attorney for the S.S. Investment Company. By 1923 he opened his own law practice. From 1929 until 1942 the Smiths rented the upstairs of their house to boarders. On December 28, 1952, Hilda died of a stroke, and in 1956 Charles passed away. Additional information on the couple's children is available by reviewing Charles' obituary, which mentioned that Hjordis attended the University of Washington. A search of yearbooks from the time she would have been in college, the late 1920s, was fruitful. She is included in the 1927 UW yearbook, listed as the secretary of Lambda Rho, an art fraternity. Photos of her are included as well.

A 1905 Sanborn map shows an architectural footprint that is very different from the current house. The front section of the house is two stories high and is longer and wider than the back section. A curved bay window and a small front porch are on the front façade. The smaller back section probably is the current kitchen, and a back porch is located to the south. This information is also substantiated by the subflooring of the main level, which can be viewed from the basement. The floorboards are laid east-west under the back section of the house, while the floorboards for the main portion of the dwelling are diagonal. The 1917 Sanborn shows a remodel has enlarged the floor plan of the house, removed the Victorian bay, and added a full-length front porch. The house underwent a massive remodeling, and since the Victorian style was no longer in fashion, the owners completely updated the house.

Victorian, Tudor Revival, Neo-Victorian?

The Victorian-Tudor Revival house, in the late 1990s.

The house as it appeared on the 1937 property record card. *Washington State Archives, Puget Sound Regional Branch*

The Victorian-Tudor Revival house, in 2004.

Sometimes just pulling the property card from Puget Sound Archives will provide sufficient information. Several years ago I visited a Seattle house that appeared to be Tudor Revival from the exterior. While typical Tudor Revival elements existed, an arched front door opening, and curved sloping roof, the house didn't quite look right from the outside. I originally thought that perhaps the building was simply a poor example of the style. An examination of the 1937 property photo showed why the house looked so odd. The house was originally a small, vernacular, hipped-roof Victorian. Slender Tuscan columns supported a front porch. A cross gable protruded from the left, covering an extension with decorated clipped corners. As charming as the original house may seem to us now, owners in the 1940s were less than enamored. The building's ornamentation must have looked outdated to them, and apparently more interior space was needed. So the porch was walled in, and the clipped corner extension was expanded into a rectangle, adding more square footage. A garage, space that a pre-automobile era house didn't offer, was added under the house. A few years ago the owners decided that the Tudor Revival remodel no longer suited their needs, and they changed the style of the house again.

Swan Hansen Residence (circa 1900)

Even the smallest houses can have interesting histories. The Swan Hansen house was a small one-story Victorian. While Victorian massing was still evident, the front porch had lost most of its character when it was partially closed in. Faux brick veneer masked the original wood siding. The house had been poorly treated over the years, serving as a rental. The landscaping was so overgrown that you could barely see the building. When the current owners acquired the house, it was close to the point of collapse. There was no foundation, so serious structural work was needed. Somewhere under all the layers of siding and paint was a Victorian house, obscured to most people. Research on the property revealed that the land was purchased by Swan Hansen in 1901, and the house was built around this time. The 1910 Polk Seattle City Directory listed him as president of the Horseshoe Mining Corporation.

In 1914 ownership of the property changed to Catherine M. Wize. Catherine's second husband was Frank Hemen. Bagley's *History of Seattle* gives a biography of Hemen. He was born in Wisconsin and moved with his family to Montana as a young boy. They next moved to Seattle, where he attended Central High School and the University of Washington, graduating in 1888. He had a number of jobs, including bookkeeper for the A. B. Stewart Company, working in the Occidental Hotel, and member of the Seattle Fire Department at the time of the 1889 fire. In 1898 he left Seattle for the Yukon, searching for gold. In 1904 he returned to Seattle, and founded the Globe Realty Company. Many of his business transactions were listed under his wife's name.

The house is currently undergoing a complete remodel. A basement was added, not only to provide a foundation for the house but also to give additional living space. While this does change the appearance of the structure, the owners have been careful to maintain as much of the home's historic character as possible. The faux brick veneer was removed, uncovering the original clapboard siding. The enclosed front porch was restored to its original condition. A new front staircase was added. Interior work uncovered spaces for sliding pocket doors. The restoration of this house is a testament to the owner's interest in preserving the past while accommodating contemporary space and system upgrades.

The Swan Hansen residence, in 2000.

Removing the faux brick veneer, in 2000. *Photo by Jenny Joyce*

The Swan Hansen residence, in early 2004.

HISTORIC REGISTERS

Many of the large houses discussed in this book are on either the local, state, or national register of historic places. While people have a tendency to associate large, ornate dwellings with this type of designation, it is equally possible for small, more vernacular structures to be on the registers. If your house is a certain age (twenty-five years for the Seattle Landmark register, or fifty years for the state and national registers), the physical integrity of the house is good, and you can provide historical documentation, then usually it can be placed on a historic register. The registers are independent from each other, so designation on one register is not a guarantee that a building will be listed on the others.

The National Register

The National Register of Historica Places, authorized under the National Historic Preservation Act of 1966, is part of a program that identifies, evaluates, and protects historic resources at the national level. Historic buildings are nominated to the National Register through the State Historic Preservation Officer (SHPO). While anyone may prepare a nomination for the register, they are usually submitted by property owners with assistance from the state's historic preservation staff or a private consultant. For a building to be considered for the National Register, it must meet one of the following criteria: association with significant historical figures, a distinctive architectural style, association with a master architect or carpenter, or association with broad-based social or cultural history. There is also a category generally used for archeological sites, where pre-historical or early historical information may be yielded from the site. Only one of these categories needs to be addressed by the building, although exceptional buildings might be contributing in all of the categories. There are some restrictions: generally properties that have been moved, or are only the birthplace of a historical figure are not eligible. Properties need to be at least 50 years old, unless they are exceptionally important.

A National Register nomination must place a property in its historical context, describing the history of the community and what role the particular building played. Properties are also evaluated for physical integrity, particularly if a building is nominated under criteria that directly relate to the substance of the structure. A Craftsman home with updated bathrooms and new wiring will probably qualify, but a Craftsman house in which the original windows have been replaced, interior woodwork was removed, and vinyl siding has been applied would not be eligible. A 100-year-old house that was substantially remodeled eighty years ago could still be eligible, since the remodeling job may have taken on historical significance in its own right.

So what happens when your property is listed on the National Register? What types of restrictions or obligations can you expect? The federal government places no restriction on property owners regarding registration. National Register designation is an honor that recognizes the importance of the property, and property owners can do anything they wish with the building. Owners have no obligation to restore the structures, open them to the public, or even maintain them. If the owner of a National Register property wanted to tear it down, no permit would be involved and the federal government can not interfere. Since being on the National Register does not offer protection for historic structures, what is the advantage? Listed properties receive special consideration in planning in federally licensed, permitted, and funded projects. This helps to ensure that the federal government does not unknowingly damage a historic building with any of its public projects.

The best benefit from National Register listing is for commercial properties. Income-producing buildings (rental properties) that are being rehabilitated may be eligible for a 20-percent tax credit, if the federal government's standards for rehabilitation are followed. These standards ensure historic integrity by encouraging preservation and restoration of historic materials instead of replacement. National Register properties may also qualify for federal historic preservation grants, if funds are available. For many homeowners, placing a house on the National Register is simply an acknowledgment of the historical value of the structure and an expression of wanting others to be aware of the building's history. Homes on the National Register may also command a higher sale price.

Washington State Register

A listing on the Washington Heritage Register, our state's historical register, is also honorary. The criteria for significance are similar to that of the federal register, and the building must be either associated with local or regional history, an important individual, or architectural style. Listing on this register does not change a property owner's rights either, nor is there protection of the property. In 1985 the Washington State Legislature passed a program allowing building rehabilitation on historic properties located in "Certified Local Governments" (Seattle is a Certified Local Government) to receive a discount in assessed property taxes, called a Special Tax Valuation. The discount applies if the structure requires substantial rehabilitation equal to at least 25 percent of the assessed value. This dollar amount is subtracted from the assessed value of the property for a ten-year period. This discount is available for both income-producing and non–income-producing buildings, so residential property is eligible. Buildings listed on the register are also given more freedom regarding building code requirements; occasionally waivers are given to preserve the integrity of the historical structure.

Local Register

The most inclusive protection for a building is listing on the local register. In Seattle this means that the building receives the designation "Seattle Landmark." The city of Seattle is more liberal in its interpretation of historic, and a structure need only be twenty-five years old for placement of the register, instead of the fifty years required by state and national registers. Eligibility is determined in much the same way: a building must be associated in a significant way with a historic event, a historical person, cultural, or political heritage, an architectural style, or a significant designer or builder. Unlike the national and state registers, listing on the local register does carry some restrictions, but the additional help and guidance offered to the property owner more than compensates. Any exterior and, in rare cases, interior changes to the property need to be reviewed and approved by the Seattle Landmarks Preservation Board. Building use may be monitored as well. However, zoning code relief is available to encourage the preservation of landmark buildings, including setbacks, landscaping, and even parking exceptions. Building code relief is also available to help maintain historic properties. Another great benefit is the Special Tax Valuation, discussed above. Staff at both the state and city level can help you establish whether your house is eligible for listing at any of these levels and how to apply. Both agencies have helpful Web sites, and can send out a package of materials to further assist in documenting your home for inclusion on a historic register.

For information on the National Register or the Washington State Heritage Register, contact:

Office of Archeology and Historic Preservation
Office of Community Development
1063 South Capitol Way, Suite 106
Olympia, WA 98501
(360) 586-3065

For information on the Seattle Landmarks Register, contact:

Urban Conservation Division
Department of Neighborhoods
City of Seattle
700 Third Avenue
Seattle, WA 98104
(206) 684-0464

HOUSE LOCATOR BY CHAPTER

Showcased houses and their addresses are organized by chapter in this list. Dates of construction and design professionals are given when available. Structures that are no longer standing or were altered beyond recognition are listed as demolished. Residences that are on the local, state, or national register are also designated. Most of these houses are private residences; please respect homeowners' privacy. Please refer to the index to locate discussions in text.

CHAPTER 1. VICTORIAN:
Italianate, Queen Anne,
and Folk Victorian

Italianate (1850–1885)

Corliss P. Stone Residence
1120 North 35th Street
circa 1870–1880
demolished

Dexter Horton Residence
Northeast Corner of 3rd Avenue and
Seneca Street
circa 1873
demolished

George W. Ward Residence
520 East Denny Way
1882
Seattle Landmark
Washington Heritage Register
National Register of Historic Places

James Bard Metcalfe Residence
823 Main Street
1890
demolished

Mills Residence
believed to be in Ballard, location
unknown
circa 1890

Italianate Victorian Residence
1414 South Washington Street
1901
Seattle Landmark

*Queen Anne and Folk Victorian
(1880–1910)*

Turner-Koepf Residence
2336 15th Avenue South
1883
Washington Heritage Register
National Register of Historic Places
altered

George C. Kinnear Residence
809 Queen Anne Avenue
1885
demolished

David Thomas Denny Residence
512 Queen Anne Avenue
1888
demolished

D. Thomas Denny Jr. Residence
2810 Eastlake Avenue East
circa 1890
demolished

Charles Harvey Lilly Residence
Northeast corner of 5th Avenue West and
Prospect Street
W. J. L. Perry, architect
circa 1890
demolished

Henry Van Asselt Residence
1621 15th Avenue East
1890
demolished

14th Avenue Housing Group
2000–2016 14th Avenue West
1890–1909
Seattle Landmark

Victor Steinbrueck Residence
2622 Franklin Avenue East
1891
Seattle Landmark

List-Bussell Residence
1630 36th Avenue
Flynn & Rockmark, architects
1892
Seattle Landmark
Washington Heritage Register

Fisher-Howell Residence
2819 Franklin Avenue East
circa 1892
Seattle Landmark

William H. Thompson Residence
3119 South Day Street
Ernest A. MacKay, builder
1894
Seattle Landmark
Washington Heritage Register
National Register of Historic Places

23rd Avenue Houses Group
812–828 23rd Avenue East
1892–1893
Seattle Landmarks
Washington Heritage Register

Yesler Residences
103, 107, and 109 23rd Avenue East
Emil Kriegel, contractor
1899 and 1902
Seattle Landmark
Washington Heritage Register
National Register of Historic Places

Ornate Queen Anne Residence
1009 East Madison
circa 1890
demolished

Cross-gabled two-story Victorian
2246 Northwest 62nd Street
circa 1890
demolished

Pyramid-roofed Folk Victorian Residence
1522 Northwest 61st Street
circa 1890
altered

Capt. M. T. Powers Residence
1230 East Fir Street
circa 1900
demolished

CHAPTER 2. CLASSICAL REVIVALS: Colonial Revival and Neoclassical Revival

Colonial Revival (1880–1955)

William C. Phillips Residence
2822 10th Avenue East
1909

William Bell Phillips Residence
711–713 East Union Street
John M. Hester, builder
1902
Washington Heritage Register
National Register of Historic Places

Caroline Kline Galland Residence
1605 17th Avenue
Max Umbrecht, architect
1903
Washington Heritage Register
National Register of Historic Places

Reginald H. Parsons Residence
618 West Highland Drive
W. Marbury Somervell, designer
1905
Seattle Landmark

David E. Skinner Residence
725 14th Avenue East
W. W. Sabin, architect
1905
altered

Edwin G. Ames Residence
808 36th Avenue East
Bebb & Mendel, architects
1906
altered

Edgar H. Bucklin Residence
1620 East Prospect Street
Frederick A. Sexton, architect
1908

Dr. Waldo Richardson Residence
2816 10th Avenue East
1912

Raymond-Ogden Residence
702 35th Avenue
Joseph S. Coté, architect
1912–1913
Seattle Landmark
Washington Heritage Register
National Register of Historic Places

Nathan Eckstein Residence
1004 14th Avenue East
1915

Dr. Albert S. Kerry Residence
1117 Federal Avenue East
Joseph S. Coté, architect
1917

Lloyd Tindall Residence
2559 5th Avenue West
Distinctive Homes Company, builder
1913

A. Morris Atwood Residence
1941 15th Avenue East
1915
altered

Neoclassical Revival (1895–1950)

Ballard-Howe Residence
22 West Highland Drive
Emil DeNeuf
1900–1901
Washington Heritage Register
National Register of Historic Places

Dr. Adolph O. Loe Residence
917 16th Avenue East
J. Harry Randall, architect
1902

Harvard Residence
2706 Harvard Avenue East
Edward J. Duhamel, architect
1903–1909
Seattle Landmark
Washington Heritage Register
National Register of Historic Places

John C. McMillan Residence
1707 16th Avenue East
Bebb & Mendel, architects
1903
demolished

Arthur E. Lyon Residence
3311 Cascadia Avenue South
Ellsworth Storey, architect
1907–1908
altered

Henry Owen Shuey Residence
5218 16th Avenue Northeast
E. S. Bell, architect
1908
Seattle Landmark
Washington Heritage Register
National Register of Historic Places

Parker-Ferson Residence
1409 East Prospect Street
1909
altered
Seattle Landmark

Richard Dwight Merrill Residence
919 Harvard Avenue East
Charles A. Platt, architect
1909–1910
located in Harvard-Belmont
Historic District

Samuel Hyde Residence
3726 East Madison Street
Bebb & Mendel, architects
1909–1910
Seattle Landmark
Washington Heritage Register
National Register of Historic Places

Horace Adelbert Middaugh Residence
15 Comstock Street
James E. Webster, architect
1901
demolished

CHAPTER 3. CRAFTSMAN (1905–1930)

Milnora de Beelen Roberts Residence
4501 15th Avenue Northeast
1904–1905
demolished

Brehm Brothers Residences
219 and 221 36th Avenue East
Ellsworth P. Storey, architect
1909
Seattle Landmark

George Fletcher Cotterill Residence
2501 Westview Drive North
Josenhaus & Allan, architects
Ira S. Harding, builder
1910
Seattle Landmark

Charles B. Ernst Residence
6323 19th Avenue Northeast
1912
altered

Mauss Residence
2303 22nd Ave East
Long Building Company, builders
1912

A. C. Schneider Residence
2218 3rd Avenue West
pre-1912
altered

E. Ryer Residence
location unknown
pre-1913
W. J. Jones, architect
G. C. Brandon, contactor, Modern
Bungalow Company

Bowen-Huston Residence
715 West Prospect Street
Harris and Coles, Bungalow Company,
designers
1913
Seattle Landmark

G. S. Shirley Residence
3309 Hunter Boulevard South
Jud Yoho, architect
George J. Lockman, builder
1913
altered

Lars Larsen Residence
1528 6th Avenue West
1914

John H. Ogden Residence
3515 Mount Baker Boulevard
S. Swansen, contractor
1914

Harry W. Cullyford
3701 East Olive Street
Coles Construction Company
1915
altered

Frederick E. Kreitle Residence
2835 Northwest 57th Street
1915
altered

Henry Larson Residence
714 West Howe Street
Emil Beck, builder
1915

Belltown Cottages
2512–2516 Elliott Avenue
William Hainsworth, designer and
builder
Seattle Landmark
1916

CHAPTER 4. ECLECTIC REVIVALS: Tudor and Exotic Revivals

Tudor Revival (1890–1940)

Stimson-Green Residence
1204 Minor Avenue
Cutter & Malmgren, architects
1898–1901
Seattle Landmark
Washington Heritage Register
National Register of Historic Places

Charles Henry Cobb Residence
1409 East Aloha Street
Bebb & Mendel, architects
1903

Eliza Ferry Leary Residence
1551 10th Avenue East
Alfred Bodley, architect
1905
Washington Heritage Register
National Register of Historic Places

William Hainsworth Residence
2657 37th Avenue Southwest
Graham & Myers, architects
1907
Seattle Landmark

Charles H. Black Residence
613 West Lee Street
Bebb & Mendel, architects
1907–1909
Seattle Landmark

Oliver David Fisher Residence
1047 Belmont Place East
Beezer Brothers, architects
1908–1909
located in Harvard-Belmont
Historic District

McFee-Klockzien Residence
534 West Highland Drive
Spalding & Umbrecht, architects
1909
Seattle Landmark

M. Hardwood Young Residence
954 Broadway Avenue East
James H. Schack, architect
1909
located in Harvard-Belmont
Historic District

Joseph Kraus Residence
2812 Mount Saint Helens Place
J. E. Douglas, designer
1911
Seattle Landmark
Washington Heritage Register
National Register of Historic Places

Perry B. Truax Residence
1014 East Galer Street
David J. Meyers, architect
1919–1920
altered

Jesse C. Bowles Residence
2540 Shoreland Drive South
1925
Arthur L. Loveless, architect
Washington Heritage Register
National Register of Historic Places

Times-Stetson & Post Model House
935 East Allison Street
Edward L. Merritt, architect
Herman Neubert, contractor
1925

Anhalt Apartments
1005 and 1014 East Roy Street
Fred Anhalt, designer and builder
1927–1930
Seattle Landmarks

William F. Prosser Residence
1000 East Garfield Street
Graham & Myers, architects
circa 1910
altered

Tudor Revival Residence
1859 Boyer Avenue East
(originally 1740 Interlaken Boulevard)
1923
altered

Small Brick Tudor Revival Residence
7523 33rd Avenue Northwest
1930

Exotic Revivals (1890–1940)

Stimson-Griffiths Residence
405 West Highland Drive
Bebb & Mendel, architects
1903–1905
Washington Heritage Register
National Register of Historic Places

Norvell Residence
3306 Northwest 71st Street
1908
Seattle Landmark

Rosen Residence
9017 Loyal Avenue Northwest
1933
Seattle Landmark
altered

CHAPTER 5. FOUR-SQUARE (1900–1925)

Clara Fraychineaud Residence
2806 Boyer Avenue East
1906
altered

W. Williamson Residence
939 18th Avenue East
1907

Thomas J. King Residence
2616 Harvard Avenue East
1909
altered

Patrick W. McCoy Residence
955 16th Avenue East
W. A. Perk, contractor
1906

Martin J. Heneham Residence
820 15th Avenue East
1904

307 and 309 Boylston Avenue East
Residences
1904
both altered

Satterlee Residence
4866 Beach Drive Southwest
1905–1906
Seattle Landmark

Robert C. Saunders Residence
2701 10th Avenue North
Frederick A. Sexton, architect
1906–1908
altered

William D. Hofius Residence
1104 Spring Street
Gribble & Skene, contractors
1902

2403 and 2407 7th Avenue West
Residences
1907
N. M. Wardall Residence
2215 41st Avenue Southwest
1907

1205 16th Avenue East Residence
1906

CHAPTER 6. SPANISH REVIVALS: Mission Revival and Spanish Eclectic

Mission Revival (1900–1920)

Flora Allen Residence
503 13th Avenue East
1905
demolished

Brace-Moriarty Residence
1709 Prospect Street
Kerr & Rogers, architects
1904
Seattle Landmark

Rolland H. Denny Residence
6601 Northeast Windermere Drive
Bebb & Mendel, architects
1907
condition unknown

James Clemmer Residence
2612 Harvard Avenue East
1909

Spanish Eclectic (1915–1940)

John Hamrick Residence
1932 Blenheim Drive
Lionel Pries, architect
1929
altered

B. C. Keeler Residence
537 North 79th Street
1925

Stanley S. Sayres Residence
3020 Mount St. Helens Place
1926

North 77th Street Residences
late 1920s
various states of preservation

CHAPTER 7. MODERN:
International Style, Minimal Traditional, and Contemporary

International Style (19250–1940)

Edwin C. Edwards
303 36th Avenue East
1936
altered

Percival K. Nichols Jr. Residence
1600 East Boston Terrace
Thiry & Shay, architects
1936

Frank J. Barrett Residence
4350 53rd Avenue Northeast
Thiry & Shay, architects
1937
altered

Minimal Traditional (1935–1950)

Seattle *Post-Intelligencer* Model Home—
Lake Forest Park
16520 Shore Drive Northeast
Thiry & Shay, architects
1935
altered

Arthur French Residence
4718 36th Avenue Northeast
1940

Seattle *Post-Intelligencer* Model Home—
Arbor Heights
1948
location unknown

Contemporary (1935–1980)

Smith Residence
536 Lake Washington Boulevard
John R. Sproule, architect
1936
altered

Paul Hayden Kirk Residence
(original owner and architect)
6216 Ravenna Avenue Northeast
1944
altered

Walter P. Coulon Residence
3607 East Republican Street
J. Lister Holmes, architect
1946
altered

Phillip A. Stewart Residence
7050 56th Avenue Northeast
1947
altered

Sam Rubinstein Residence
5818 South Eddy Street
J. Lister Holmes, architect
1947
demolished

Harold Mayer Residence
1353 East Boston Street
Tucker, Shields & Terry, architects
1948

Rader-Revere Residence
8504 43rd Avenue Northeast
Chiarelli & Kirk, architects
1948
altered

Dr. John Lehmann Residence
8041 32nd Northwest
Roger Gotteland, architect
1950
undergoing massive alterations/
demolition

CHAPTER 8. HOUSE TALES:
Researching Your Home's History

Charles McInnis Residence
6539 Earl Avenue Northwest
circa 1895
Victorian/Craftsman

Victorian-Tudor Revival Residence
2852 Northwest 62nd Street

Swan Hansen Residence
2436 Northwest 60th Street
circa 1900
Victorian
altered

HOUSE LOCATOR BY NEIGHBORHOOD

Houses that are still standing have been grouped according to neighborhood (see map on following page) and are listed in alphabetical order of street name or numerical sequence of street. Please refer to the index to locate discussions in text.

DOWNTOWN, DENNY REGRADE, BELLTOWN, EASTLAKE

Belltown Cottages
2512–2516 Elliott Avenue
William Hainsworth, designer and builder
Seattle Landmark
1916
Craftsman

Victor Steinbrueck Residence
2622 Franklin Avenue East
1891
Seattle Landmark
Queen Anne

Fisher-Howell Residence
2819 Franklin Avenue East
circa 1892
Seattle Landmark
Queen Anne

QUEEN ANNE, MAGNOLIA

A. C. Schneider Residence
2218 3rd Avenue West
1912
altered
Craftsman

Lloyd Tindall Residence
2559 5th Avenue West
Distinctive Homes Company, builder
1913
Colonial Revival

Lars Larsen Residence
1528 6th Avenue West
1914
Craftsman

2403 and 2407 7th Avenue West Residences
1907
Four-Square

14th Avenue Housing Group
2000–2016 14th Avenue West
1890–1909
Seattle Landmark
Queen Anne

Ballard-Howe Residence
22 West Highland Drive
Emil DeNeuf, architect
1900–1901
Washington Heritage Register
National Register of Historic Places
Neoclassical Revival

Stimson-Griffiths Residence
405 West Highland Drive
Bebb & Mendel, architects
1903–1905
Washington Heritage Register
National Register of Historic Places
Exotic Revival (Swiss Chalet Revival)

McFee-Klockzien Residence
534 West Highland Drive
Spalding & Umbrecht, architects
1909
Seattle Landmark
Tudor Revival

Reginald H. Parsons Residence
618 West Highland Drive
W. Marbury Somervell, designer
1905
Seattle Landmark
Colonial Revival

Henry Larson Residence
714 West Howe Street
Emil Beck, builder
1915
Craftsman

George Fletcher Cotterill Residence
2501 Westview Drive North
Josenhaus & Allan, architects
Ira S. Harding, builder
1910
Seattle Landmark
Craftsman

Charles H. Black Residence
613 West Lee Street
Bebb & Mendel, architects
1907–1909
Seattle Landmark
Tudor Revival

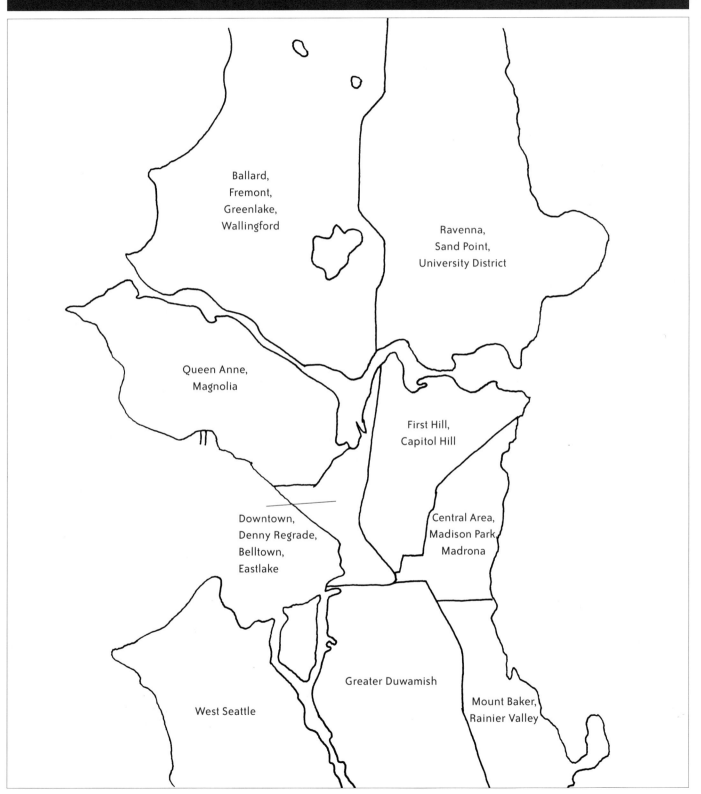

Ballard,
Fremont,
Greenlake,
Wallingford

Ravenna,
Sand Point,
University District

Queen Anne,
Magnolia

First Hill,
Capitol Hill

Central Area,
Madison Park,
Madrona

Downtown,
Denny Regrade,
Belltown,
Eastlake

Greater Duwamish

West Seattle

Mount Baker,
Rainier Valley

Brace-Moriarty Residence
1709 Prospect Street
Kerr & Rogers, architects
1904
Seattle Landmark
Mission Revival

Bowen-Huston Residence
715 West Prospect Street
Harris and Coles, Bungalow Company,
designers
1913
Seattle Landmark
Craftsman

BALLARD, FREMONT, GREENLAKE, WALLINGFORD

Dr. John Lehmann Residence
8041 32nd Avenue Northwest
Roger Gotteland, architect
1950
undergoing massive alterations/
demolition
Contemporary

Small Brick Tudor Revival Residence
7523 33rd Avenue Northwest
1930
Tudor Revival

Frederick E. Kreitle Residence
2835 Northwest 57th Street
1915
altered
Craftsman

Swan Hansen Residence
2436 Northwest 60th Street
1900
Victorian

Pyramid-Roofed Victorian Residence
1522 Northwest 61st Street
circa 1890
altered
Victorian

Victorian-Tudor Revival Residence
2852 Northwest 62nd Street

Norvell Residence
3306 Northwest 71st Street
1908
Seattle Landmark
Exotic Revival (Swiss Chalet Revival)

North 77th Street Residences
Near Greenlake
late 1920s
various states of preservation
Spanish Eclectic

Keeler Residence
537 North 79th Street
1925
Spanish Eclectic

Charles McInnis Residence
6539 Earl Avenue Northwest
circa 1895
Victorian/Craftsman

Rosen Residence
9017 Loyal Avenue Northwest
1933
Seattle Landmark
altered
Exotic Revival (Scandinavian Revival)

RAVENNA, SAND POINT, UNIVERSITY DISTRICT

Henry Owen Shuey Residence
5218 16th Avenue Northeast
E. S. Bell, architect
1908
Seattle Landmark
Washington Heritage Register
National Register of Historic Places
Neoclassical Revival

Charles B. Ernst Residence
6323 19th Avenue Northeast
1912
altered
Craftsman

Arthur French Residence
4718 36th Avenue Northeast
1940
Minimal Traditional

Rader-Revere Residence
8504 43rd Avenue Northeast
Chiarelli & Kirk, architects
1948
altered
Contemporary

Frank J. Barrett Residence
4350 53rd Avenue Northeast
Thiry & Shay, architects
1937
altered
International Style

Phillip A. Stewart Residence
7050 56th Northeast
1947
altered
Contemporary

Paul Hayden Kirk Residence
(original owner and architect)
6216 Ravenna Avenue Northeast
1944
altered
Contemporary

Seattle *Post-Intelligencer* Model Home—
Lake Forest Park
16520 Shore Drive Northeast
Thiry & Shay, architects
1935
altered
Minimal Traditional

Rolland H. Denny Residence
6601 Northeast Windermere Drive
Bebb & Mendel, architects
1907
condition unknown
Mission Revival

FIRST HILL, CAPITOL HILL

Eliza Ferry Leary Residence
1551 10th Avenue East
Alfred Bodley, architect
1905
Washington Heritage Register
National Register of Historic Places
Tudor Revival

Robert C. Saunders Residence
2701 10th Avenue East
Sexton, architect
1906–1908
altered
Four-Square

Dr. Waldo Richardson Residence
2816 10th Avenue East
1912
Colonial Revival

William C. Phillips Residence
2822 10th Avenue East
1909
Colonial Revival

David E. Skinner Residence
725 14th Avenue East
W. W. Sabin, architect
1905
altered
Colonial Revival

Nathan Eckstein Residence
1004 14th Avenue East
1915
Colonial Revival

Martin J. Heneham Residence
820 15th Avenue East
1904
Four-Square

A. Morris Atwood Residence
1941 15th Avenue East
1915
altered
Colonial Revival

Patrick W. McCoy Residence
955 16th Avenue East
W. A. Perk, contractor
1906
Four-Square

Dr. Adolph O. Loe Residence
917 16th Avenue East
J. Harry Randall, architect
1902
Neoclassical Revival

1205 16th Avenue East Residence
1906
Four-Square

Caroline Kline Galland Residence
1605 17th Avenue
Max Umbrecht, architect
1903
Washington Heritage Register
National Register of Historic Places
Colonial Revival

W. Williamson Residence
939 18th Avenue East
1907
Four-Square

Mauss Residence
2303 22nd Ave East
Long Building Company, builders
1912
Craftsman

Times-Stetson & Post Model House
935 East Allison Street
Edward L. Merritt, architect
Herman Neubert, contractor
1925
Tudor Revival

Charles Henry Cobb Residence
1409 East Aloha Street
Bebb & Mendel, architects
1903
Tudor Revival

Oliver David Fisher Residence
1047 Belmont Place East
Beezer Brothers, architects
1908–1909
located in Harvard-Belmont
Historic District
Tudor Revival

John Hamrick Residence
1932 Blenheim Drive
Lionel Pries, architect
1929
altered
Spanish Eclectic

Harold Mayer Residence
1353 East Boston Street
Tucker, Shields & Terry, architects
1948
Contemporary

Tudor Revival Residence
1859 Boyer Avenue East
(originally 1740 Interlaken Boulevard)
1923
altered
Tudor Revival

Clara Fraychineaud Residence
2806 Boyer Avenue East
1906
Four-Square

307 and 309 Boylston Avenue East
Residences
1904
both altered
Four-Square

M. Hardwood Young Residence
954 Broadway Avenue East
James H. Schack, architect
1909
located in Harvard-Belmont
Historic District
Tudor Revival

George W. Ward Residence
520 East Denny Way
1882
Seattle Landmark
Washington Heritage Register
National Register of Historic Places
Italianate

Dr. Albert S. Kerry Residence
1117 Federal Avenue East
Joseph S. Coté, architect
1917
Colonial Revival

Perry B. Truax Residence
1014 East Galer Street
David J. Meyers, architect
1919–1920
altered
Tudor Revival

William F. Prosser Residence
1000 East Garfield Street
Graham & Myers, architects
circa 1910
altered
Tudor Revival

Richard Dwight Merrill Residence
919 Harvard Avenue East
Charles A. Platt, architect
1909–1910
located in Harvard-Belmont
Historic District
Neoclassical Revival

James Q. Clemmer Residence
2612 Harvard Avenue East
1909
Mission Revival

Thomas J. King Residence
2616 Harvard Avenue East
1909
altered
Four-Square

Harvard Residence
2706 Harvard Avenue East
Edward J. Duhamel, architect
1903–1909
Seattle Landmark
Washington Heritage Register
National Register of Historic Places
Neoclassical Revival

Stimson-Green Residence
1204 Minor Avenue
Cutter & Malmgren, architects
1898–1901
Seattle Landmark
Washington Heritage Register
National Register of Historic Places
Tudor Revival

Parker-Ferson Residence
1409 East Prospect Street
1909
altered
Seattle Landmark
Neoclassical Revival

Edgar H. Bucklin Residence
1620 East Prospect Street
Frederick A. Sexton, architect
1908
Colonial Revival

Anhalt Apartments
1005 and 1014 East Roy Street
Fred Anhalt, designer and builder
1927–1930
Seattle Landmarks
Tudor Revival

William D. Hofius Residence
1104 Spring Street
Gribble & Skene, Contractors
1902
Four-Square

William Bell Phillips Residence
711–713 East Union Street
John M. Hester, Builder
1902
Washington Heritage Register
National Register of Historic Places
Colonial Revival

CENTRAL AREA, MADISON PARK, MADRONA

Turner-Koepf Residence
2336 15th Avenue South
1883
State Heritage Register
National Register of Historic Places
altered
Italianate–Queen Anne

Yesler Residences
103, 107, and 109 23rd Avenue East
Emil Kriegel, contractor
1899 and 1902
Seattle Landmark
Washington Heritage Register
National Register of Historic Places
Queen Anne

23rd Avenue Houses Group
812–828 23rd Avenue East
1892–1893
Seattle Landmarks
Washington Heritage Register
Folk Victorian

Raymond-Ogden Residence
702 35th Avenue East
Joseph S. Coté, architect
1912–1913
Seattle Landmark
Washington Heritage Register
National Register of Historic Places
Colonial Revival

Edwin C. Edwards Residence
303 36th Avenue East
1936
altered
International Style

Brehm Brothers' Residences
219 and 221 36th Avenue East
Ellsworth P. Storey, architect
1909
Seattle Landmark
Craftsman

Edwin G. Ames Residence
808 36th Avenue East
Bebb & Mendel, architects
1906
altered
Colonial Revival

List-Bussell Residence
1630 36th Avenue
Flynn & Rockmark, architects
1892
Seattle Landmark
Washington Historic Register
Queen Anne

Percival K. Nichols Jr. Residence
1600 East Boston Terrace
Thiry & Shay, architects
1936
International Style

William H. Thompson Residence
3119 South Day Street
Ernest A. MacKay, builder
1894
Seattle Landmark
Washington Heritage Register
National Register of Historic Places
Queen Anne

Smith Residence
536 Lake Washington Boulevard
John R. Sproule, architect
1946
altered
Contemporary

Samuel Hyde Residence
3726 East Madison Street
Bebb & Mendel, architects
1909–1910
Seattle Landmark
Washington Heritage Register
National Register of Historic Places
Neoclassical revival

Harry W. Cullyford Residence
3701 East Olive Street
Coles Construction Company
1915
altered
Craftsman

Walter P. Coulon Residence
3607 East Republican Street
J. Lister Holmes, architect
1946
Contemporary

Italianate Victorian Residence
1414 South Washington Street
1901
Seattle Landmark
Italianate

MOUNT BAKER, RAINIER VALLEY

Arthur E. Lyon Residence
3311 Cascadia Avenue South
Ellsworth P. Storey, architect
1907–1908
altered
Neoclassical Revival

G. S. Shirley Residence
3309 Hunter Boulevard South
Jud Yoho, architect
George J. Lockman, builder
1913
altered
Craftsman

John H. Ogden Residence
3515 Mount Baker Boulevard
S. Swansen, contractor
1914
Craftsman

Joseph Kraus Residence
2812 Mount St. Helens Place
J. E. Douglas, designer
1911
Seattle Landmark
Washington Heritage Register
National Register of Historic Places
Tudor Revival

Stanley S. Sayres Residence
3020 Mount St. Helens Place
1926
Spanish Eclectic

Jesse C. Bowles Residence
2540 Shoreland Drive South
1925
Arthur L. Loveless, architect
Washington Heritage Register
National Register of Historic Places
Tudor Revival

WEST SEATTLE

William Hainsworth Residence
2657 37th Avenue Southwest
Graham & Myers, architects
1907
Seattle Landmark
Tudor Revival

N. M. Wardall Residence
2215 41st Avenue Southwest
1907
Four-Square

Satterlee Residence
4866 Beach Drive Southwest
1905–1906
Seattle Landmark
Four-Square

GLOSSARY

Addition: an added platted town section.

Art Nouveau: a late nineteenth-century style of architectural and applied art decoration that focused on organic, nonhistorical forms. Most common in France and Belgium. Famed stained glass and jewelry artist Louis Tiffany is one of the best known American practitioners.

ashlar masonry: rectangular blocks of stone, sawed so they are square on all sides.

awning window: a rectangular window that is hinged at the top and swings outward.

balustrade: a series of balusters (short pillars or upright design elements) that are held in place by a coping or handrail on the top and by a bottom rail; used on porches, balconies, and staircases.

bay: a regular subdivision on a façade.

Beaux Arts: elaborate monumental architecture associated with the École des Beaux Arts in Paris during the nineteenth century. Formal in design and symmetrical, showcasing paired columns, garlands, and quoins.

block modillion: a block-shaped horizontal bracket on the underside of a cornice. Commonly decorates Classical Revival buildings.

board and batten: timber construction where the exterior cladding is made from closely placed vertical boards. Joints are covered by narrow wood strips.

braced-frame: heavy wood structural framing that uses supports mortised (embedded) into solid posts.

brackets: projecting members that either support or appear to support an overhanging cornice or eave.

broken pediment: a pediment where the sloping (or curving) sides end before reaching the highest point. The resulting opening is often filled with an urn. Found in Neoclassical and Colonial styles.

builders' row houses: a row of houses constructed by a builder that share one or more side walls with neighboring houses.

canted corners: commonly found on Victorian houses where building corners were "clipped," allowing for angled end windows and ornate gingerbreading or scroll work.

casement window: a window containing a casement sash that opens on a vertical edge.

clapboard: horizontal exterior wood siding in which the boards overlap.

clinker brick: the darkly glazed, irregularly shaped bricks, originally discarded as waste, used to create picturesque wall surfaces in Craftsman and Tudor Revival houses. The term "clinker" comes from the heavier, deeper sound these bricks make when struck together.

colonnade: a series of evenly spaced columns supporting a band of horizontal molding.

coping: a protective cap that covers the top of a wall. Originally designed to provide protection from rainwater, usually found in Spanish or Mission Revival buildings.

corbelling: a series of projecting blocks, each stepped out farther than its predecessor. Commonly found on Tudor Revival chimney stacks.

Classical: a term used to refer to the arts, including architecture, of the ancient world of Greece and Rome.

Colonial: architecture transplanted from the mother countries to overseas colonies. Usually applies to seventeenth-century English architecture in North America.

Colonial Revival: the reuse of Colonial designs in the United States at the end of the nineteenth and beginning of the twentieth centuries.

colossal order: an architectural order (columns) that is more than one story in height.

Contemporary: an architectural style common in the 1940s through 1960s. Two main subtypes, flat roofed and gabled. The flat-roofed subtype is similar to International Style structures but lacks the exterior white stucco walls and utilizes various combinations of wood, brick, or stone. The gabled-roof subtype has overhanging eaves, often with exposed beams. Traditional ornamental detailing is absent, with visual appeal provided by wood, brick, and stone.

Corinthian: a Classical architectural order (columns) with ornate capitals carved with acanthus leaves and small scrolls. The columns are fluted.

cornice: the horizontal projection at the top of a wall met by the roof edge.

cottage style windows: windows on which the top sash is proportionately smaller than the lower sash, usually a 1-to-2 or a 1-to-3 ratio. Commonly found in early twentieth-century residences. Upper sashes usually have multiple lights.

cove ceilings: a ceiling with a concave molding where the wall transitions to the ceiling.

Craftsman: an American style of house most popular in the early 1900s. Usually includes a nonsymmetrical façade, often sheathed with wood, and having square piers, exposed (or even decorative) "structural" members, and a low-pitched roofline with wide overhanging eaves and exposed roof rafters.

crenellations: an alternating system of squared masonry and open spaces that simulate medieval defensive architecture. Commonly found on brick Tudor Revival homes.

cross gable: a gable whose face parallels the main roof ridge.

dado: the lower portion of an interior wall, usually finished with wood paneling. Sometimes referred to as wainscoting.

dentil: one in a series of small square blocks that ornament cornices and moldings. Most common on Neoclassical and Colonial Revival buildings.

Doric: a Classical order (columns) with a plain capital and plain, unfluted columns.

dormer: a window projecting out from a roof. It is framed separately from the main roof and provides daylight into the attic or living spaces.

double-hung window: a window with two sashes, each of which can slide vertically.

eave: the part of a roof that projects beyond the walls.

Eclectic Revival: a term used to describe a number of historical revival styles, including Tudor Revival, Spanish Eclectic, Mission Revival, and Exotic Revival, constructed in the late nineteenth and early twentieth centuries.

Empire Revival: American Empire Revival (a type of Neoclassicism) furniture that became popular in the early 1800s and was still appearing in design magazines by the early 1900s. Empire furniture is known for its simple, massive curves. Mahogany was generally the wood of choice.

entablature: a horizontal member at the top of a wall divided into horizontal bands, including the frieze, which often has Classical carved decoration, and the cornice, the capping element that projects and is detailed with modillions or dentils.

eyebrow dormer: a low dormer lacking angled sides; the roofing curves over the small window.

Exotic Revival: architectural historical revival styles that favored designs of exotic origins, such as the Near East, Asia, and Switzerland.

façade: the exterior elevation of a building, usually referring to the front side.

fanlight: a fan-shaped or semicircular window often located over an entrance door. Most commonly found in Neoclassical or Colonial Revival houses.

fenestration: the design and arrangements of windows in a building.

Flemish bond: a brick pattern in which each row consists of alternating stretchers (the long side of a brick) and headers (the short end). Each stretcher is centered against the header on the preceding row.

Folk Victorian: a type of folk, or vernacular, architecture common in the United States from 1870 until 1910. Characterized by use of machine-made gingerbreading and spindlework, and occasionally details borrowed from the Italianate style.

Four-Square: a house style in which there are four rooms, one in each corner, and a pyramidal roof.

Free Classic: a substyle of Queen Anne architecture known for its subdued ornamentation and use of Classical design forms.

frieze: the middle horizontal section of a Classical entablature, directly below the cornice, often decorated with carved design or sculptural elements.

gable roof: a roof with a single slope on each side of a central ridge, forming triangular ends.

gambrel roof: a roof with two pitches on each side, often used on barns. Commonly found on Dutch Colonial houses.

gingerbreading: decorative lathe-turned or jigsaw-carved woodwork. Most commonly found on the exterior of Victorian houses.

glazing: a window or door that has been filled with sheets of glass.

Gothic Revival: a architectural design movement from the eighteenth and nineteenth centuries that revived decorative Gothic forms, including pointed arches, quatrefoils, heavy masonry, and interior vaulting.

half-timber: a construction technique where supporting timbers were in-filled with brick, mud plaster, or wattle and daub. In the late nineteenth and twentieth centuries, examples of half-timbering were ornamental. Commonly found in Tudor Revival homes, and occasionally Craftsman residences.

hipped roof: a roof where all four sides slope upward and join onto a single ridgeline.

hooded window: a small decorative covering over a window, or occasionally doors. Most commonly found on Italianate windows, and Colonial Revival doors.

horseshoe arch: a rounded arch with a curve slightly greater than a semicircle, forming a narrower opening at the bottom. Sometimes called a Moorish arch.

International Style: an architectural style developed in Western Europe and the United States during the early twentieth century, in which the structures are devoid of historical ornamentation or regional forms. Common design elements are steel interior frames, smooth white walls, metal-cased windows flush with the exterior wall, and flat roofs.

Ionic columns: a classical order whose column capitals have opposing spiral designs (volutes.) Columns are fluted.

Italianate: an architecture style loosely based on Italian villa design during the mid to late nineteenth century. Design details include low-pitched, bracketed roofs, and square towers.

jack arch: a flat arch.

keystone: the wedge-shaped stone that anchors the center of an arch.

light: a pane of glass in a window.

loggia: a porch with an arcade or colonnade that is part of a larger structure.

Minimal Traditional: a mid-twentieth-century architecture style based on scaled-down Tudor Revival designs. Gabled roofs are common. The style lacks most decorative detailing, and in extreme examples, massing and form are so simplified that the term "cottage" is occasionally used.

Mission: a form of Spanish Colonial architecture of the American Southwest. Often found in church complexes. Characteristics are adobe brick walls, stuccoed exteriors, low-pitched roofs with multicurved parapets, and massive carved wood doorways.

Mission Revival: a style of architecture common in the southwestern United States during the early twentieth century, loosely based on the Mission style.

Modern: an architecture term used loosely to describe a number of twentieth-century building styles, including International Style and Contemporary.

muntin: a secondary framing member that holds panes of glass. A muntin can be vertical or horizontal. Vertical members are often referred to as mullions.

newelpost: a tall and often ornamented post at the foot of a stair, supporting the handrail.

Neoclassical: a style of the arts, including architecture, that was especially popular in Europe during the time of Napoleon, the late eighteenth and early nineteenth centuries, in which Classical orders and ornamentation were used to evoke the grandeur of the eras of ancient Greece and Rome. Andrea Palladio, an Italian Renaissance architect (1508–1580), was one of the earliest practitioners of the style; the Palladian window design is sometimes attributed to him.

Neoclassical Revival: an architectural style favored in the United States from the late nineteenth and early twentieth centuries that used monumental orders and Classical ornamentation.

ogee arch: a pointed arch formed by concave upper curves and convex lower curves.

one-over-one window: a window made of two sections, one directly above the other, each containing a single pane of glass.

oriel window: a bay window, located above the first floor, that projects out from a wall.

Palladian window: a large three-part window, in which the central section is arched at the top, and the windows on either side are narrower and rectangular. Particularly favored in Neoclassical architecture design.

parapet: a low wall or protective railing used around a balcony.

pediment: a triangular section used as a crowning element on doors and windows. Most commonly found in Colonial and Neoclassical Revival houses.

pilaster: a pier or pillar attached to a wall, and decorated to represent a classical order.

porte cochere: a covered entrance that projects across a driveway so automobiles can pass under it.

portico: a porch supported by columns over a building's entrance.

quatrefoil: a four-lobed pattern like a four-leaf clover typically found in Gothic Revival or Tudor Revival architecture.

Queen Anne: a style of Victorian architecture in the late nineteenth century, misnamed after Queen Anne. Its forms were based on English country estate and cottage architecture, sometimes blended with Tudor Gothic and Colonial Revival forms.

quoins: flat emphasized masonry used on a building's corners. Quoins have a different color, size, or texture than surrounding masonry.

rafter tails: the part of a rafter that overhangs the wall.

ridge crest: an ornamental strip along the ridge of a roof.

Roman brick: bricks that are elongated, emphasizing a building's horizontal nature. Roman bricks were often used on post-World War II houses.

roofline: the horizontal top ridge of the roof.

row house: See builders' row houses

sidelight: a framed area of glass along the side of a door opening. Usually fixed (doesn't open).

soldier brick: a brick positioned vertically with the narrow side showing.

Spanish Eclectic: a revival of Spanish of Spanish Colonial architecture in the United States, of both domestic and religious (Mission) designs, in the late nineteenth and early twentieth centuries.

Spanish Revival: a revival of Spanish and Spanish Colonial forms in the late nineteenth and early twentieth centuries, particularly common in the southwestern United States.

stacked bond: a brick pattern used for decorative sheathing where the facing bricks are laid with all vertical and horizontal elements aligned.

Stick style: an eclectic American architectural style in the late nineteenth century characterized by design elements that express a frame construction.

stretchers: bricks laid so their long, thin sides are parallel with the wall.

stringcourse: a band of masonry or wood on an exterior wall used to break up a large expanse of wall surface.

Sullivanesque: a term to describe the architectural style and organic decorative panels of Chicago architect Louis H. Sullivan. Commonly found on buildings from 1890 until 1920.

transom: a horizontal window, directly above a door. Often fixed (doesn't open).

Tudor: a form of late English Gothic architecture characterized by its use of masonry and Medieval architectural forms, including pointed arches.

Tudor Revival: a revival of Tudor architecture in the United States, most common during the early twentieth century.

Tuscan columns: a Classical order that is similar to Doric but with fewer moldings and with unfluted columns.

tympanum: the space between the cornice of a pediment and the sloping sides of the pediment.

vergeboard: a board that hangs from the gable end of a roof, sometimes carved. Occasionally called a bargeboard.

vernacular: folk architecture heavily based on pattern books and readily available mass-produced decorative elements, or common regional forms and materials.

Victorian: a term that can loosely cover the ornate architectural styles names for the reign of Queen Victoria from 1840 until 1910, including Folk Victorian, Queen Anne, and Italianate forms.

wainscoting: decorative wood paneling on the lower surface of an interior wall.

BIBLIOGRAPHY

PRIMARY SOURCE MATERIAL

Architect and Biography Files, Special Collections, Suzzallo Library, University of Washington, Seattle, Washington.

Architect and Style Files, Office of Archaeology and Historic Preservation, Olympia, Washington.

Bungalow Magazine, 1912–1917.

Landmark Files, City of Seattle, Washington.

Polk Seattle City Directories, 1887–1960.

Washington Heritage Register Forms and National Register Forms, Office of Archaeology and Historic Preservation, Olympia, Washington.

OTHER SOURCES

Abercrombie, Stanley. *A Century of Interior Design, 1900–2000*. New York: Rizzoli, 2003.

Anglin, Rob. "Briefing Paper on Bungalows in Seattle." Unpublished paper, submitted to the Seattle Landmarks Board, 1982.

Axelrod, Alan. *The Colonial Revival in America*. New York: W. W. Norton, 1985.

Bagley, Clarence. *History of Seattle: From the Earliest Settlement to the Present Time*. Chicago: S. J. Clarke, 1916.

———. *Pioneer Seattle and its Founders*. Seattle, n.p., 1925.

———. *History of King County, Washington*. Chicago: S. J. Clarke Publishing Company, 1929.

Best, Brook V. *Celebrating 150 Years: Architectural History of West Seattle's North End*. Vashon, Washington: Capturing Memories, 2003.

Boris, Eileen. *Art and Labor: Ruskin, Morris, and the Craftsman Ideal in America*. Philadelphia: Temple University Press, 1986.

"Bungalow: Landmark Nomination," Vols. I–III. City of Seattle, Office of Urban Conservation (unpublished), 1982.

Calvert, Frank, ed. *Homes and Gardens of the Pacific Coast*, Vol. I. Seattle: Beaux Arts Society, 1913.

Cigliano, Jan. *Bungalow*. Salt Lake City: Gibbs-Smith, 1998.

Comstock, William C. *Turn-of-the-Century House*. New York: Dover Press, 1994. (Originally published as *Suburban and Country Homes*. New York: William T. Comstock, 1893.)

Comstock, William Phillips, and Clarence Eaton Schermerhorn. *Bungalows, Camps, and Mountain Houses*. New York: Comstock and Company, 1915; reprint, Washington, DC: American Institute of Architects, 1990.

Conover, C. T. *Mirrors of Seattle*. Seattle: Lowman and Hanford, 1923.

Crowley, Walt. *National Trust Guide, Seattle*. Washington: Preservation Press, 1998.

Cumming, Elizabeth, and Wendy Kaplan. *The Arts and Crafts Movement*. New York: Thames & Hudson, 1991.

Dietz, Duane. "Architects and Landscape Architects of Seattle: 1876–1959 and Beyond." Special Collections, University of Washington, Seattle, Washington, 1993.

Doherty, Erin M. "Jud Yoho and the Craftsman Bungalow Company: Assessing the Value of the Common House." Unpublished Master's Thesis, University of Washington, 1997.

Dorpat, Paul. *Seattle Now and Then*, Vol. 2. Seattle: Tartu Publications, 1984.

Ficken, Robert E., and Charles P. LeWarne. *Washington: A Centennial History*. Seattle: University of Washington Press, 1989.

Goff, Lee. *Tudor Style: Tudor Revival House in America from 1890 to the Present*. New York: Universe Publishing, 2002.

Gordon-Van Tine Homes. *Gordon-Van Tine Homes*. Davenport, Iowa: Gordon-Van Tine, 1923; reprint, New York: Dover Publications, 1992.

Gottfried, Herbert, and Jan Jennings. *American Vernacular Design, 1870–1940*. Ames: Iowa State University Press, 1985.

Gowans, Alan. *The Comfortable House: North American Suburb Architecture 1890–1930*. Cambridge: MIT Press, 1986.

Graf, Jean, and Don Graf. *Practical Houses for Contemporary Living*. New York: F. W. Dodge, 1953.

Grant, Frederic James. *History of Seattle, Washington*. New York: American, 1891.

Green, Betsy J. *Discovering the History of Your House and Your Neighborhood*. Santa Monica, California: Santa Monica Press, 2002.

Hanford, C. H., ed. *Seattle and Environs, 1852–1924*. Chicago: Pioneer Historical, 1924.

Harris, Cyril M., ed. *Illustrated Dictionary of Historic Architecture* (1977). New York: Dover, 1983.

Harris, Cyril M. *American Architecture: An Illustrated Encyclopedia*. New York: W. W. Norton, 1998.

House and Garden. *House and Garden's Book of Building*. New York: Condé Nast, 1952.

Jackson, Lesley. *'Contemporary:' Architecture and Interiors of the 1950s*. London: Phaidon, 1994.

Jennings, Jan, and Herbert Gottfried. *American Vernacular Interior Architecture 1870–1940*. New York: Van Nostrand Reinhold, 1988.

Kitchen, Judith L. *Caring for Your Old House*. Washington, DC: Preservation Press, 1991.

Kreisman, Lawrence. *Apartments by Anhalt*. Seattle: Office of Urban Conservation, 1978.

Lancaster, Clay. *The American Bungalow: 1880-1930*. New York: Abbeville, 1985.

Light, Sally. *House Histories: A Guide to Tracing the Genealogy of Your Home*. Spencertown, New York: Golden Hill Press, 1989.

Loeb, Carolyn S. *Entrepreneurial Vernacular: Developers' Subdivisions in the 1920s*. Baltimore: John Hopkins University Press, 2001.

Loizeaux, J. D. *Classic Houses of the Twenties*. New York: Dover, 1992; reprint, Loizeaux's Plan Book No. 7, 1927.

London, Mark. *Masonry: How To Care for Old and Historic Brick and Stone*. Washington, DC: Preservation Press, 1988.

Lucie-Smith, Edward. *Furniture*. New York: Thames & Hudson, 1979.

Maddex, Diane, and Alexander Vertikoff. *Bungalow Nation*. New York: Harry N. Abrams, 2003.

Matthews, Henry C. *Kirtland Cutter: Architect in the Land of Promise*. Seattle: University of Washington Press, 1998.

McAlester, Virginia and Lee. *A Field Guide to American Houses*. New York: Knopf, 2000.

——. *A Field Guide to America's Historic Neighborhoods and Museum Houses: The Western States*. New York: Alfred A. Knopf, 1998.

Moss, Roger W. *Lighting for Historic Buildings*. Washington, DC: Preservation Press, 1988.

Mutter, William E. "Builder Housing: A Seattle Survey." Unpublished Master's Thesis, University of Washington, 1988.

Naeve, Milo M. *Identifying American Furniture*, 2nd Ed. New York: W. W. Norton, 1989.

National Fire Proofing Company. *The Natco Bungalow*. Boston: Rogers and Manson, 1913.

Nylander, Jane C. *Fabrics for Historic Buildings* (Rev. Ed.). Washington, DC: Preservation Press, 1990.

National Park Service. *Respectful Rehabilitation*. Washington, DC: Preservation Press, 1982.

Nylander, Richard C. *Wall Papers for Historic Buildings* 2nd Ed. Washington, DC: Preservation Press, 1992.

Ochsner, Jeffrey Karl, ed. *Shaping Seattle Architecture*. Seattle: University of Washington Press, 1994.

Passport to Ballard. Seattle: Ballard *News Tribune*, 1988.

Phillips, Steven J. *Old House Dictionary*. Washington, DC: Preservation Press, 1992.

Rhoads, William B. *The Colonial Revival*, Vols. I and II. New York: Garland, 1977.

Rosenberg, Casey. *Street Car Suburb: Architectural Roots of a Seattle Neighborhood*. N.c., Fanlight Press, 1989.

Salkin, Andrew H. "The Influence of the Region: A Comparison of Seattle and Portland Residential Architecture, 1900–1960." Unpublished Master's Thesis, University of Washington, 1982.

Schwantes, Carolos Arnaldo. *The Pacific Northwest* (1989). Rev. ed., Lincoln: University of Nebraska Press, 1996.

Seattle Building and Investment Company. Catalogue of house plans. Seattle: Building and Investment Company, n.d., in University of Washington Library.

Shivers, Natalie. *Walls and Molding: How To Care for Old and Historic Wood and Plaster*. Washington, DC: Preservation Press, 1990.

Shoppell, R. W., et al. *Turn-of-the-Century Houses, Cottages, and Villas*. New York: Dover, 1983.

Smeins, Linda E. *Building and American Identity: Pattern Book Homes and Communities 1870–1900*. Walnut Creek, California: Altamira Press, 1999.

Snowden, Clinton A. *History of Washington*. New York: Century History Company, 1911.

Standard Homes Company. *101 American Houses*. Washington, DC, 1921.

Standard Homes Company. *Planbook of Modern American Homes*. Washington, DC, 1921.

Stevenson, Katherine Cole, and H. Ward Jandl. *Houses by Mail: A Guide to Houses from Sears, Roebuck and Company*. Washington, DC: Preservation Press, 1986.

Stickley, Gustav. *More Craftsman Homes* (1912). New York: Dover, 1982.

——, ed. *Craftsman Bungalows*. New York: Dover, 1988.

Von Rosenstiel, Helene. *Floor Coverings for Historic Buildings*. Washington, DC: Preservation Press, 1988.

Voorhees, Victor W. *Western Home Builder*. Seattle: V. W. Voorhees, [1910?].

Walter, Lester. *American Shelter, Revised Edition*. Woodstock, New York: Overlook Press, 1996.

Woodbridge, Sally B., and Roger Montgomery. *A Guide to Architecture in Washington State*. Seattle: University of Washington Press, 1980.

INDEX

DESIGNED